# Together We Begin Again

A Community of Faith Rebuilds
Week by Week

The Rev. Mary Vano
The Rev. Michaelene Miller
The Rev. Cindy Fribourgh

St. Margaret's Episcopal Church
Little Rock, Arkansas

With special guests
The Rt. Rev. Larry Benfield
Dr. Greg Garrett
The Rev. Rob Leacock

*Edited by Dr. Donnal Walter*

## St. Margaret's
EPISCOPAL CHURCH

20900 Chenal Parkway
Little Rock, AR 72223

**ISBN 979-8-9926350-1-0 (Paperback)**
**ISBN 979-8-9926350-0-3 (Hardback)**
**ISBN 979-8-9926350-2-7 (eBook)**

Published by St. Margaret's Episcopal Church
20900 Chenal Parkway, Little Rock, AR 72135
http://stmargaretschurch.org

Cover design: St. Margaret's Episcopal Church

Because sermons at St. Margaret's are grounded in the Revised Common Lectionary[1], readings appointed for the day are listed with each sermon. Our hope is that readers will take time to read the companion scriptures along with the sermons.

Unless otherwise noted, the Scripture quotations contained herein are from the New Revised Standard Version Bible, copyright © 1989 by the Division of Christian Education of the National Council of Churches of Christ in the U.S.A. Used by permission. All rights reserved.

All citations from the Book of Common Prayer are from Episcopal Church. (1979). The Book of Common Prayer and administration of the sacraments and other rites and ceremonies of the church: together with the Psalter or Psalms of David, according to the use of the Episcopal Church. Seabury Press.

We dedicate this book to the steadfast
community of spiritual seekers at
St. Margaret's Church,
who meet each challenge united in spirit.

# FORWARD

Like many church congregations during the pandemic, St. Margaret's Episcopal Church closed its doors to protect one another, learning to worship, study, pray, and support each other online or by phone for many months. When it became safe to meet in person, we couldn't wait to gather again and return to our familiar routines and practices. Yet, it felt like a whole new beginning. How does a scattered parish become a vibrant church community once more? And how long would that take?

We knew renewal wouldn't happen overnight, despite our hope and enthusiasm. We also understood that rebuilding required the efforts of everyone—listening individually for God's call and seeking His direction as a congregation. This process of renewal was, and remains, a communal effort.

It also required leadership from the church vestry and staff, particularly from our rector, Rev. Mary Vano, who had already shepherded us through the wilderness of separation. In an early in-person worship service, Rev. Vano called us together with the stirring words of St. Benedict: "Always we begin again." Then, alongside our new associate rector, Rev. Michaelene Miller, and our faithful deacon, Rev. Cindy Fribourgh, they guided us from the pulpit, Sunday after Sunday. Their sermons inspired us in our spiritual practices and expanded our collective vision for our church, community, and the world.

As an acolyte for the 8:00 a.m. service, I had a front-row seat for these sermons each week. Seated directly before the pulpit, I was struck by three things: the uniformly high quality of the sermons, the complementary approaches and styles of our preachers, and the recurring themes of new beginnings woven throughout the church calendar. I often wished I could revisit not only that day's sermon but also those from previous weeks.

While St. Margaret's YouTube channel serves as a treasure trove of worship services, I am a literary learner—I read. One day, it occurred to me: Why not compile these sermons into a book? So, I simply asked. Mary, Michaelene, and Cindy graciously allowed me to collect and arrange their manuscripts.

This book was not planned in advance, so no unifying theme was intentionally developed from week to week—except for this: in the months following Rally Day 2022, the parish of St. Margaret's began again. This process is ongoing, just as Christians have done for centuries. The church calendar itself is filled with new beginnings. The journey of renewal undertaken by St. Margaret's following the pandemic is one that congregations everywhere, in all times, may recognize as their own.

– Dr. Donnal Walter

# ALWAYS WE BEGIN AGAIN

THE REV. MARY VANO
Proper 19 – Rally Day, September 11, 2022

*Jeremiah 4:11-12, 22-28*
*Psalm 14*
*1 Timothy 1:12-17*
*Luke 15:1-10*

Rejoice with me! It is so good to be together today. It has been a few years since we've been able to celebrate a big Rally Day, and I love it. I love that we can eat together. I love that we can see all the people and ministries serving to the glory of God. I love that we can choose from new opportunities for spiritual growth and renewal. It is a good day to be together.

So, rejoice with me! Because Jesus has given us to one another.

Today, we read again those familiar parables of the lost sheep and the lost coin. On more than one occasion in the Gospels, Jesus uses sheep and shepherd imagery to reveal God's heart to us. Because of that, I think we sometimes conflate the lessons and miss what Jesus is doing in this particular parable. Here, Jesus invites us into the role of the shepherd:

> *Which one of you, having a hundred sheep and losing one of them, does not leave the ninety-nine in the wilderness and go after the one that is lost until he finds it? When he has found it, he lays it on his shoulders and rejoices.*

For today's lesson, you are neither the lost sheep nor one of the ninety-nine. Instead, Jesus asks you to stand in the shepherd's place—to look out across God's flock, to see its fullness, and to consider that God has entrusted you with the care of others. God has given us to one another—to tend and to keep, to feed and to nurture. So, rejoice with me! Because from here, we can see the surpassing value of every soul.

When I was in college, my roommate's parents owned a small ranch. It wasn't too far from campus, so I was occasionally invited to visit. One day, out of curiosity, I asked, "How many cows does your dad own?"

Her answer surprised me. "I couldn't tell you that." Not knowing anything about ranching, I assumed she meant there were too many to

1

count—so many that individual numbers didn't really matter. But I was wrong. She explained that her parents had taught her never to answer that question because it was like asking how much money they had in their bank account. I had committed a cowboy faux pas! Every single animal had value. They knew exactly how many were in their care, but it wasn't something they shared lightly.

Jesus wanted the righteous Pharisees to know that God values sinners just as much as he values them, and vice versa. He wanted the scribes to understand that God cares for the tax collectors as much as he cares for them, and vice versa. This is even clearer in the second parable:

> *What woman, having ten silver coins, if she loses one of them, does not light a lamp, sweep the house, and search carefully until she finds it?*

A silver coin is valuable, no matter how old or dirty it may be. It does not lose its worth simply because it is misplaced. When she loses one, she searches for it—not because it is more important than the others, but because each one matters.

By stepping into the shepherd's role and the woman's perspective, we come to see God more clearly. We worship a God who values each of us so much that he is willing to take risks—to light the lamps, to sweep and to search, and to sacrifice—even for just one.

So, rejoice with me! Because that, after all, is what we are here to do. Jesus told these parables because the Pharisees and scribes were grumbling—grumbling because Jesus was eating with tax collectors and sinners. These were the same religious leaders who had criticized Jesus even when he ate with them. No wonder he preferred the company of those who at least knew how to enjoy a meal!

More importantly, Jesus knew that in God's kingdom, the more, the merrier. God desires that no soul be lost. So, he gives us to one another—to tend, to care for, to rejoice in. And he reminds us that we should celebrate every spiritual victory: each soul that glimpses heaven, each moment of peace, each small act of healing—even a paper cut!

Let us celebrate! Yes, we carry the responsibility of caring for one another, but we are not here to be weighed down by the burdens of duty.

We are here because it is good to be whole. We are here because it is good to be together. We are here because it is good to be healed in love. We are here because it enriches our lives to be counted among God's beloved. We are here because this is where we belong.

This day of celebration makes me reflect on the last two and a half years of pandemic. It has been such a difficult time for everyone, and I know some have suffered far more than I have. Yet, I have to say—of my nineteen years in ordained ministry, these have been the hardest.

- We have lost a lot.
- We have been separated from one another.
- We have lost our peace.

Fear, division, and isolation—though not invented by the coronavirus—were certainly magnified. There were days when I forgot that I wasn't alone. Days when I forgot that we belong to one another. Days when I held myself back, thinking my contribution wasn't valuable. Days when responsibility and obligation overwhelmed my ability to rejoice. But thanks be to God—today is a new day!

"Always, we begin again."

That phrase comes from St. Benedict—the 6th-century monk and father of Western monasticism. His *Rule of St. Benedict* was written as a guidebook for monks living in community, but for centuries, it has been treasured by all Christians seeking a deeper spiritual life. For all of us, Benedict offers this wisdom:

"Always, we begin again."

Because our Shepherd holds us dear, every day is an opportunity to start fresh. Because we hold each other dear, there is gracious space for each of us to find our place and begin again. As we journey through this wilderness, we will always encounter loss, but—by God's goodness—we will always find something even greater to celebrate.

"Always, we begin again."

So, please—rejoice with me

# THE CALL FROM CRISIS TO SOLIDARITY

THE REV. MICHAELENE MILLER
Proper 20 – September 18, 2022

*Jeremiah 8:18-9:1*
*Psalm 79:1-9*
*1 Timothy 2:1-7*
*Luke 16:1-13*

Good morning!

A moment of honesty, y'all—I'm not used to preaching this regularly. In previous calls I've had, "preaching regularly" meant preaching once a month. I'd dive deeply into the scriptures here, surface for a bit, and then dive again over there. But this—preaching every other week—has me truly immersed in the text. It's challenging me to stay in the nitty-gritty and keep pace with Jesus' movement. It's stressful. It is tough, walking right along with Jesus as he travels toward Jerusalem. It is not an easy road.

One thing I'm learning, though, is that I need to read ahead—to try to catch a closer glimpse of where the lectionary is taking us next. Because, when I preached two weeks ago, I opened by saying that *that* gospel passage was difficult. Ooph. If only I had read ahead, I would have saved that line for this week!

Because now, NOW we are faced with a difficult passage from Luke that ends with a line that lingers with a sizzle: *"You cannot serve both God and wealth."*

Our Gospel passage today states it plainly: *"No one can serve two masters; for you will either hate the one and love the other, or be devoted to the one and despise the other."*

Ooph. In some ways, this line from Jesus should not surprise us. It echoes that haunting line from two weeks ago where Jesus said, *"None of you can become my disciple if you do not give up all your possessions."*

4

While Jesus has changed who he is talking to, he hasn't really changed topics. Today's passage continues a longer conversation pointing to a central theme in Luke's Gospel—a focus on wealth and poverty, framed by Mary's song where the mighty are brought down and the lowly are lifted up in God's vision of making everything level.

Jesus has been traveling from Jericho to Jerusalem, teaching about God's kingdom—by word and example. He has been telling parables, healing folks, and eating with tax collectors and sinners. This last activity caused a lot of grumbling among the religious elite who traveled with Jesus to keep a close eye on him.

Their grumbling makes some sense if we understand their hopes for the Messiah. If Jesus were to fulfill the messianic expectation of restoring Israel to the Davidic royal line and liberating them from Roman oppression, then he would certainly need to climb the ranks—not hang out with those on the lowest rung of societal standards.

Instead of directly addressing their grumbling, Jesus tells three parables—one about a lost sheep, one about a lost coin, and one about a lost son (often referred to as the prodigal son). Jesus uses these parables to reframe our minds, to challenge how we devalue those we consider "other" or "less than," and especially those labeled as "lost."

Right after these parables, Jesus tells two more—the first of which we hear today—addressing where we place our value and what we hold above human life: wealth.

It is important to state that wealth, in and of itself, is not inherently bad. It is a neutral power. Its moral stance is determined by how it is used and distributed among people.

If we serve wealth, the goal will always be to create more wealth, regardless of the cost to human life and the natural world. This mindset flies in the face of a God who sees all of creation as good. We cannot serve God and honor the inherent value and dignity of creation while also devaluing and exploiting it in the pursuit of wealth.

5

When we serve God, we take all that we are and all that we have—gifts from God's abundance—and work toward the restoration of God's vision of the inherent dignity and value of all life.

In today's parable, Jesus introduces us to a rich man who owns property and employs a manager. The manager's role is to make the rich man more money by enforcing and collecting taxes from poor farmers who labor on the land.

When the rich man hears the manager has been squandering his property, he immediately fires him. The manager, realizing his precarious position, shifts his mindset from exploitation to solidarity. He reduces the debts of those who owe the rich man, possibly by removing his own commission, choosing to help his neighbors rather than serve the absentee landlord.

In this shift, Jesus invites us to awaken to the systems of exploitation we're caught in and to recognize the crises we face today—the climate crisis, mental health crisis, racial violence, violence against the LGBTQ community.

Serving wealth has led to dangerous divisions and destruction. But God's vision of a world created good, where all is valued and there is enough to share, dismantles that mindset.

Each individual crisis is overwhelming to contemplate and terrifying to face, so how and where do we even begin? Notice that the manager does not get stuck in this space of "what should I do?" He asks the question, acknowledges what he is not capable of, and then, rather than allow perfectionism to paralyze him, he simply decides to do something uniquely within his power to do, and acts. We can take heart from the manager's example.

In looking at the news this week, we find another example of someone doing something new and creative with the resources in their care in the time they have left. Yvon Chouinard, the founder of Patagonia, gave the entire company to a trust and non-profit that will turn all of their profits towards the effort of saving the planet. He turned his for-profit company into a for-purpose movement.

Chouinard said, "As of now, Earth is our only shareholder." He continued, "If we have any hope of a thriving planet—much less a thriving business—fifty years from now, it is going to take all of us doing what we can with the resources we have ... this is another way we've found to do our part."

What is your part? Where is God inviting us to act in the midst of the many different crises we face today? What is the part that we will play here at St. Margaret's? Facing these crises will require participation from us all. It will require us to examine what we are capable of, and to dream and discern together what we can do, and then we must bravely step forward and act with God's big, abundant love. How will we respond creatively with what we have, in the time that we have?

# WE ARE THE LIVING

THE REV. MARY VANO
Proper 21 – September 25, 2022

*Jeremiah 32:1-3a, 6-15*
*Psalm 91:1-6, 14-16*
*1 Timothy 6:6-19*
*Luke 16:19-31*

Today, Jesus asks us to listen carefully to a tale of two souls, set wide apart in this life and the next.

First, there is Lazarus. His name means "God has helped"—which is fitting, for it seems that no one else was going to help him. Jesus describes Lazarus sitting at the gate of a rich man, covered with sores and longing for the scraps that fell from the rich man's table. He had no food, shelter, or healthcare. Though he was the rich man's neighbor, a great chasm existed between them.

Then there is the rich man, sometimes known from the Latin as "Dives." Who is he? He is a man who lives inside a gated community. His expensive purple clothes suggest that he may even be of royal standing. He eats well and wants for nothing—and probably doesn't notice or think much about the man at his gate.

Though they are neighbors, the gap between them is enormous. Dives owns a grand home, while Lazarus can claim only a dusty patch by the roadside. Dives can take a warm bath and satisfy his nutritional needs from his own pantry; Lazarus has no food or bath, no doctor to tend to him, and his body wastes away as dogs lick his sores. Though a gate might separate them, the greatest barrier is the failure of compassion—the rich man's indifference to his neighbor's suffering.

Yet, Lazarus and Dives are not entirely different. They share a common humanity, and both meet the fate that awaits us all: death. On the other side of death, the chasm between them widens, and their fortunes are reversed. Dives suffers in torment while Lazarus is carried by angels to be with Abraham. Even as Dives gazes upon Lazarus in the bosom of

Abraham, he withholds any compassion, his parched voice pleading, "Fetch me some water, boy."

The rich man still clings to his old-world order—where he is on top and Lazarus is on the bottom. Though he has died, he has not experienced the kind of death that leads to resurrection. Only by dying to oneself can one step into the life on the other side of the chasm, where God reigns.

Who is Lazarus? He represents those abandoned to suffer by their fellow humans until, at last, they are welcomed into paradise. Who is the rich man? He is the one who, by creating an impassable gap between himself and others in this life, discovers that there is also a chasm between himself and God in the next. And who are we? Jesus tells this parable not for our entertainment, but for our engagement. He invites us to find our place in the story so that we may ultimately shape the ending of our own lives.

We are not Lazarus—we may take comfort in knowing that God loves us even when the world does not, but none of us here suffers the abject poverty of Lazarus. We have neighbors who do. We are not the rich man, though we might share some traits with him. There is one very important quality that distinguishes us from both Lazarus and Dives: we are still living.

At the very end of the parable, Jesus challenges us. The rich man calls to Father Abraham, "*I beg you to send Lazarus to my father's house—for I have five brothers—so that he may warn them, so that they will not also come into this place of torment.*" There we are—the Living. We are the ones who have opportunities each day to cultivate compassion and to bridge the gap, moving toward the other side where we are united with all of God's children.

This parable is an apocalypse—a story meant to reveal the cosmic mystery into which we are all drawn and toward which we are headed. It is symbolic, and while I caution against taking it entirely literally, its purpose is clear.

Imagine, if you will, a game show like "Let's Make a Deal," with Jesus stepping into the role of Monty Hall. Picture a set of doors: behind one door is suffering, behind another, comfort; behind another, the chasm of isolation, and behind yet another, connection. Unlike Monty Hall, Jesus shows us exactly what lies behind each door. He asks us to choose—not waiting until the end of our story, but to choose now, to choose our future today.

The chasms in our lives are very real. In 2021, for example, the top 10% of Americans held nearly 70% of the wealth, while the bottom 50%—roughly 63 million families—held just 2.5%.[2] That's a staggering gap. And this chasm is not solely a product of economic injustice—it is deepened by our widespread failure of compassion. The gap widens every time we pass by a homeless person without a second thought, every time a business prioritizes profit over a living wage, and every time lawmakers reduce social services to favor the wealthy. Each neglect of our neighbor digs a deeper chasm between us and God.

These are serious problems with difficult solutions. Yet, Jesus makes the choice clear. In the parable, Abraham reminds the rich man—amid his suffering—that the guidance we need is right in front of us. He points to Moses and the prophets, saying, "If they do not listen to Moses and the prophets, neither will they be convinced even if someone rises from the dead."

Everything we need to close the chasm between ourselves, our neighbors, and God is written in Holy Scripture. Consider these words:

- **Deuteronomy 15:11:** *"There will always be poor people in the land. Therefore, I command you to be openhanded toward your brothers, the poor and needy in your land."*
- **Micah 6:8:** *"What does the Lord require of you but to do justice, love kindness, and walk humbly with your God?"*
- **Psalm 82:3-4:** *"Defend the cause of the weak and fatherless; maintain the rights of the poor and oppressed. Rescue the weak and needy; deliver them from the hand of the wicked."*
- **Proverbs 21:13:** *"If a man shuts his ears to the cry of the poor, he too will cry out and not be answered."*
- **1 Timothy 6:17-19:** *"As for those who are rich in this present age, command them not to be haughty, nor to trust in uncertain riches but in God,*

*who richly provides us with everything for our enjoyment. They are to do good, to be rich in good works, and to be ready to share, storing up for themselves the foundation for the future, so that they may take hold of the life that is truly life."*

The Bible contains over 300 verses on the poor and social justice— a clear call to compassion and action. It's more than any other topic in scripture. Everything we need to know to close the chasm between ourselves and our brothers and sisters, and between ourselves and God is there. And not only do we have the clear voice of scripture calling us to compassion, we have Jesus Christ. Jesus showed us what compassion looks like. He exhibited for us God's passion for His people. And Jesus never stopped giving. With his own life, he bridged the gap between God and humanity, and between death and life. And he was raised from the dead so that we do not have to share the torment of the rich man.

We are the living. Now is the time. Listen.

# SITTING WITH GRIEF

THE REV. MICHAELENE MILLER
Proper 22 – October 2, 2022

*Lamentations 1:1-6; 3:19-26*
*Psalm 137*
*2 Timothy 1:1-14*
*Luke 17:5-10*

> *How lonely sits the city, that once was full of people! How like a widow she has become ... She that was a princess ... has become a slave. She weeps bitterly in the night, with tears on her cheeks; ... she has no one to comfort her ... Judah has gone into exile with suffering.* (Lamentations 1:1-3)

Our Old Testament reading for today comes from the Book of Lamentations. In recent weeks, we have been reading through the Book of Jeremiah, and Lamentations is often seen as an extension of that prophet's voice—or at least a reflection of that moment in history.

Biblical Theologian Ellen Davis acutely captures their relationship: If "Jeremiah charts [Jerusalem's] long descent into the pit of destruction," then "Lamentations might be the scream at the bottom ... Together, they offer an immediate, insider's view of the decline and fall of Jerusalem—a different perspective from that of the Book of Kings, which views those same events from arm's length in the manner typical of a historical account. Jeremiah and the poet(s) of Lamentations express overt anguish over the destruction of the city that they name in distinctly personal, even familial, terms (as Daughter Zion) ... These poetic voices enlarge the space for lament within the Bible."[3]

The Book of Lamentations is short—it consists of only five chapters (or poems) that describe in agonizing detail the aftermath of Jerusalem's destruction, its military occupation, and the deportation of its citizens by King Nebuchadnezzar and the Babylonian Empire in 586 BCE. It teaches us how to give voice to shared grief while confronting God with honest anger, soul-wrenching questions, and painful uncertainty.

Today—this is the only Sunday in our three-year lectionary cycle that we encounter these six verses. They are the opening lines of a grief-filled book that we would otherwise only hear in our public liturgy during a Tenebrae Service or on Holy Saturday. Those services invite us to linger in sorrow, without yet turning toward hope; they call us to wait with Jesus in the shadow of the valley of death or to simply sit with Christ in the tomb.

So why am I inviting us to sit with these verses now? They bring us back to the scene of devastation[4]—look at how she sits, all alone! Jerusalem was changed forever. For us, these verses cut through the rush to leave the past behind. As our church community and society's calendar quicken, I hear Lamentations cry out: "Do NOT rush past all that has happened! Remember how we sat, all alone!"

The timing is hauntingly appropriate. I am joining you as you return to this faith community—many of you emerging from a time of enforced distance. Today, even as we gather and rejoice, we are reminded that it is also right to hold space for our weeping. Even amid abundant gratitude and renewed community, we must allow ourselves to weep bitterly in the night with tears on our cheeks. Lamentations calls us to the holy practice of naming and processing our grief together—to remember the exile of the last two years.

To remember and name all that was lost to Covid—the interrupted expectations, the lost plans, the lost time, and the lost loved ones.

To remember that in recent years, life has been confusing. In many ways, we find ourselves living in a new reality. The pandemic of Covid-19 disrupted the patterns of life as we knew them, forcing us into new practices of communal care. We wrestled with what it meant to live while pausing, and how to start again under such different circumstances. We had to learn new expressions of love—wearing masks, standing apart, gathering outdoors in the heat or cold, attending school via screen, sacrificing personal comfort and connection for mutual health, and even sacrificing mental health for physical safety. The epidemic of loneliness intensified.

In addition to COVID-19's grip on our lungs in 2020, many began to see America's original and ongoing pandemic of white supremacy—kneeling squarely upon the necks of our Black siblings. We passed a point of no return in the climate crisis. Children continued to die even in the supposed safety of their school buildings. Our young experiment in democracy is straining at its limits. There is no shortage of grief for the poets to lament, and they invite us back to that scene of devastation.

I used to lead the corps members of the intentional Christian community I directed in St. Louis through an Examen practice each week. I would invite them to reflect on the past week—remembering both moments of gratitude and moments of regret and grief. We named these emotions out loud and held them together.

It was a difficult, yet holy, practice. It made our community brave and real. They were invited to show up and share with one another before God. Today, I invite you to join in a similar practice. It is okay if you feel uncomfortable—we, as a society, are often out of practice in noticing and naming our grief. For now, with the poets of Lamentations, simply hold these realities up to God.

### Weekly Examen: Gratitude and Grief

As we prepare for this practice, I invite you to reflect on the past few years—this time of exile—and notice the moments of gratitude and grief that have come together.

First, bring your attention to your breathing and your body. This will help us arrive together in the present moment. Our minds may wander to the past or future, but our bodies are always here. Sit comfortably upright with your feet on the floor. Close your eyes if you are comfortable, or simply lower your gaze.

Take a moment to feel your body in the chair, your feet grounded on the floor, right here in the present. Let the weight of your body relax and settle. For a few moments, focus on your breathing—it will naturally deepen as you pay attention.

As you breathe, relax the muscles of your face and head—the areas where tension often builds. Relax your neck and throat, your jaw and mouth, your eyes and the muscles around them. Soften your forehead, your cheeks, and even your chin. Allow your ears and scalp to relax.

Now, breathe into your heart space and sense the Divine Love that surrounds you—always present, always inviting you more deeply into relationship and community. With God's help, we step forward as a community that invites each other to show up, share, and hold one another—as we are, wholly (holy) as we are, even in our brokenness.

Begin to examine the past for moments of gratitude: With your hand on your heart, ask God's Spirit to bring forth memories that were life-giving. Allow your heart—not your head—to find these moments. If you could relive one moment from these past two years, what would it be? When were you most able to give and receive love? When did you feel deeply connected to God's Stable Presence, to others, or simply at one with yourself? Remember what made that moment special, and let its energy fill your heart. Offer these memories to God in prayer with gratitude.

Next, examine the past for moments of grief: Again, with your hand on your heart, ask God to bring forth memories that drained you. Were there times when you grieved the inability to give or receive love? When did you feel separated or distant from God's Sustaining Spirit? When did loneliness or isolation overwhelm you? Be with the energy of those moments. Without trying to change or fix anything, take a few breaths and allow God's love to fill your heart. Trust that God can hold our anger and intimately knows our pain, and offer those moments to God in prayer with grief.

Now, pause and name your needs. Ask God to help you reflect on and remember what you need for the coming week. What emotions do you hold? What need lies beneath those emotions—the joy, the tight feeling in your chest, or the weight upon your shoulders? Ask God for the courage to share and request help, whether for big or small things. Also, ask the Spirit to help you recognize the needs of others, so you can offer assistance in return.

As we close with Peace, remember that God's peace—the peace that surpasses all understanding—does not erase our gratitude or our grief. We give thanks for the clarity that has emerged, for the vulnerable truths named before God and offered in prayer. Thank you for exploring this Examen practice together.

Afterward, as we turn toward the table and prepare to return to the swiftness of life, I invite you to share what arose—both gratitude and grief—with someone before you leave. Whether you share with someone at the table, with your family on the drive, or by calling a friend or loved one (especially someone who might be alone), extend this practice of sharing. With God's help, we step forward as a community that continues to invite each other to show up, share, and hold one another—as we are, wholly and holy, in our brokenness.

# GOD IS NOT ELSEWHERE

The Rev. Mary Vano
Proper 23 – October 9, 2022

*Jeremiah 29:1, 4-7*
*Psalm 66:1-11*
*2 Timothy 2:8-15*
*Luke 17:11-19*

God is not elsewhere. Let's just ponder that for a moment—God is not elsewhere but right here.

Last week, we read from the Book of Lamentations, and in her sermon, Michaelene gave us time to acknowledge and observe our collective grief over these past few years, as well as to reflect on what is happening in our world and our lives now. Following this, I come to this week's Gospel story of Jesus healing the ten lepers, feeling a new solidarity with them. I might not be as outcast as they were, or afflicted with a skin disease, but I know that I am in need of healing. I know that we all are. Like those ten lepers, it seems that in one way or another, the whole world is now crying out, "Have mercy on us!" "Mercy!"

We cry out loudly for help, not realizing that God is not elsewhere. When I came across the phrase "God is not elsewhere" in my reading this week, it was a little "aha" moment for me—perhaps the great insight of the tenth leper. He turned back because he realized that if he kept running, he would miss his chance to give thanks and praise to God, who was right there in the person of Jesus Christ. Of the ten, he was the only one who saw it: that God was not elsewhere.

Now, this phrase "God is not elsewhere" comes from Esther de Waal, a contemporary writer and teacher of Benedictine and Celtic spirituality. She uses it to sum up the teachings and practices of St. Benedict of Nursia—the sixth-century monk and father of Western monasticism. Benedict developed a rhythm of life built around work, prayer, and study—a pattern focused on discovering the divine in the ordinary, in the small acts that make up our everyday life. As Esther de Waal says, it is a life rooted in the acknowledgment that God is not elsewhere.

Benedict's rule of life was, in many ways, a contrast to the conditions of the previous century. The context of fifth-century Italy was characterized by volatility, uncertainty, complexity, and ambiguity—conditions described by the acronym VUCA. (Originally coined in the 1980s to understand the breakdown of the political order after the Cold War, these terms also capture the upheaval of the fifth century after the fall of the Roman Empire.) In many ways, that era is not too far removed from what we are experiencing now.

That time of upheaval gave rise to a new kind of monk, known as the gyrovagues—literally, "one who wanders in circles." These monks moved from monastery to monastery, searching for something better—a better community, better food, a better abbot.[5] They were constantly on the move, always looking for God elsewhere. But God was not elsewhere.

The insight of Benedict—to find God right where you are—was also the great discovery of the tenth leper: that God is never far away.

In today's story from the Gospel of Luke, Jesus is on his way to Jerusalem—traveling through the borderlands between Galilee and Samaria—when he meets a group of ten lepers who cry out to him for mercy. Because leprosy was so contagious, these people were forced to live apart from their families and outside their communities. They were, in a sense, refugees who, without the opportunity to work, had to rely on the kindness of strangers. On the day they encountered Jesus, they cried for mercy. I don't know what they expected to receive, but I suspect it was far less than what he gave them. Following Jesus' instruction, it is only when they are already on their way to the priests that they look back and discover they are healed.

For all ten of them, it is an amazing gift. Their diseased skin is renewed. With the clearance of the priests, they can return home—restored to their communities and able to work and be useful once again. This gift is so tremendous that it's hard to imagine any one of them being ungrateful, which makes me wonder if this story is perhaps more than it appears.

It isn't about simple gratitude—writing thank-you notes or posting on Facebook about our blessings. What we see in the tenth leper goes beyond that. His gratitude is life-changing.

It is much more than simply saying thank you. It begins with truly seeing. The Gospel tells us that something happens to this man when "he saw that he was healed." It wasn't just about clear skin; what he saw was an act of God—a loving God at work in his life. His eyes were open enough to recognize that he had just encountered divine mercy So the tenth leper responds by turning back. As anxious as he might have been to reach the priests or return home to his family, he allows his path to be diverted—he turns back to the one who has given him this gift. And he responds by praising God out loud. I don't know if he was singing, shouting, or laughing, but he did not keep his joy to himself. His love, gratitude, and joy were expressed for all to hear. Then, upon returning to Jesus, the tenth leper kneels down—expressing reverence and trust in God's goodness, reminding himself that God is greater. Having seen, turned, praised, and knelt, he finally gives thanks to Jesus.

The Gospel then reminds us that this tenth leper was a Samaritan—a foreigner, considered by some to be a fool and an enemy, not to mention a diseased, unworthy outcast. Yet, Luke tells us, among the ten who were healed, it was the Samaritan who truly knew how to give thanks and praise to God. He is the outsider from whom we need to learn. Nine of the lepers obediently returned to their old lives—improved, yes, but still lives marked by wandering and searching. Only the tenth man, upon realizing that God is not elsewhere, claimed the new life offered to him in Jesus Christ.

We, too, are living through a time of volatility, uncertainty, complexity, and ambiguity. Violence erupts in our cities, our country, and around the world. Change is rapid, and we live with such uncertainty that it's often difficult to discern truth from falsehood. Our world is both beautifully diverse and overwhelmingly complex, revealing just how interconnected we all are. Yet, with such divergent opinions and interpretations of our times, our sense of ambiguity can undermine our courage to act.

We need healing. We need mercy. Yet perhaps we need not shout our prayers, but rather whisper them into the ear of God—who is not elsewhere, but right here with us. Following the example of the tenth leper, can we see the good that God is doing in our lives? Can we turn back—not merely rushing to reclaim what was, but pausing to discover what is? Will we raise our voices in praise of God—with singing, shouting, and laughter—even amid a broken world? Will we kneel together in holy reverence? Will we give thanks and claim the new life offered to us in Jesus Christ?

Wherever we go from here, it must begin with the realization that God is not elsewhere, but ever walking with us.

# THE WIDOW'S WAY, BOLD AND FOOLISH

THE REV. MICHAELENE MILLER
Proper 24 – October 16, 2022

*Jeremiah 31:27-34*
*Psalm 119:97-104*
*2 Timothy 3:14-4:5*
*Luke 18:1-8*

Today, in our gospel passage, we encounter Jesus as he continues teaching his disciples on the way to Jerusalem. At this point, they are drawing closer. Before we dive into today's passage, it's important to consider what came immediately before—even though our lectionary skips that section. Examining the context helps us see how Luke arranged his account of the Good News for his community and understand what Jesus is responding to, as we wonder why he tells this story about a persistent widow who acts boldly—and perhaps even foolishly—for justice.

As Jesus nears the end of his journey with the disciples, the end of his earthly ministry, he speaks to them again about the "end of time" and the coming of the Kingdom of God. He explains that suffering and rejection will precede its full arrival. The kingdom of God is already among them—his birth and ministry have begun to break in, unfolding the Realm of God in their midst—but the world will not be fully transformed until the Child of Humanity returns at the end of the age.

After hearing this, Jesus seems to know his disciples need reassurance. Or perhaps it is Luke, exercising his artistic license because he knew the community well—a community living through great persecution amid the delay of Christ's return, discouraged in their longing for an era of justice, peace, and joy in a world filled with insurmountable challenges. They naturally wondered, "What do we do in the meantime? What about the injustice, hardened hearts, and sorrow of our present world? What does faith look like now?"

Indeed, Luke introduces today's parable very directly. Jesus tells his disciples a parable about the need to pray always and not lose heart. He speaks of a city with a judge who neither fears God nor respects people, and of a widow who persistently seeks justice from him.

This parable is often known as the Parable of the Unjust Judge. When we examine the character of this judge in contrast with the nature of God, we are encouraged not to lose heart. By this point in Luke's Gospel, we have already heard Jesus say in chapter 11, *"If you, who are evil, know how to give good gifts to your children, how much more will your heavenly Father give the Holy Spirit to those who ask him!"* And in chapter 12, *"If God so clothes the grass of the field, which is alive today and tomorrow, will be thrown into the oven, how much more will he clothe you!"*

It is even more encouraging, then, to see that if a judge with an unchanging heart—who still does not revere God or care for his neighbor—can be moved to show mercy in the face of a persistent woman, how much more merciful is God, who loves us, created us, and knows every part of our being. We are urged: do not lose heart. God is faithful, knows us intimately, reaches out to us, and chooses us every moment.

I have also seen this parable called the Parable of the Persistent Widow. Its focus is to encourage us to pray faithfully—day and night. It clarifies what Luke wanted his community to understand about prayer in this interim time, when the kingdom of God is already here but not yet fully realized. We can look to the widow in today's story and strive to persist—persist, persist, and persist—in seeking justice.

The term "persistent widow" should not obscure the full range of her experience. She might equally be called the rejected widow, the tired widow, or the angry widow. I imagine each of these descriptions captures part of her reality.

In fact, the original Greek text explaining why the unjust judge eventually grants her request is more accurately translated as: "Because this widow causes trouble for me, I will give her justice, so that she may not, in the end, give me a black eye by her coming." In her unending fight for justice, she is prepared to show the full force of her desire and desperation.

Through this character, Jesus acknowledges that God's kingdom—where true justice changes hearts, transforms relationships, and ripples throughout the world—is not yet fully here. Nevertheless, he urges his disciples to remain active, faithful, and boldly, even foolishly, persistent for God. No matter how long it takes, keep calling on God for justice; keep demanding it like a tireless, fierce, and even bothersome widow. Jesus highlights her persistence.

Can you imagine this widow? I picture her waking before dawn, too restless and weary to sleep in, wondering each day if it will be worth the humiliation and cost to set out once more—to walk to the courthouse and knock on a judge's closed, hardened heart. Can you imagine her?

I have been pondering her all day. Yesterday, at the Central Arkansas Pride event at Argenta Plaza in North Little Rock, as I joined in celebrating the diversity of God's creation, I found myself thinking about this widow. I wondered if she—or those living out her story in real life—had a community in which to gather, a place of shared identity and understanding where she could find the strength and encouragement to persist in her fight for fair treatment and care.

I don't know—the story does not tell us. But I would guess that this widow knew of at least one place to turn for strength. In ancient Israel, it was common teaching that if not on earth, she had an ally in God. Time and again, Scripture testifies to God's special care for widows, orphans, and strangers. Both the Old and New Testaments make it abundantly clear that God calls us to protect and care for the most vulnerable among us.

As she readies herself for the day under the morning stars, I imagine her turning to God in prayer. In doing so, she unites her fight with God's fight. She seeks protection and justice for the most vulnerable, striving to transform her world—her particular place in society. Aligned with God, she goes to the courthouse. In Luke's Gospel, prayer is faith in action.

And God does not merely hear her cry—God is in her cry. God is with the most vulnerable. God is that persistent widow crying for justice, knocking on our hardened hearts to awaken our care, to help us see, and to prompt us to act on her behalf. The way of the widow is the way of

God: boldly and, if need be, foolishly persisting for justice and transformation. God's way is that bold, seemingly foolish persistence—showing up, reaching out in relationship, and choosing us again and again despite our hardness. The question is, will we choose God back?

At the end of today's passage, Jesus wonders aloud, *"When the Son of Man comes, will he find faith on earth?"* Will Jesus find us walking the way of the widow? Will he find that we turn to God in prayer and unite ourselves with both God and our neighbor? Will we choose God back, aligning ourselves with God as we respond to and cry out with the most vulnerable? Will we have the faith of the widow to persist—boldly and, if necessary, foolishly—against seemingly insurmountable obstacles? Will we trust that, eventually, the Child of Humanity will return, that God's dream for creation will be fulfilled on earth, and that the kingdom of God will fully break through, transforming our hearts and our world?

In the meantime, let us pray:

> May God bless us with a restless discomfort
> at easy answers, half-truths, and superficial relationships,
> so that we may seek truth boldly and love deeply in our hearts.
> May God bless us with holy anger
> at injustice, oppression, and exploitation,
> so that we may work tirelessly for justice, freedom, and peace
> among all people.
> May God bless us with the gift of tears to shed with those
> who suffer from pain, rejection, starvation, war, or the loss of all
> that they cherish,
> so that we may reach out to comfort them
> and transform their pain into joy.
> And may God bless us with enough foolishness
> to believe that we truly can make a difference in this world,
> so that, with God's grace, we are able to do what others claim
> cannot be done.[6]

Amen.

# PRAYER POSTURES

THE REV. MICHAELENE MILLER
Proper 25 – October 23, 2022

*Joel 2:23-32*
*Psalm 65*
*2 Timothy 4:6-8, 16-18*
*Luke 18:9-14*

Good morning! Again, we are presented with another parable to ponder. Just like last week's parable of the persistent widow and the unjust judge, today's parable is also about prayer. Last week, the Evangelist of Luke's Gospel helped us understand that the parable was about our need to pray always and not to lose heart.

We took a close look at the persistence of the widow in her fight for justice and, in doing so, caught a glimpse of how the way of the widow is the way of God—who boldly and even foolishly persists for justice and transformation, who continuously shows up, reaches out in relationship, and chooses us again and again despite our hardness of heart and forgetfulness.

At the 9 o'clock service, I invited everyone into a prayer posture that helped us understand how God is always reaching out to us with bold love—calling us back into relationship time and time again. Thankfully, our relationship with God is not reduced to a mere contract or a handshake—a business deal easily broken when we forget to be in relationship. No, thanks be to God; God establishes and invites us into a covenant relationship, one that can be symbolized by a wrist grasp—an embrace that goes beyond holding our hand, inviting us instead to grasp God back.

In covenant, God moves past our forgetfulness and embraces us fully as beloved creations. This understanding reminds us that even when we let go, God is still holding onto us, always calling us to repent and return. If we were to adopt this wrist-grasp posture in prayer, it would both embody our belief and serve as a constant reminder that God is ever-present—even when we forget. God persists in calling us back into relationship, choosing us and inviting us to choose God in return.

As we set up today's parable, the Evangelist of Luke again gives us a hint of where Jesus is leading us. Jesus told this parable to those who trusted in themselves as righteous and regarded others with contempt. In the parable, we encounter two contrasting characters—a Pharisee and a tax collector—each depicted in distinct prayer postures that remind us to put our trust in God, to close the distance between ourselves and God, and thereby, the gap between ourselves and our neighbor. Jesus presents us with a Pharisee who stands alone in prayer and a tax collector who stands at a distance.

Much of our communication is nonverbal. In this case, our prayer posture speaks volumes about our beliefs and the actions we intend to take. Within our own worship, there are many opportunities to explore and practice different prayer postures—what some might jokingly call "pew aerobics." Yet, each movement is an opportunity to explore and embody our faith.

As we move through our liturgy—bowing our heads in reverent prayer, sitting to listen to the ancient stories of our faith, standing during the Gospel reading as we turn toward Jesus, kneeling humbly in confession, making the sign of the cross over ourselves in a prayer for blessing, or opening our hands to receive Christ at the Communion rail—we embody our faith. Each of these postures brings God into our world and makes our faith incarnational.

There is a theology behind our prayer postures—a belief and relationship with God articulated and practiced through these movements. The postures of both the Pharisee and the tax collector in today's parable, along with their words, help reveal their character and their understanding of God.

First, consider the Pharisee, who stands alone in prayer. To Jesus' first audience, this man—by virtue of his position and role in society—would have been regarded with great respect as righteous and in good standing with God. Pharisees were religious leaders and moral exemplars who served God with strict devotion and disciplined obedience under Jewish law.

I imagine this Pharisee standing tall in the crowded temple, arms open wide, eyes gazing upward, praying with a loud voice: "Thank you, God, that I am not like other people!" Perhaps he even projected his voice over his shoulder, seeking not only God's attention but that of those around him.

Other translations tell us that the Pharisee prayed to himself, boasting about his own righteousness while comparing his good works to the sins of others—such as the tax collector. Though he begins by acknowledging his blessings, he quickly turns to judge the shortcomings of those around him. St. Augustine once remarked that instead of confessing his sins to the great Physician, this religious leader merely "compared his own health to the diseases of others."[7] In doing so, he missed an opportunity for true healing and connection. By staying fixed in his own place—standing alone, self-satisfied—he separated himself from both God and his neighbor, hiding his inner insecurities behind a façade of perfectionism.

In contrast, consider the tax collector—a figure immediately recognized by Jesus' audience as a sinner and traitor. Tax collectors worked for the Roman Empire and enforced an economic system of exploitation. Their reputation for dishonesty and greed was well known.

The prayer posture of the tax collector speaks for itself. Unlike the Pharisee's boastful stance, the tax collector's posture declares his unworthiness. Standing at a distance, separated from God and others by his own sin, he does not look up to heaven but bows his head in humility. With a slow, measured tone and a hand beating his chest, he pleads, "*God, be merciful to me, a sinner!*" Each beat of his chest reminds him of his desperate need for God's mercy. His posture, steeped in brokenness and humility, draws him back into a right relationship with God.

Herein lies the great leveling of Luke's Gospel—where the mighty are brought low and the lowly are lifted up. Jesus makes it clear: those who exalt themselves will be humbled, and those who humble themselves will be exalted.

While the tax collector, initially distant because of his sins, returns to God with a deep awareness of his own need for mercy, the Pharisee remains isolated by his self-righteousness, offering nothing but a self-serving prayer that distances him further from both God and his neighbor.

The religious practices of praying, fasting, and tithing are not meant to elevate us above others but to draw us closer to God and to one another. They are meant to help us see the opportunities for connection that surround us.

How might we notice when we are standing apart from God and our neighbor? When have we forgotten to be in relationship with both? Where are the spaces in our lives where we could step in, draw near, and reconnect? What spiritual practices draw you nearer to God and deepen your ties with the community at St. Margaret's?

There are many ways to explore this. Whether it's sitting with God in the House of Prayer, walking a labyrinth in God's creation, worshiping in community, participating in a fellowship group or formation class, or practicing trust in God's abundance by giving your time, talent, and treasure—the list goes on. Take time this week to explore how you are being called to step toward God and your neighbor, trusting that God is already reaching out to us and always ready to meet us in relationship.

# WHAT STEWARDSHIP SHOULD LOOK LIKE

THE REV. MARY VANO
Proper 26 – October 30, 2022

*Habakkuk 1:1-4; 2:1-4*
*Psalm 119:137-144*
*2 Thessalonians 1:1-4, 11-12*
*Luke 19:1-10*

My list of starring roles in grade-school productions is notably short. In kindergarten, I was Little Orphan Annie—the little girl with curly hair, wearing a red dress with a white belt, singing "Tomorrow." In fourth grade, I was chosen from among my girl-school classmates to play Zacchaeus—yes, that wee little man. I think I was typecast.

After all, I know what it means to be short. The very worst place for a short person is in a crowd, where you lose your line of vision and get pushed around—or even elbowed in the nose—by people who overlook you because you are below them. The perils of being short are something I share with Zacchaeus, but there's more.

I also know a little about what it means to be wealthy. To be wealthy is to have everything you need and still sense that something is missing—something that money cannot buy. To be wealthy is to be admired by some while others reduce your worth to that of a dollar bill, or even hold you in disdain simply because you have more than they do.

And then there is what it means to be a sinner. In this case, Zacchaeus was a "taker"—a "chief tax collector," as the Gospel tells us. In the eyes of many of Jesus' followers, he was "sinner in chief." He seized every opportunity to get ahead, even at the expense of others. He took all he could from hard-working individuals and families, knowing that the more he collected for Rome, the more he could pay himself. When the crowd prevented him from seeing what he wanted to see, he climbed into a tree so that he could catch a glimpse of Jesus. And he got more than he bargained for. Expecting only to see the top of Jesus' head, he instead saw His eyes—looking right back at him.

Thanks to that familiar song—"Zacchaeus was a wee little man."—I always thought this was simply a story about how Jesus loves sinners—even the short ones! That seemed like sufficiently good news to me. But I later realized I, like everyone else, had overlooked the rest of the story beyond the part where Jesus and Zacchaeus head off together. I didn't notice that, faced with the disdain of others, we catch a glimpse of Zacchaeus' incredible conversion. Standing there, he declares to the Lord, *"Look, I will give half my income to the poor, and if I've cheated anyone, I will pay them back fourfold."*

"I will give half my income" – he becomes generous.

"to the poor" – he becomes compassionate.

"if I've cheated anyone, I will pay them back fourfold" – Zacchaeus becomes honest.

Zacchaeus went from being a taker to a giver, a hardened tax collector to a compassionate soul, a cheater to a man of integrity—all because Jesus turned His clarifying gaze upon him and saw him: not as short, but as whole; not as rich, but as valuable; not as a sinner, but as a child of Abraham. In that moment, his heart was transformed. This is the day of his salvation! No longer did he need to push his way to the front; he now knew he had a place. No longer did he feel ashamed of who he was or what he had, for he recognized his true worth. No longer did he feel compelled to take more than he needed—his soul was free to give generously, even beyond the expectations of others. Not only was his life changed, but the effects of his generosity rippled out to bring healing and life to those around him.

This, I believe, is what stewardship is meant to look like. I know that when many of you hear the word "stewardship," you may think first of the church's request for next year's giving estimate, or worry about balancing the needs of the church budget with those of your household. But in this season, I choose instead to reflect on how God turns my heart around and fills it with joy.

You see, I know what it is to feel small—not in terms of my stature, but in every way that our culture and economy whisper that we do not have enough, that we are not enough. You all hear these messages—in commercials urging you to buy more, from bosses with unreasonable expectations, or in the pressure to provide nothing but the best for your family. This is the experience of feeling too small in too large a crowd—losing sight of who you are and getting pushed around by forces beyond your control.

Most of us here know something about what it means to be rich. I have a house, cars, children receiving a quality education, health insurance, and a savings account—more than many around the world can even dream of. And yet, I know—and I suspect you do too—what it feels like to have all that and still feel insecure, afraid that there won't be enough tomorrow.

I know what it's like to receive far more than I can ever give, yet still worry that nothing is ever enough.

Thanks be to God, I have also come to understand what it means to be seen by Christ. Through my own journey and struggles, I have learned about stewardship. Before I became a steward of what I have, God was a steward of me. God created me. God has seen me—not as short or tall, but as whole; not as wealthy or poor, but as valuable; not as a sinner or saint, but as a beloved child.

I don't know exactly how it went for Zacchaeus, but I do know that for me, the journey isn't over. Just like the bills that arrive each month, there are times when worry still creeps in. Yet every month, my tithe to the church feels like a victory—a reminder that I have placed my trust in God, who sees me, who knows me, and who calls me. Because I know I am made whole by the Spirit, because I know that I have value in the Body of Christ, and because I know I am God's child, I will be a steward. I will give—not until it hurts, but until I am filled with joy. I will do my part to build the kingdom and trust that there will be enough.

Every year, when we send out the pledge cards at St. Margaret's, my prayers are simple: That we'll have enough estimated giving to support and grow the ministries of our church. I believe that Christ works through the Church to bring grace into our lives and to heal a hurting world. I support that work, and I invite you to join me in that support.

But my deeper prayer goes far beyond next year's budget. I pray for each one of you—that your lives may be transformed. Like Zacchaeus, I pray that you will meet Christ and that your hearts may be turned by a generous spirit. I pray that gratitude will lift you up, that the fears haunting you will subside, and that you may live fully and freely, just as God has dreamed for you.

Do not doubt that God dreams for you—dreams of healing, peace, and joy. Salvation will come to your house too, "For the Son of Man came to seek and to save the lost." He is looking for you, as well.

# BEATITUDES

THE REV. CINDY FRIBOURGH
All Saints Sunday, November 6, 2022

*Daniel 7:1-3, 15-18*
*Psalm 149*
*Ephesians 1:11-23*
*Luke 6:20-31*

How odd. Blessed are you who are poor, hungry, and stressed out. When people hate you, exclude you, and insult you because of your beliefs, you are blessed. Be joyful. What?

Woe to you who are rich, have plenty to eat, are deliriously happy, and are held in high regard by others. Your future is bleak. What?

Love your enemies. Be gracious, kind, and giving to those who hate you. Bless those who abuse you. And when they do horrific things to you, invite them to do it again. And how about those who steal from you—bless them, too. When they do, offer everything else. What? Are you crazy?

Before the Sermon on the Plain, Jesus repeatedly offended the religious authorities. He spoke favorably about despised Gentiles, touched lepers, mingled with tax collectors, relaxed fasting requirements for his disciples, and even allowed them to work on the Sabbath. And, speaking of which, Jesus himself was guilty of healing on the Sabbath—after all, some argued that one should not do the work of God on the Lord's Day.

The scribes and Pharisees were furious with Jesus' violations of traditional law. They were not open to a different way to see, interpret, and live out the love of God, nor were they willing to allow him to undermine their power and authority—or to make them look foolish.

In this conflicted setting, Jesus chose his twelve apostles, gathered folks from across the region, and began to preach—starting with the passage we heard today, known as the Beatitudes. "Beatitude" comes from the Latin *beatitudo*, meaning blessedness. In Jesus' day, the expression "blessed are ..." carried the promise of divine joy and perfect happiness.

You, who are poor, hungry, grieving, excluded, and oppressed for your faith, you are blessed. But what about those who are rich, full, happy, and held in high esteem? Not so much.

Perhaps Jesus' underlying message was not just to assure the oppressed that they too are worthy of God's love and divine happiness, but also to challenge those who live abundantly. It calls us to pause, examine our good life and our identity, become meeker, offer ourselves to God's service, and be radically generous to everyone.

Bestow blessing with wild abandon—just like Jesus. Bless everybody, even those you think "don't deserve it." There's always at least one person or entity you can think of that "doesn't deserve it."

Blessed are the drug dealers, wicked politicians, owners of sweatshops, and leaders of oppressive nations—those who make evil choices, who murder, steal, lie, cheat, commit adultery, covet their neighbor's possessions, curse, and forget all about the Sabbath.

It hurts to say that out loud. Dear sweet Jesus—don't bless them. Not them. But whether we like it or not, blessed are all children of God.

Even those who do horrific things—those who seemingly "don't deserve it"—and when we really get down to it, "those who don't deserve it" includes us. We are all notorious sinners in some way. But God loves us anyway. God forgives us, offers redemption through Jesus Christ, and grants us eternal life. God accepts our sinful selves just as we are. That is grace, and God's grace has no boundaries or stipulations.

Grace is bestowed on you and me—and everyone— including those who have brought horror into others' lives, those with differing political views, and anyone who may not be "just like us" in one way or another.

The Beatitudes are more than a series of blessings; they are a challenge for us to reflect on our own blessings and sins—and to be a blessing for others. They call us to be the church, to make Jesus present, visible, and manifest in the dark corners of the world, and to be the voice of Jesus when others try to silence those who speak the truth.

Martin Luther King Jr. wrote in his "Letter from a Birmingham Jail:"

There was a time when the church was very powerful—in the time when the early Christians rejoiced at being deemed worthy to suffer for what they believed. In those days, the church was not merely a thermometer that recorded the ideas and principles of popular opinion; it was a thermostat that transformed the mores of society ... If today's church does not recapture the sacrificial spirit of the early church, it will lose its authenticity, forfeit the loyalty of millions, and be dismissed as an irrelevant social club with no meaning.[8]

The Beatitudes are a call to be that powerful, transformative church—and to know that what we say, think, and do matters.

It does matter. Do we bless the poor, hungry, and grieving—or look the other way? Do we assume someone else will take care of it? Are we so overwhelmed by the extent of poverty, hunger, and grief that we decide we can't make a difference, and so we melt down and do nothing?

It does matter. It matters that we rise up and be the saints of Jesus Christ.

This Sunday, we celebrate All Saints Day, as well as the first anniversary of our ministry resettling our Afghan refugee family. Blessed are the saints who work with the displaced and the homeless.

This All Saints Day, we also lift up those who share a meal with the veterans of St. Francis House, who fill the Little Free Food Pantry, and who pack our children's backpacks with food for neighbors who are struggling. Blessed are the saints who feed the hungry.

We lift up those who visit the sick and elderly, those in prison, those with terminal illness, and those who grieve. Blessed are the saints who offer the gift of presence in lonely, painful times.

We lift up those who give so generously of their time and talent to make our worship beautiful and meaningful, who teach, serve in the leadership of our church—those who gather for prayer, reside in our hearts, or join us in spirit.

Blessed are we, the simultaneous sinners and saints of God—blessed so that we may, in turn, bless others.

35

# LOVE WILL LEAVE ITS MARK

THE REV. MARY VANO
The Feast of St. Margaret's – November 13, 2022

*Ephesians 3:16-21 (specially appointed reading)*

As you know, a group of us took a pilgrimage to Scotland this past summer to visit and explore the home of St. Margaret. It was a journey through space and time—a chance to encounter the God who is with us here and now. Before we saw St. Margaret, we traveled back to the origins of Christianity in Scotland. We journeyed to the year 563, when St. Columba established a mission on Iona. We traveled by land and sea to reach that tiny island from which the Christian mission began. Like thousands of pilgrims over the centuries, we walked among the ruins of the old Benedictine nunnery and worshiped in the rebuilt abbey on the very site where Columba first gathered his monks.

From Iona, we crossed Scotland and moved into the 7th century to meet St. Aidan and St. Cuthbert at the Holy Island of Lindisfarne. Between Iona and Lindisfarne, most of the pagan populations of Scotland and England embraced Christ. At Holy Island, we again walked among the ruins of a once-magnificent monastery and joined the Anglican churchgoers for Sunday communion.

Finally, we traveled into the 11th century to find the home of Queen Margaret at Dunfermline. Although the capital later moved across the Firth of Forth to Edinburgh, Dunfermline is where Margaret became queen when she married Malcolm. It was there that she fed the hungry from her own banquet hall and invited Benedictine monks to establish a priory—an effort to unite the Christians of Scotland with the rest of the world. At Dunfermline, we gathered around Margaret's shrine, toured the hollowed remains of the abbey she built, and stood within the church founded on the very foundation she laid.

On this holy pilgrimage, I couldn't help but notice the marks of destruction at each of the places we visited. These ancient churches and abbeys by time; they were ravaged by people. Viking raiders tore through in the 8th and 9th centuries, at one point murdering 68 monks at Iona. Then, in the 16th century, the Protestant Reformation brought its own violence: monasteries were closed, treasures were seized to fund the state, and buildings were destroyed. Yet, despite these marks of deconstruction and violence that have faded over time at Iona, Lindisfarne, and Dunfermline, the deep presence of God remains. Ministry still springs forth. The Good News of God's kingdom is still proclaimed. The indelible marks of faith, hope, and love remain.

Even as human tendencies toward destruction have brought raids, warfare, greed, and conflict, they could not stop the power of God working through those saints in ways they could scarcely imagine—beyond anything they had asked for. Violence did not stop the church from giving glory to God from generation to generation. I returned from that pilgrimage fortified for our own time.

Looking around today, I see forces of destruction that will leave their mark on our society for years to come—bad religion, growing secularism, apathy and contempt toward our neighbors, gun violence and war, systemic racism, and environmental degradation. These forces are evident even now: we see churches being hollowed out, and the nightly news tells of a culture crippled by animosity and marked by grave memorials to those lost through violence, abuse, and poverty. And we are living with the impacts of our ailing planet. All these forces are leaving their mark.

... and I wonder ... what mark will we leave?

At St. Margaret's Episcopal Church in Little Rock, in the Episcopal Diocese of Arkansas, within the Protestant Episcopal Church of the United States of America, we are part of the worldwide Anglican Communion. As such, we share a common commitment to the mission of God—a mission that, by its very nature, leaves marks. Here is how we articulate the Five Marks of Mission:

1. To proclaim the Good News of the Kingdom.
2. To teach, baptize, and nurture new believers.
3. To respond to human need with loving service.

4. To transform unjust structures in society—to challenge all forms of violence and pursue peace and reconciliation.

5. To strive to safeguard the integrity of creation and to sustain and renew the life of the earth.

Regarding this mission, the late Archbishop Desmond Tutu once said it makes us all aware of the incredible love God has for us. It reminds us: you don't have to earn God's love. God loves you, period. Everything flows from there. In the midst of destructive forces, we have something life-giving to offer. In contrast to those who proclaim a condemning God, we proclaim the Good News of God's extraordinary love shown in Jesus Christ. For those who are hungry and lost without true faith, we can teach and walk with them on the way of love. In a world where apathy leaves so many in need, we can take action and serve with love. Together, we have the power to transform unjust structures, to challenge violence, and to pursue peace. And even now, we have opportunities to safeguard creation and renew the life of the earth. Love will always leave its mark.

So, what are we faithfully asking of God? Are we asking for more new believers? To heal creation? To restore hope? God's answer is already yes—if we, in turn, say yes to what God is asking of us: to proclaim the Good News, to teach, nurture, and serve others, and to make bold changes.

Can you imagine a future of peace and reconciliation? Can you envision the next generation of faithful believers? Can you see a restored creation? God can—and He invites us to imagine it, too. We cannot help create what we cannot imagine.

As we celebrate this St. Margaret's Day, I pray that we will ask God faithfully—ask for our needs, our hopes—and cast a vision for the kingdom of God in our own hometown and our own time. Imagine what is possible in love. And know that God can do infinitely more in love.

Nearly two thousand years ago, the letter to the Ephesians was written to encourage Christians. I wonder if its author knew that his prayer for us would echo through every generation. Today, as we face our own challenges, we are reminded to place our trust in God, "whose power working in us can do infinitely more than we can ask or imagine." This is how we will leave a mark that outlasts deconstruction and violence: by giving "glory to God from generation to generation in the church, and in Christ Jesus forever and ever." This is how our love will leave its mark.

# MARKS OF HOPE

The Rev. Michaelene Miller
Proper 29 – Christ the King, November 20, 2022

*Jeremiah 23:1-6*
*Canticle 16*
*Colossians 1:11-20*
*Luke 23:33-43*

Well, we made it! We have reached the end of another year—at least, it's the end of the church calendar year. Liturgically, today marks the last Sunday before the new year. In our calendar, today is a hinge point between this long, Ordinary season after Pentecost and the coming Advent weeks of preparation, celebrated as Christ the King Sunday.

On this day, we recenter our lives around Jesus before we join in midwifing what is being born into the world this Advent. As we celebrate the reign of Christ as King, we take an intentional pause to remember what His kingship means for our lives as Christians. What kind of king is Jesus? What does it mean to live and thrive under His rule?

To see Jesus clearly, we must first set aside our earthly expectations of royalty—kings of power, self-serving privilege, and rigid monarchies that merely preserve the status quo. Once we do that, we can begin to recognize Jesus' messiahship at work all around us and catch a glimpse of the holy in our midst.

Unlike the first disciples, we have the benefit of hindsight and the convenience of studying the Gospel of Luke, which repeatedly reveals the unexpected and counter-cultural nature of Jesus' kingship. Throughout this long season, we journeyed with Jesus toward Jerusalem: He gathered crowds, ate with sinners, and healed the sick—breaking the rules to care for and love those around Him.

Last week, on St. Margaret's feast day, we read in Luke that Jesus is the anointed King who brings good news to the poor, proclaims release for the captives, restores sight to the blind, and sets the oppressed free. And then, with a jolt of transition in today's Gospel passage, we see where this earthly ministry led Him: we find Him hanging, crucified on a criminal's cross, flanked by two others—men who likely fought for freedom and dared to dream of a world beyond Roman domination.

It is in this scene that we encounter Christ today on this feast day. As Christians, we proclaim that Christ is the ultimate lens through which we see and experience the world. Jesus—who brought good news, liberation, and clarity—is our King, even as He endures the cross.

Today, we celebrate that Jesus, this unexpected type of King, is our compass and guide through life. Encountering Him now reminds us that we can turn to Jesus in ordinary moments, celebrations, times of expectation, and especially in times of despair.

This resilient faith amid despair is powerfully illustrated by the criminal crucified beside Jesus. While a crowd watched, religious leaders scoffed, soldiers mocked, and another criminal derided, this one man caught a glimpse of the holy kingdom and the truth Jesus had preached all His life. In his moment of extreme desperation, he saw past the imminence of death—both his own and Jesus'—to embrace the hope that shone even on the cross.

He had eyes to see the act of grace unfolding beside him, and ears to hear the truth in the taunts. Jesus, being executed on a cross, was indeed the "Messiah of God, His chosen one," the "King," and Savior of all.

In that most desperate hour, when worldly powers and earthly judges threatened to take everything, when his own dream of revolution was dying, this criminal recognized the dream of God revealed by Jesus. He pleaded, *"Remember me when you come into your kingdom,"* and Jesus answered, *"Today, you will be with me in Paradise."* In that moment, God's active, transformative mission was made clear—a mission that continues to work in the world today.

Even on the cross, Jesus brought release and restored vision. The criminal's eyes were transformed; in that unlikely setting, he read a message of hope—a message that reminds me of the ancient stepwells of India.

41

Stepwells—perhaps an unfamiliar term for many in the western hemisphere—are ancient man-made irrigation tanks built in the 1100s in and around Western India. These structures, dug deep into the earth, were created to collect and store rain during the monsoon season so that communities could survive long, dry spells. Their designs vary from modest pits with simple descending steps to grand, intricately carved chambers that span vast underground spaces.

My husband, who visited New Delhi in high school, described these stepwells as an upside-down version of the great pyramids—an apt image for the role-reversing, status-quo-flipping kingship of our King, Jesus the Messiah.

Jesus taught that those who are last will be first and the first last. He made it clear that He did not come to be served but to serve. He is our upside-down King.

These stepwells did more than just store water. In the wet season, they brimmed like abundant lakes. Yet, their true beauty emerged as the waters receded. As the source of life dwindled, messages of hope—carved by ancestors—appeared on the walls, reassuring the people that others had endured and survived even the worst droughts.

The work of those carvings, done in times of fear and despair, passed on a message of hope: even in the deepest drought, there is an invitation to create hope. As the waters recede, instead of being overcome by fear, the people are able to read a story of hope on the walls: others have been here before, and they survived.

Understood here, is the duty of the community to continue to mark out a map of hope for future generations if the waters were to ever recede below the last message. That in that moment of deepest despair and drought, their eyes might see an invitation to do the work of hope, to make their own mark, and become a profession for future generations.

For many, these days might feel like dry times if not a time of full-on drought. Especially in our home state of Arkansas, I know there are many who worry about their bodily autonomy. I know there are families who worry that their marriage will not be protected. And I know there are those who wondered and worried about the literal drought that brought on a burn ban across the state that lasted much further and longer into the Fall than usual.

So, what do we do in these or other dry times? From the creators of the stepwells, we learn that we can't become petrified. We must constantly turn towards the creative practices that connect us. They didn't know what the next moment of their lives would hold, but they had some kind of hope that what they carved into the well wall at that moment could possibly bring a message of hope to future generations who might end up at that same depth of despair. Making creative marks upon the walls of the wells in times of uncertainty—this was their spiritual practice of hope.

What are the creative and spiritual practices that connect you to God and one another? How do you leave signs and directions for future generations who may face their own droughts? For some, it might be as simple as posting a status update or revisiting a cherished memory on social media. For others, it is the faithful act of gathering each Sunday—participating in the apostles' teaching, breaking bread, and praying together. These practices leave their mark. They write the creative signatures of our faith on the walls of our lives.

In today's Gospel story of the crucifixion, we catch a glimpse of the holy, creative mark God left on the cross—a mark that transforms even the violence of the world into resurrection, love, and healing. This is the message of hope we center on every time we gather for worship and the Eucharist.

What are your personal creative practices that move you toward holy hope, toward God and each other with care? As we turn toward the Advent season of preparation, let us renew and recommit to those spiritual practices that help us midwife hope into the world. What signs will we leave behind for future generations?

# PREPARING FOR THE LIGHT

THE REV. MARY VANO
First Sunday of Advent – November 27, 2022

*Isaiah 2:1-5*
*Psalm 122*
*Romans 13:11-14*
*Matthew 24:36-44*

A few months ago, I read a news article[9] about a Canadian couple, Edith and Sebastian, and their four children: Mia, Leo, Colin, and Laurent. Mia, now 12, is the oldest, and when she was just three years old, Edith and Sebastian noticed she was having trouble with her vision. They took her to see a specialist, and after several years, she was diagnosed with retinitis pigmentosa—a rare genetic disorder that causes gradual vision loss. Although one sibling remains unaffected, the other three will almost certainly be impacted. *"But about that day and hour, no one knows."*

Jesus said, *"Keep awake therefore."*

Edith and Sebastian had no choice but to come to terms with the diagnosis and its implications. With no effective treatment or cure available, they cannot predict how quickly the disease will progress in their children—but they expect that blindness may come by mid-life.

*"Therefore,"* Jesus said, *"you also must be ready."*

Remaining hopeful, yet accepting that darkness is inevitable, these parents decided they must prepare their children for it. When Mia's doctor suggested helping her build a cache of "visual memories," an idea was born. They began saving money and planning to spend a year together touring the world.

What better way to focus on the light than to intentionally go out and see the beauty of the world? Edith says she wants her children to experience the beauty that surrounds us—and she shares it with the rest of us. I follow her on Facebook along with more than 30,000 others, and in the months they have been traveling, I've seen breathtaking images from

Mongolia, Malaysia, scuba diving, surfing, and more. With great intention, they are traveling to witness the light in the world.

Creating visual memories is only one goal for their year of travel. They also hope to build resilience in their children. Mia, Colin, and Laurent face challenges ahead. While they can anticipate some of the difficulties that accompany vision loss and eventual blindness, they cannot plan for everything. So, they are approaching their journey in a flexible way. They left home in March without a detailed itinerary. Instead of planning every step, they arrange loose plans about a month ahead and otherwise go with the flow. They expect unwelcome surprises, unintended detours, delays, and disappointments. In this way, travel itself becomes a teacher—helping their children build the resilience needed to handle the unexpected.

By building resilience and seizing the opportunity to see the beauty of the world while they can, Mia, Colin, and Laurent are preparing for the darkness—and, I suspect, transforming it. Along the way, they are also deepening family bonds. As they explore together, learn together, and go on adventures, they create a small community with shared experiences and a common vision. They come to know the intimate details of each other's personalities and perspectives, learning to trust and rely on one another. Their shared knowledge of the light, combined with the resilience they develop and the deep bonds of love within the family, will make the dark a lot less daunting.

On this first Sunday of Advent—the first Sunday of the Church Year—we take our Gospel reading from the 24th chapter of Matthew. These few verses, drawn from what is essentially Jesus' last sermon in this gospel, are prompted by the sense that disaster is imminent. Jesus told his disciples that the temple would be destroyed, and they longed to know when it would happen and what signs would reveal that Jesus was coming to set all things right. In response, Jesus emphasizes that hard things will occur. Some of these challenges we cannot prevent or even plan for We must expect the unexpected and be prepared for suffering. But—do not give up hope! In fact, we should dive even deeper into hope. We're not just preparing for the darkness, which will come for all of us; we're preparing for the light—the ultimate end toward which we are headed.

As Paul wrote to the Romans, "*For salvation is nearer to us now than when we became believers; the night is far gone, the day is near.*" It is the light we are preparing for, even as we work to transform the darkness.

So, as we embark on a new year, I wonder if we might take Edith, Sebastian, and their family as our tour guides. When Jesus calls upon us to "keep awake, therefore," I suspect He means that we should do what they are doing on their world tour. Keep awake:

- Go and see the light of the world. Learn to look for the beauty, the goodness, the joy, and the love. This is how we learn to see God at work in the world. It is how we discern the light even on the dark days.

- Build your resilience. You don't have to travel the world or seek out trouble, but you will likely need to take risks—trusting that God will hold you when things do not go as planned. Your risks might include pursuing a vocation, starting a new relationship, volunteering for a cause, or even letting go of something no longer needed. Whatever risks you choose, anchor your trust and resilience in God's unfailing love.

- Don't go alone. The Church has always been the community with which we journey in faith. It is worth intentionally cultivating deep bonds of love. Sometimes it is easier to see the light when a friend points it out. We are much more resilient and hopeful when we know we are not alone. As Jesus calls us to keep awake at the beginning of another year, it is a call to remember to get together, to eat together, to learn together, to pray together, and to serve together.

By doing all these things, we not only transform the darkness—we prepare for the light.

# REPENT AND REFINE

THE REV. MICHAELENE MILLER
Second Sunday of Advent – December 4, 2022

*Isaiah 11:1-10*
*Psalm 72:1-7, 18-19*
*Romans 15:4-13*
*Matthew 3:1-12*

The Second Sunday of Advent always brings us back to the banks of the Jordan River and to John the Baptist. In our Gospel reading from Matthew, we are taken back to those days when John the Baptist appeared in the wilderness of Judea proclaiming, *"Repent, for the kingdom of heaven has come near."*

All four Gospel narratives include John in the story of Jesus Christ, yet I can't recall a single church nativity pageant that includes John the Baptist on its casting list. If we did include him, he would surely be depicted as the most disheveled and grumpiest character—wild hair, wilder eyes, mumbling incessantly about sin and righteousness. He'd likely end the show by crying out to the audience about their need to repent and be cleansed.

Imagine the final scene, set 30 years into Jesus' life—it would probably end with some dramatic asperges, as John would cast water from the stage to remind everyone to live out their baptism. He'd send us home drenched, wide awake, and alert. Even though we rarely include John in our Christmas Eve services, all four Gospel writers agree: there is no Gospel of Jesus without John the Baptist.

Every Second Sunday of Advent, we are called to pay attention to this fact. Today, we are reminded that the proper unfolding of the season's holy drama depends on the disheveled baptizer's opening act. Today, we focus our attention on John.

John took his role—to declare the imminent arrival of the coming Messiah—very seriously. He knew his part well. He is the one of whom the prophet Isaiah spoke: *"The voice of one crying out in the wilderness: 'Prepare the way of the Lord, make his paths straight."* And he delivered his lines clearly and unflinchingly. Entering the scene on cue, appearing in the wilderness, John proclaims: Repent! Because God's kingdom has come close.

It helps to read about John across the different Gospels. In each, we catch another glimpse of his proclamation; together, they give us the fullest picture and the clearest message. In Matthew's and Mark's Gospels, we receive his well-known physical description—a picture of an eccentric, wide-eyed wilderness prophet, eating locusts and wild honey and wearing camel's hair with a leather belt around his waist. In the Gospel of John, we encounter him as the Witness, bravely pointing to Jesus and testifying to his faith in Him as the Christ, the Messiah—even amid intense scrutiny and questioning by the religious elites.

Perhaps it is John's location in the wilderness—far from the power, security, and comforts of the city—that allows him to be so rooted, clear-minded, and unwavering in his faith. The wilderness is a place of danger and testing. There, one must remain alert and prepared; it is a place of vulnerability that quickly strips away any illusions of self-sufficiency and control.

It was also in the wilderness that Israel was formed. During their years of wandering, the people came to know God and were prepared to receive His promises. It was in the wilderness that they learned to see and hear God's call more clearly.

John the Baptizer, that witness in the wilderness, saw clearly and called others to do the same. On this Second Sunday of Advent, he calls us to the wilderness—to come into a place where we see clearly our dependence on God and our constant need to repent and return to that relationship.

Dependent solely on God, John was not swayed by power or intimidated by authorities. In the wilderness, he existed beyond the reach and control of the empire. In our Gospel passage for today, we see him calling out to the power and authority in his midst. John denounces the Pharisees and Sadducees who come for baptism, declaring, *"You brood of vipers! Who warned you to flee from the wrath to come? Bear fruit worthy of repentance."*

When we read across Luke's Gospel, we, too, hear ourselves called out by John and drawn into this conversation about repentance. In Luke, he addresses the entire crowd gathered before him—and, by extension, us as we gather here now. *"You brood of vipers! ... Bear fruit worthy of repentance. Do not presume to say to yourselves, 'We have Abraham as our ancestor'"* John calls the Sadducees, Pharisees, and all who listen to wake up and realize that their claim as descendants of Abraham (or, in our case, disciples of Christ by title alone) will not save them from the coming judgment. Neither a brief moment of ritual nor mere birth status can substitute for true repentance and an ongoing conversion of life.

John is clear: Bear fruit worthy of repentance. More is required. Using the metaphor of a tree that bears good fruit, he describes the need for ethical reform—where one's lifestyle and external actions reveal the genuine transformation of the heart. John gives the Sadducees, Pharisees, and the entire listening crowd an opportunity to wake up to their unexamined assumptions. He calls them to repent. They must be capable of reform. This is good news.

It is also in the Gospel of Luke that we receive the most complete account of John's preaching. Luke extends John's sermon, and as the crowd begins to wake up and realize that their original plan is insufficient, they ask him, *"What then should we do?"* Tax collectors ask, "Teacher, what should we do?" Soldiers ask, "And we, what should we do?" To these seemingly simple, even mundane, questions, John prescribes lessons reminiscent of childhood: share your extra coats and food, and do not take what is not yours.

The repetition of this question underscores that each context in life may require a different response. One group is to give, another to receive; one is to be empowered, another to relinquish power. These actions, these fruits, are what John calls "worthy of repentance."

For John, repentance is not merely the Old Testament practice of donning sackcloth and ashes. He does not call the people to radical acts of revolution—denouncing their ties to the Empire to retreat into the desert. Instead, John calls for individuals to address the needs of others through everyday, mundane acts of love. His prescriptions reveal that the work of repentance and reconciliation in the world begins with the individual.

John prophetically calls the crowd into a lifestyle—a way of living that, though unique to each context, reflects genuine repentance. In this way, each person will discover a life of Baptismal integrity, where outward actions reveal the inward transformation of identity. John calls us to sacramental living. It may seem a modest transformation—simply sharing and avoiding the abuse of power—but its ripples are profound. This is good news.

And then John declares that the Messiah, *"who is more powerful than I am, is coming."* God is drawing near, and Christ is coming into the world. With fire, He will refine; He will separate the wheat from the chaff— burning away all that is not good in us and in the world. God is breaking in and making all things new. Good news indeed.

So, what is John's role in our lives this Advent? In these days, how does John prepare us for God's continued eruption into the world? First, John still calls out to us today to awaken from our own assumptions and narratives that separate us from God and prevent us from loving our neighbor. It is not a condemnation—it is an invitation. He invites us to reorient and return to God.

These days, John still warns us against becoming stuck in separation. He calls us to reorient ourselves toward God, time and again, to close the distance and return to right relationship with both God and our neighbor. He makes it clear that this must be the unending rhythm of our lives.

Each day, we must ask ourselves: What should I do? What fruit am I bearing today? Who is being transformed by my love? What does turning toward God and neighbor look like in my life today? In these actions, we join John the Baptizer—the witness in the wilderness—in preparing and transforming the world, for God is near and calls out: the kingdom of heaven has come near.

# STAND STILL

THE REV. MARY VANC
Third Sunday of Advent – December 11, 2022

*Isaiah 35:1-10*
*Psalm 146:4-9*
*James 5:7-10*
*Matthew 11:2-11*

The only person stranger than John the Baptist is Jesus himself—which is saying a lot. In last week's sermon, Michaelene reminded us just how strange John the Baptist was. Everything about him—from his clothing to his diet to his choice of location—was wild. Like the ancient prophet Elijah, John wore camel hair and a leather belt, a far cry from first-century fashion. Like the Israelites who wandered the desert before him, he ate locusts and wild honey. And he preached mostly by the Jordan River, on the borderlands between the wilderness and the Promised Land.

All of this is strange, yet the highest mark of his strangeness was his willingness to speak truth to power. He not only called out the Sadducees and Pharisees for their hypocrisy, but he also publicly criticized the king for his inappropriate marriage. This boldness is why we find him today—in the eleventh chapter of Matthew's Gospel, in prison. And what is John wondering about in prison? "Why is Jesus so strange?"

Jesus is not what John expected. I can imagine him pacing his cell—eight steps toward one wall, eight steps back toward the other—pounding an ever-deeper groove in the ground as he wonders where things went so wrong. John always knew he was not the chosen one—never the Messiah—but he had passionately embraced the role he believed God had called him to. He was the one crying out in the wilderness, "Prepare the way of the Lord." He wandered around the Jordan, boldly proclaiming a message of repentance. He called people to a new kind of purity—a purity that transcended ritual and tribal boundaries, a purity of spirit and soul. He baptized the repentant with water for a new life, and the crowds came to see and hear him.

But had it all been for naught? Had he wasted all that time wandering in the wilderness and eating locusts so that people might receive a little water—only to sin again? John had pointed everyone to Jesus, whom he expected to baptize with fire, to wield a winnowing fork that would gather the wheat and burn the chaff with unquenchable fire, thereby changing the world.

Yet, some months after Jesus' baptism—and sometime after John ended up in jail—he finds himself alone and confined. And not only confined but confused. Where is the Messiah to overthrow these ungodly rulers and set him free? Where is the judgment? Where is the fire? Why must we wait for the kingdom of heaven to be realized? Pacing his cell, John wonders if he has chosen the wrong Messiah, if he has wasted his life and best efforts. With doubt and disillusionment, he sends a message to Jesus: *"Are you the one who is to come? Or are we to wait for another?"*

While out teaching, Jesus receives John's message. His audience now includes the tax collectors, prostitutes, and other sinners whom Jesus had befriended even before they repented. Though Jesus' teachings have been challenging, He has not yet wielded a winnowing fork nor brought down fire. In response to John's question, Jesus sends back messengers to report on what they have seen and heard. It is exactly as the prophet Isaiah envisioned: the blind receive their sight, the lame walk, the lepers are cleansed, the deaf hear, the dead are raised, and the poor have good news brought to them. Jesus adds, *"Blessed is anyone who takes no offense at me."*

Blessed is John—even though he doubts because reality has not met his expectations, because God has not met those expectations. And blessed are we, too. Blessed are we, even when we doubt, because life in the present moment often fails to live up to our hopes, and we are unsure where God is in this messy life. Yet, we are blessed, beloved. John is blessed, even though he didn't quite get everything right; he thought he knew what the Messiah would be, only to find that he was mistaken on some points. Blessed are we, too, even when we don't get everything right. We are blessed not because we are perfect, but because God loves us.

Perhaps it is a little odd on the third Sunday of Advent to ponder John the Baptist's disappointments. Yet for many, the weeks leading up to Christmas are filled with doubt, disappointment, and grief. John is not alone in feeling that the expectations upon which he built his life have led him astray. He is not alone in feeling estranged from the hope that once sustained him, or in feeling that the new world he was promised was nothing but a sham.

He was not alone—and that is precisely the Good News Jesus sent to him by return messenger: "*The blind receive their sight, the lame walk, the lepers are cleansed, the deaf hear, the dead are raised, and the poor have good news brought to them.*" Isaiah's vision is that those isolated by blindness will be restored, those left behind will walk again, and those imprisoned by illness, deafness, or even death will be set free. John is not alone, because the mission of the Messiah—the purpose of God incarnate in Jesus Christ—is to meet us in our pain, in our suffering, and in our loneliness, and to restore us. God at Christmas took on human flesh so that He might meet us in our darkest prisons and lead us from death to life. John is not alone. And neither are we.

There is a poem by David Wagoner called "Lost":

Stand still. The trees ahead and bushes beside you
are not lost. Wherever you are is called Here
and you must treat it as a powerful stranger.[10]

I read this poem this week in a book by Pádraig Ó Tuama. In his book *In the Shelter*, the author writes, "In the world of Wagoner's poem, it is the rooted things—trees and bushes—that tell the truth to the person who is lost, the person with legs and fear who wishes to be elsewhere. The person must stand still, feel their body still on the ground where they are, in order to learn the wisdom."[11]

"Stand still," the poet says. "Go and tell what you see and hear," Jesus says. Though much of the kingdom of heaven is not yet realized, if we look and see what God has done—and is doing—we can find hope for what is to come. We can look back on our lives and see the marks of grace left by a God who has been at work for our healing. We can see how, even in these dark times, people bring the light of God through acts of kindness and generosity. If we listen carefully, we can hear the love that draws us closer to God and transforms us.

Perhaps this is the strangest message of all, but let this be your hope, dear friends: you are not alone in the dark. God is with you and for you. And when you can't see from your own vantage point, send out messengers who will bring back good news. Stand still and listen to the voice of the powerful stranger in our midst.

# ALL IN WITH GOD

The Rev. Michaelene Miller
Fourth Sunday of Advent – December 18, 2022

*Isaiah 7:10-16*
*Psalm 80:1-7, 16-18*
*Romans 1:1-7*
*Matthew 1:18-25*

In the hurriedness of this final week of Advent—when cultural cues seem to propel us toward Christmas with relentless force—I invite you to try and linger. Maybe you're already bursting with anticipation and ready to skip ahead to the next beloved chapter of this story. I know I'm finding it hard to wait, but I invite all of us to pause, to linger together on this Fourth Sunday of Advent, and to lean into the story we encounter in the Gospel of Matthew.

Linger we must, even if the place we are called to dwell is not easy or restful. This space may be fraught with its own problems, scandals, and anticipatory anxieties, but in our lingering, we find an opportunity to encounter the deep love of this season—a love of courageous commitment that leads to compassion, care, and living a life that is truly ALL IN with God.

For the past few weeks of Advent, we have journeyed with John the Baptist in the wilderness, where he prepared the way for the Lord along the Jordan River—first amid bustling crowds, then later alone in jail, with only disillusionment and questions for company.

This week, however, as we draw ever closer to the arrival of God enfleshed in Jesus the Christ child, we are transported backward in the Scripture story, back to chapter 1, where we are invited to worry, to dream, and to take a life-changing step alongside Joseph.

On this final Sunday of Advent, we return to the beginning to remember what it takes to prepare. We remind ourselves once again that it takes our whole self to bring new life, light, and renewal into the world.

Our passage encompasses a tense moment—a rare occasion in Scripture and our lectionary when the focus is on Joseph, a descendant of the House of David and Mary's betrothed, who is too often sidelined as a supporting character in the nativity story.

In the midst of learning that his betrothed is pregnant—and finding himself in a situation he did not create—we are told that Joseph is also a righteous man, one who knows and follows the law. Likely, he is a man who does not relish stirring up trouble or drawing attention to himself. With all that is unfolding, we can infer that Joseph was likely struggling, frightened, and desperate to save face in a messy situation.

Our Gospel of Matthew sets the scene: the birth of Jesus, the Messiah, took place in this very way. Although the moment of birth is fleeting in Matthew's narrative, the Gospel effectively introduces us to a newborn named Jesus and Emmanuel—"The God Who Saves, Is With Us."

There are several things I try to hold in my biblical imagination when I think about Jesus. First and foremost, that Jesus is God incarnate—God enfleshed, God come close, God with us. And this is central to our passage today. After recounting Joseph's dream, the Gospel author explains that all this happened to fulfill the prophecy: *"Look, the virgin shall conceive and bear a son, and they shall name him Emmanuel,"* meaning "God is with us." In Jesus, God does something entirely new—he breaks every rule by putting on flesh and coming near.

I also hold in my mind that God chose to enter the world through Jesus—a brown-bodied Palestinian Jewish man born into a working-class family that once fled across borders as political refugees. I picture Jesus as a tiny, fussy, vulnerable baby, learning how to latch and nurse, how to walk and talk, scraping a few knees and grappling with the Scriptures and laws that would guide His life.

Yet, there is more that I often forget to mention: this passage from Matthew also tells us that Jesus was adopted. Likely, it was Joseph—his righteous, all-in stepparent—who, convinced by God's calling, embraced Jesus as his own, passed on his knowledge of the law, and provided the family legacy needed to legitimize Mary's child as the Messiah, connecting Jesus to the line of David.

Biblical commentator Debby Thomas reminds us:

> Interestingly, in the genealogy of Jesus's ancestors, [the Gospel author] mentions Abraham—the patriarch who abandoned his son, Ishmael, and twice endangered his wife's safety in order to save his own skin. He mentions Jacob, the trickster usurper who humiliated his older brother. Mentions David, who slept with another man's wife and then ordered that man's murder to protect his reputation. He mentions Tamar, who pretended to be a sex worker, and Rahab, who was one. These are just a few representative samples.
>
> Notice anything? Anything like messiness? Complication? Scandal? Sin? How interesting that God, who could have chosen any genealogy for his Son, chose a long line of brokenness, imperfection, dishonor, and scandal. The perfect backdrop, I suppose, for his beautiful works of restoration, healing, hope, and second chances.[12]

It is from this very mess that Joseph emerges, and it is into another blended, complicated family system that he is called.

After resolving to make the cleanest, quietest decision he could imagine to extricate himself from this scandal, Joseph is visited by a messenger of God in a dream. The angel of the Lord says, "Do not be afraid, Joseph, son of David! You have a role to play in this new thing God is doing: to welcome the child into your lineage by embracing him as your own, naming him your heir, helping to form and raise him, and supporting Mary every step of the way." The angel calls out, "Take courage, go all in, and love!"

This opening story of the Good News of Jesus Christ is an account of Joseph being called to go all in—to courageously commit, to embrace a mess he did not create but was called to care for by God. And Joseph chose God back. When he awoke, he did exactly as the Angel commanded.

57

Joseph names Jesus, legally adopting him as his heir, and goes all in on what would become one of history's most complicated, blended families: Mary, Joseph, Jesus, and God. It would not be an easy, quiet path, but Joseph knew they would not be alone—God was with them.

Through all of this, Joseph had to set aside his previous understanding and the prevailing interpretations of God's will and law in favor of this new Word of God growing within Mary's womb. In doing so, we catch a glimpse of how Jesus was not only born of Mary but also became Joseph's son in every meaningful way—how Joseph became a parent, imparting his wisdom and faith to Jesus.

As the story continues, we see Joseph beginning to live into the tension of "you have heard that it was said, but I say to you," a tension that recurs throughout the Gospel of Matthew and which Jesus would further unfold in His ministry.

Like Joseph, we are called into this all-in lifestyle—a messy, blended family of the Body of Christ. We are invited into the mess, even if we aren't fully ready.

I don't imagine Joseph or Mary were ever completely prepared for the mess that awaited them as Jesus' parents. I don't know any parents who are. Nor could the disciples of Christ have fully prepared for what was to come. At some point, we must commit and go all in with God—courageously entering the mess, because God did and does every day.

God did not wait. Madeleine L'Engle, in her poem *First Coming*, writes:

> He did not wait till the world was ready,
> till men and nations were at peace.
> He came when the Heavens were unsteady,
> and prisoners cried out for release.
>
> He did not wait for the perfect time.
> He came when the need was deep and great.
> He dined with sinners in all their grime,
> turned water into wine.

He did not wait till hearts were pure.
In joy he came to a tarnished world of sin and doubt.
To a world like ours, of anguished shame
he came, and his Light would not go out.

He came to a world which did not mesh,
to heal its tangles, shield its scorn.
In the mystery of the Word made Flesh
the Maker of the stars was born.

We cannot wait till the world is sane
to raise our songs with joyful voice,
for to share our grief, to touch our pain,
He came with Love: Rejoice! Rejoice![13]

So, beloved and blended family of God, even as we linger here, let us know and trust that God already came—and will come again—daily into our hearts, our messy lives, and our complicated world. Let us trust that God is all in, not waiting for the mess to clear or the problems to be solved. And so, as we prepare and try, with Joseph as our model for courageous love and compassionate care, let us embrace the holy mess and go all in with God, helping to bring new life, light, and renewal to this world.

# UNTO YOU A CHILD IS BORN

THE REV. MARY VANO
Christmas Eve – December 24, 2022

*Isaiah 9:2-7*
*Psalm 96*
*Titus 2:11-14*
*Luke 2:1-14(15-20)*

*"For unto you, a child is born ..."*

It's incredible, isn't it? Shocking. *"For unto you, a child is born."* My favorite little nativity set comes from the collection by the artist Lori Mitchell. They are handcrafted metal and resin figures of Mary and Joseph and the baby Jesus, and what I love best about them is the look of utter surprise on their faces. They are wide-eyed and slack-jawed—all three of them! Joseph's little wire arms hang at his side as if he has no clue what to do now. The tilt of Mary's raised eyebrows suggests some worry that she didn't get that swaddle quite right. And even little Jesus looks up at his parents as if to say, "Whoa, who could have expected this?!" In contrast to all those peaceful, sweet nativity scenes, this artist has captured the shock of it all. *"For unto you, a child is born."* What do we do now?

It is not unlike how I felt almost twenty years ago, when Stephen and I were sent home from the hospital with our first-born son and an overwhelming feeling that maybe the doctors and nurses were being negligent in letting us take this child home! How could they possibly trust that we knew what to do with this kid?! Beyond a few babysitting gigs, we had never taken responsibility for a newborn human life. What did we know? Not much at all.

We had taken some of those infant care classes, in which we learned a few useful things. We learned the proper technique for swaddling—just like the mother of Jesus, we knew how to wrap our newborn child in such a way as to help him feel secure so that he could rest. It is crucial knowledge that gets you through only the first few months. You have to let the swaddle go as the child grows and find other ways to make them feel safe. Then we learned all the ins and outs of diapering, which turned out to be more complicated than expected. I remember realizing that with super-absorbent 21st Century diapers, at first, I couldn't tell when they were wet. I needed some experience to realize that you could tell by the weight of them. And then there were all the things about nutrition to learn. How to nurse, how often, when to transition to solid foods, and what to do when things weren't working. There was so much to learn, and only a fraction of it could be taught in a classroom!

But the best wisdom I received came from my mother. Mom is an early childhood educator and later received additional training in infant and toddler development. She is the one who taught me that newborns come wired for connection. You might miss a diaper change, or there may be complications when it comes to feeding. But more than anything else, a child needs relationship. They need love. When babies are not held, and when they're not tenderly cared for, it can create a heartbreaking failure to thrive. A baby needs love. It is both the easiest and the most demanding thing of all—the child born unto you needs you.

Whether you are a parent or not, no matter your age, marital status or family situation, Christmas comes again and announces that unto you a child is born, and tonight we will send you home with that newborn love. Each Christmas is our celebration of God incarnate in Jesus Christ. We celebrate tonight that God is with us. We remember the child born and laid in a manger two thousand years ago, and we recognize that divine, sacred love enters into our lives over and over again, with new opportunities all the time to nurture, tend, and grow the love that heals the world. So, yes, tonight we send you home with a newborn love, and it is up to you to figure out what to do next.

How will you nurture love in its infancy? Will you swaddle it tight? Such security is important for the newborn, but it must be shed as love grows. That security is simply the foundation upon which a healthy love will develop and learn to walk and talk. The freedom and purpose of love must begin in a safe and warm embrace.

How will you feed this love? Love needs wholesome nutrition. St. Paul taught us to feed love with patience, kindness, and truth. Patience, because love takes time. Kindness, because irritability, resentment, and spite are like toxic junk food. Truth, because anything we try to build upon lies and half-truths will ultimately fail. With a steady diet of patience, kindness, and truth, love *"bears all things, believes all things, hopes all things, and endures all things."* (1 Corinthians 13:7)

How will you keep love clean and healthy? Not unlike diapering, love requires attentiveness to deal with the waste. We've got to be ready and willing to notice, repenting when we have missed the mark of love and offering forgiveness when others have. It's the only way not to sit in the filth of sin and guilt, but to clean it away and to move ahead in good health.

This is how you might think about caring for the love that God gives you: nurturing it with a balance of security and freedom, nourishing it with patience, kindness, and truth, and tending to it with regular repentance and forgiveness. Perhaps that's as much of an instruction manual as anyone could ever provide for a life of love. But even then—thanks to this child who was born, who lived to be Jesus of Nazareth, who would teach, and heal and call disciples, who would give his life for ours—our faith is not a checklist that indicates failure if any one step is missed or neglected. There's room for error, and a lot of room for grace, because the one most important thing that love asks of us is ourselves. The easiest and most demanding thing of all—the God who comes to you, the love that is born in you, needs you. Like a new child in your life, it doesn't really matter how full your schedule is, or how much you'd rather be watching Netflix. Sacrifices will need to be made, and they will be 100% worth it! God needs you in all your brokenness and vulnerability, in all your amazing talent and beauty. Love came down at Christmas. Love is going home with you. And love needs you. What will you do now?

# WITNESSING GOD ENFLESHED

The Rev. Michaelene Miller
Christmas Day – December 25, 2022

*Isaiah 9:2-7*
*Psalm 96*
*Titus 2:11-14*
*Luke 2:1-14 (15-20)*

Good morning and Happy Feast Day of the Incarnation of our Lord and Savior, Jesus Christ! Merry Christmas Day! I give thanks that we have twelve whole days to focus on the gift and allow the hope of the Incarnation in Christ Jesus to truly find a home in our hearts.

The poet Mary Oliver writes:

> The spirit likes to dress up like this. It needs the body's world,
> ten fingers, instinct
> ten toes, imagination
> shoulders, and all the rest and the dark hug of time
> at night sweetness
> in the black branches and tangibility
> in the morning    to be understood,
> in the blue branches to be more than pure light
> of the world, that burns
> It could float, of course, where no one is —
> but would rather so it enters us —
> plumb rough matter. In the morning
> Airy and shapeless thing, shines from brute comfort
> it needs like a stitch of lightning;
> the metaphor of the body, and at night
> lime and appetite, lights up the deep and wondrous
> the oceanic fluids; drownings of the body like a star.[14]

Mary Oliver: "The spirit likes to dress up like this." And the poet author of John's Gospel declares:

*And the Word became flesh and lived among us, and we have seen his glory,*
*full of grace and truth.*

In that 14th verse of the prologue, we encounter John's Gospel Christmas story. As we begin to celebrate the season of the Incarnation—Christmas—we remember, aided by Mary Oliver's vivid words, that the human body is the metaphor God delights in employing.

In other words, God taking on flesh and blood not only helps us understand God but also allows God to understand us. It is through witnessing this body, fully human and fully God, that we come to see God's love at work in the world.

And so, the Word became flesh. Yet enfleshment is a messy process. In a contemporary response to medieval attempts to render Jesus' birth nonphysical (as seen in the decisions of the Council of Trent), Rachel Marie Stone writes in her book *Birthing Hope*:

> The scandal of the incarnation is that God became a human not
> by being beamed down from on high but by being born in the
> usual way—clinging as a bundle of cells to the blood-rich inner
> wall of Mary's womb, floating in the amniotic bubble inside her
> uterus, that astonishingly strong and expanse-full muscle making
> room in her body—her hospitable body—for God the Son to de-
> velop limbs, heart, brain, fingernails, earlobes, eyelashes ... The
> scandal of the incarnation is that a woman—we might even be
> tempted to refer to Mary as a girl she was so young—was in labor
> with God. A girl was in labor with God.[15]

We meet the infinite, boundless, eternal Word—the holy origin through which all things came into being—in the soft, fragile, finite body of a newborn babe. A particular babe born to a particular Jewish, Palestinian family, surviving under Roman occupation and grappling with the chaos that accompanies a new life. In the midst of that messy, young family, we receive the tremendous gift of the Incarnation! God came into the world in order to be known by us.

Enfleshed, the Word lived among us. By coming into the world in flesh, God did not come merely to be loved and known but to love us and

64

understand our labor. Becoming human involves growing pains—both physical (first steps, bruised knees, puberty, achy joints) and emotional (awkward interactions, broken hearts, falling in love, joy and anger, gratitude and grief, pleasure and pain). God's coming in Christ means that these messy human experiences are the very places where God meets us. God meets us in the mess—and the mess does not overcome God.

And in the Word, clothed in flesh and living among us, we have seen His glory. God became something tangible—a living body—that we can see and recognize. In Jesus, our ultimate way of knowing God, we witness the glory of God's love for the world.

In this Gospel, we also learn how to witness the Incarnation. John is not called "John the Baptizer" here but "John the Witness," for he sees the light revealed in Jesus and proclaims it so that others might know. John is our model.

We are to witness this metaphor—to see it, to open ourselves so that we may know it and be known by it. In our witness of the Incarnation, we are transformed, and we are called to tell the story. Moreover, because God chose to come to us in a form we recognize—a human body like our own—we are empowered to reach out: to call and connect, to FaceTime, to feed and heal—to make contact with the bodies surrounding us. The Incarnation establishes a relationship that draws God toward us and us toward God, propelling us toward our neighbor.

The enfleshed Word is a glorious revelation, full of grace and truth. Jesus shows us an alternative way of being—of being bodies in this world with God and neighbor. As a poor member of a religious minority and a refugee living under an oppressive empire, Jesus continuously treats the needs of people as sacred. He heals those in need of relief, reaches out to those marginalized by a hierarchical society, and breaks bread with those in need of redemption. God chose to become human as a member of a vulnerable, oppressed, and even hated group so that we might see God in those who are vulnerable, oppressed, and despised.

We, the church, are the body of Christ at work in the world now. We continue to read and witness the life of Christ—a life that reveals God's glorious love—as we also proclaim and strive to enact that very love in the world, birthing it anew in our own lives and in those around us, day after day, year after year.

After all ...

The spirit likes to dress up like this

ten fingers,

ten toes,

shoulders, and all the rest.

The Spirit dresses in bodies like ours so that we might see each other as bearers of the holy—with needs that are sacred.

So, as we begin this Christmas season and continue our mad rush toward a new calendar year (and may it be a year full of glorious revelation, grace, and truth), I invite you to reflect: How is God at work in your life? What is God doing in this community of living saints? In our nation? In the world? What holy need is God calling you to meet? How can you join in the labor of God?

# NAMING GOD

THE REV. MARY VANO
The Holy Name – January 1, 2023

*Numbers 6:22-27*
*Psalm 8*
*Galatians 4:4-7*
*Luke 2:15-21*

How do you name the Son of God? This is the daunting task Mary and Joseph faced just eight days after the birth of their child. They had to give a name to the Son of God. Perhaps, like any parents, we might imagine they were beset with typical challenges: Should they use a family name? Will the other children tease him? Can both Mary and Joseph agree on a name they love? But unlike ordinary parents, Mary and Joseph had to name the divine—God incarnate. For faithful Jews, this was a serious, weighty task.

It's serious because, throughout the long story of the covenant people, names hold profound significance. Names reveal character and foreshadow an individual's purpose. For example, Abram's name was changed to Abraham, meaning "father of a multitude." Isaac was named "he laughs" because his mother laughed. Later, Jacob, whose name means "supplanter" or "deceiver," was renamed "Israel" after wrestling with God—signifying "prince with God." And then we have Joshua ("God Saves") and David ("hero"). For their new baby, Joseph and Mary needed a name with such significance—a name that could encompass the character and purpose of God.

Adding to the challenge is the sheer power of names. In recent years, I've become all too aware of this when con artists send emails or texts in my name. Because my title includes "The Rev.," they exploit the trust and respect associated with it, hoping to trick people into giving money. Our names are keys to our identity, and in the ancient world they were often fiercely protected—especially, God's Name.

According to Hebrew tradition, the name of God should not be spoken; God is too great to be tethered by a name. So when God self-identifies to Moses, He reveals a name meaning something like "I am." In the Hebrew scriptures this is written with a four-letter abbreviation (YHWH, or Yahweh), but it is never pronounced; the covenant people instead refer to God as LORD.

The power of God's name is evident in today's reading from Numbers: "*The LORD bless you and keep you; the LORD make his face to shine upon you, and be gracious to you; the LORD lift up his countenance upon you, and give you peace.*" This familiar blessing is followed by a line often overlooked: "*so they shall put my name on the Israelites, and I will bless them.*" God's mysterious name is a powerful source of blessing for the covenant people—even for Mary and Joseph.

Thus, Mary and Joseph were given a profound task: they had to look into the eyes of this infant—the Son of God, the Great I AM—and give Him a name.

This task is not new. From the very beginning, God entrusted human beings with the responsibility to name creation. God created the land, sea, sky, plants, animals, and finally human beings, yet He did not name any of it; that privilege was reserved for Adam. The naming of the holy child is likewise a privilege bestowed upon humanity.

Fortunately, Joseph and Mary had divine guidance. The angel of God directed them: "*You will name him Jesus, for he will save his people from their sins.*" Thus, the child foretold by the prophet Isaiah—who would be called "wonderful, counselor, Almighty God"—was given the name Jesus, the most common, ordinary name a Jewish boy could have. (Jesus is a form of Joshua, meaning "God saves.") Under Roman rule, Jewish parents hoped for deliverance by naming their sons after the ancient hero who led their ancestors into the Promised Land. So, Jesus—our Jesus, the salvation of the world—began his life with a Jewish name, a name so ordinary it did not immediately set him apart.

And yet, in the ordinary, the holy is revealed. The Incarnation and the naming of God in human form change everything. First, through Jesus, human beings can call God by a personal name. Though God remains transcendent and beyond our wildest imaginations, He is also with us, known intimately through Jesus. Through Jesus, God experienced human pain and suffering; He lived as a member of a family and a community—He touched the sick and dined with friends and sinners. Even thousands of years later, we remain part of that community. We have been touched by Him; we have dined with Him. We know God by name.

Second, the Incarnation teaches us that if God can take on ordinary flesh, then God is present in the world around us. It becomes our task, as people of faith, to recognize and name the divine wherever we encounter it. This is the serious task we now share with Mary and Joseph. While no human being can be God as fully as Jesus, God is present in every person we meet. Imagine if we, with reverence and deliberate intent, named that divine presence in those around us—what a transformation that could bring! What if we looked into the eyes of our neighbor, even our enemy, and said, "God is with you?" How might the world change if we acknowledged the divine presence in our cities, in the ghetto, in communities far and wide?

This act of naming is the most powerful task God gives to human beings. God creates, and it remains our privilege to name. In this New Year, I pray that we may all witness and experience the divine in our lives and give it a name so that all may know it—the Holy Name of Jesus.

# GOSPEL OF OUR LIFE

THE REV. MICHAELENE MILLER
The Baptism of our Lord – January 8, 2023

*Isaiah 42:1-9*
*Psalm 29*
*Acts 10:34-43*
*Matthew 3:13-17*

Good morning! I once heard a bishop preach at a baptism that "the gospel of our life may be the only gospel ever read by our neighbors in this world."

> ... The gospel of our life may be the only gospel ever read by our neighbors in this world ...

Some words seem to cling to your heart, and I'm still carrying them years later. Perhaps it was the bishop's foot-stompin' and pulpit-shaking delivery of that urgent message to the congregation gathered to witness a baptism—a message that renewed and reiterated the well-known words of the Baptismal Covenant. But I think it was also how that statement laid bare the implications of our Christian faith: It matters how we live.

Every year, on the first Sunday following the Feast of the Epiphany—which we celebrated just this past Friday, remembering that God's light is revealed to all people in every place—we come together to remember and celebrate the Baptism of our Lord, Jesus Christ. According to the Book of Common Prayer, this feast day is one of four Sundays especially appropriate for baptisms or, when there are no new candidates, for the renewal of our Baptismal Vows. And that is exactly what we will do in just a moment: we will remember and recommit ourselves to our resolutions of discipleship.

But before we do that, we have our first encounter with Jesus as an adult in the Gospel of Matthew—at the moment of His own Baptism. And this moment can be a bit confusing. It even embarrassed the early church. After all, why would God's incarnate Son need a baptism of repentance? Wasn't He sinless? Wasn't He perfect?

70

Yet, Jesus approaches John and says, "Let it be. This is what will fulfill all righteousness." This act—wading into the waters of the world; stepping into the midst of the trials and errors of all the people of Jerusalem and Judea who came to John at the Jordan River to confess their sins—fulfills all righteousness because it unites the incarnate God with all creation. At that very moment, Jesus steps in beside us.

This step into solidarity with broken people is immediately blessed by God's affirming voice. Emerging from the water, Jesus sees the heavens torn apart and the Spirit descending like a dove upon Him. Then a voice from heaven proclaims, *"This is my Son, the Beloved, with whom I am well pleased."*

In that moment, the author of Matthew's Gospel introduces and affirms Jesus' public ministry with a Trinitarian formula. In that parting of water and sky, Matthew shows us what it means for God to break into the world. From then on, Jesus embarks on His public ministry, revealing the relational nature of God and teaching us how to live a life of love here on earth.

It is crucial to notice that before we fully come to know Jesus and His ministry of solidarity and transformation, we first encounter His precursor—John the Baptist—who appeared in the wilderness of Judea proclaiming, *"Repent, for the kingdom of heaven has come near."* In preparing the way for God, John emphasized that the people must first confess their sins.

The order matters. The Gospel does not go straight from Jesus' birth to His baptismal moment of peace and the invitation into new life with God. Before there is new life, there is the death of repentance Before healing and transformation, there is the turning of reconciliation. This is the order of God's unfolding into the world.

We see this pattern in our baptismal liturgy as well. If you have a Book of Common Prayer nearby, I invite you to turn to page 302. At that moment in the Rite of Baptism, there are three questions of renunciation and three questions of affirmation. With our bodies, we enact what our words express. Often, the priest will have candidates answer the first three questions of renunciation while facing west, toward the horizon of the setting sun. This process of renunciation is an exercise in truth-telling—a recognition of evil as a force in the world.

As the baptismal candidate renounces Satan and all the rebellious spiritual forces, they acknowledge, on a cosmic level, the existence of structural systems of oppression that corrupt God's creatures. Finally, on a personal level, they confess their own sinful desires that pull them away from the love of God.

Only after confessing the truth does the candidate turn to face east—toward the rising sun—to affirm their new life. In affirming that they will turn to Jesus Christ, accept Him as their Savior, place their whole trust in His grace and love, and promise to follow and obey Him as Lord, the candidate commits to a new way of living—a way of life and transformation.

If you have the BCP open, turn the page and look through our Baptismal Covenant, or refer to your worship bulletin. This is the Episcopal Church's succinct teaching on what a Christian believes and how a Christian resolves to live, both within and beyond the church walls. In just a brief moment, we will read and renew our commitment to these resolutions of our faith.

As you read these statements, if it does not immediately become clear that our faith makes great demands upon our lives as baptized, committed Christians, I encourage you to take your bulletin home today or spend some time with your own BCP, reading these statements slowly. And as you do, I invite you to be honest and share the truth of your limitations with God.

Several places in the Baptismal Covenant remind us that we are to see Christ in every person and strive for justice for all. It also reminds us that whenever—not if—we fall into sin, we are to repent and return to the Lord. In reality, each of us has a limit to our "all." We will mess up, need to ask for forgiveness, and must turn back into relationship with God and our neighbor.

That is why our response to these vows is, "I will, with God's help." We live to find the limits of our "all," and then, with God's help, we transform those limitations to bring transformation into the world. We expand, move, and live through and beyond our growing edges.

If you feel a desire to connect more deeply with these radical demands on our lives, I suggest using the vows of the Baptismal Covenant as a guiding structure—a rule of life—for your daily living. St. Benedict once said that a Rule of Life is "simply a handbook to make the very radical demands of the gospel a practical reality in daily life." These resolutions are radical demands, and with God's help, we commit to living them every day.

For each question, write down one or two ways you hope to live into that vow more deeply. Consider your relationship with God, with yourself, with others, and with creation as you reflect.

For example, one might continue in the apostles' teaching and fellowship, in the breaking of bread, and in prayer by regularly attending Sunday worship, intentionally lingering after service to engage in fellowship over coffee and a snack, and exploring different service opportunities and ministry groups at St. Margaret's to deepen one's faith in community.

To seek and serve Christ in all people—to love your neighbor as yourself—you might strive to break boundaries by making eye contact with everyone you pass, acknowledging each person regardless of age, race, gender, or sexuality with an engaged "hello" that affirms their humanity; a "hello" that communicates, "I see you. You are a beloved creation of God."

After all, do you remember these haunting words? "The gospel of our life may be the only gospel ever read by our neighbors in this world."

The Church—the Body of Christ—is vast, composed of many members. It is a body that has, at times, contributed to many dark moments in history. And those dark moments, for all of us who claim the Christian identity, are ours to bear in confession and repentance. This is to be the pattern of our lives: We repent, and then we live further into and extend the invitation to transformation. We are to proclaim this alternative way of life in Christ, as our third Baptismal vow clearly states—in both word and action.

It matters how we live in the world—in relationship with God, with God's Creation, and with our neighbors (human, plant, and animal alike). Our lives are meant to testify to God's justice to all who have eyes to know the truth. As I come to understand this Christian ethic and its demands on my life, I am reminded of Eleanor Roosevelt's words, that rights begin

> in small places, close to home-so close and so small that they cannot be seen on any map of the world. Yet they are the world of the individual person: The neighborhood he lives in; the school or college [she] attends; the factory, farm, or office where [they work]. Such are the places where every [adult] and child seeks equal justice, equal opportunity, and equal dignity without discrimination. Unless these rights have meaning there, they have little meaning anywhere. Without concerted citizen action to uphold them close to home, we shall look in vain for progress in the larger world.[16]

The Christian life is a radical life. It matters how we live. Remember, the gospel of our life may be the only gospel ever read by our neighbors in this world. As our collect for today encourages us, I pray for all of us who are baptized into Christ's Name that we may faithfully keep the covenant we have made.

# WHAT ARE YOU LOOKING FOR?

THE REV. MARY VANO
Second Sunday after the Epiphany – January 15, 2023

*Isaiah 49:1-7*
*Psalm 40:1-12*
*1 Corinthians 1:1-9*
*John 1:29-42*

In the Gospel of John, the very first words spoken by the Word made flesh form a simple question: "What do you seek? What are you looking for?"

The two people to whom He speaks are clearly seekers—and yet they seem unable to answer. Perhaps they felt as I do whenever I walk into a hardware store. I'm looking for something, but I don't know what it is called; I just know I have a problem and need something to fix it. I've encountered more than one bewildered salesperson who insists that I must know exactly what I need before they can even help me—directing me, for example, straight to aisle 13.

But Jesus is undeterred by their uncertainty. Even though they haven't yet named what they seek, He knows that whatever it is, they are looking for it in Him. Perhaps, along the way, they will discover exactly what they are seeking.

So, what are you looking for? As I ponder this question, I realize that people answer in many different ways. Some of you might say you want to be needed—you desire to help others in ways that give you purpose. Others may declare that you seek success, achievement, or accomplishment. Some of you might be willing to take risks—to be creative—but ultimately, you long to be understood as unique individuals in this world.

What are you seeking? I know some thirst for knowledge. With knowledge, you gain independence and are seen by others as capable and competent. Others seek security above all else—a deep connection with those around them to work for a common good that provides safety.

What are people looking for? I have a good friend who wants to embrace life fully—taking in relationships, adventure, love, and laughter, and capturing every joyful moment. Another friend is constantly fighting injustice, striving to lead others to work at their best. And yet others simply yearn for peace and harmony.

And what am I seeking? If you ask me, I would say that I seek a better world—one that aligns with God's will, an Eden restored.

For those familiar with the Enneagram, you might notice that I've described needs reminiscent of the nine types found in that tradition. Unlike many personality typing systems, the Enneagram addresses what motivates us; it asks, "What are you seeking?" This is an important question because what we seek in this life will shape the journey of our search.

When we first encounter Jesus in the Gospel of John, and He begins by asking, "What are you looking for?" it tells me that Jesus cares deeply about who we are and what we need. Whatever answers those first disciples might have given, Jesus invites them to find what they are seeking in Him.

"Come and see," Jesus says. "Come and see how this world needs you. See how your unique gifts and skills can accomplish great things and make the world a better place. Come, beloved, because God knows you and loves you just as you are."

- If you thirst for knowledge, Jesus invites you to find wisdom.
- If you seek safety from the storm, He offers to calm the waters.
- If you desire beauty, joy, and laughter, the richest of these experiences can be found in God's love.
- For those called to fight injustice, let Jesus lead you; and if it is peace you seek, be still and know that He is God.

God sees all our needs, and to meet them, God gives Himself in Christ and then gives us to one another. Here is the crucial point: to find what we are seeking, we need each other. We need one another to notice, to share, and to invite.

Consider the pattern in this Gospel. First, John the Baptist witnessed Jesus' baptism—He saw the Holy Spirit descend on Him, then proclaimed, *"Here is the Lamb of God who takes away the sins of the world!"* John noticed, shared what he had seen, and then invited others by declaring, "Look! Here He is."

Jesus does the same. He notices the seekers coming to Him, exchanges questions with them, and extends the invitation, "Come and see." Next, Andrew goes to his brother Simon and tells him, "We have found the Messiah." Simon then receives that invitation—"come and see." This pattern continues from John to Jesus, from Andrew to Peter and the disciples, and onward to us.

This cycle of seeing, sharing, and inviting is what we call evangelism—a message of good news. It is good news because we all need something, and what we need can be found when we see truth, share love, and invite others to experience it for themselves. All our needs—for love, acceptance, and fulfillment—are met when we see Jesus, share our joy, and invite others to join us on the path. The more we walk together—seeing, sharing, inviting—the more we discover that every need is met in the perfect love of God.

Whoever you are, whatever your needs, whatever you are seeking ... keep seeking, because Jesus extends the invitation and the promise: *"Seek, and you shall find."*

# HALF A SHADE BRAVER

THE REV. MICHAELENE MILLER
Third Sunday after the Epiphany – January 22, 2023

*Isaiah 9:1-4*
*Psalm 27:1, 5-13*
*1 Corinthians 1:10-18*
*Matthew 4:12-23*

> "The place God calls you to is the place where your deep gladness and the world's deep hunger meet."

These words may sound familiar if you joined the ECW/DoK joint book study of Parker Palmer's *Let Your Life Speak* this past fall. I still recall sitting in the computer lab at Hendrix College during my sophomore year when I first encountered this quote from Frederick Buechner. I was moments away from an interview with the Hendrix chaplains and a few professors, applying for a spot on the Miller Center's mission trip to Cuba. Scanning the Miller Center's website for solid talking points, I was still trying to discern what exactly it meant to be the Center for Vocation, Ethics, and Calling. In that research, I was captivated by the clarity and directness of Buechner's words.

"The place God calls you to is the place where your deep gladness and the world's deep hunger meet." These words definitely came up in my interview and so many other conversations I had with the Hendrix chaplains over the next three years.

Buechner's formula for discernment suggests that one's vocation—one's call—is the work God gives or invites you to do as your fullest, most authentic, God-ordained self. This work is found at the intersection of (a) what you need most to do and (b) what the world most urgently needs done. At that intersection, we find our life's vocation and purpose.

We are all created to discern this intersection. While the Episcopal Church has a formalized process for those exploring a call to ordained ministry, the truth is that God invites every one of us to engage in discernment as a lifestyle—to routinely seek our vocation and purpose in our daily lives, discovering not just what we must do, but how we are to be in this world.

Discernment is a process of open listening. According to Buechner, it means listening inward for God's call and outward for the ever-unfolding needs of the world. Eventually, this process leads to an opportunity to respond.

As the poet David Whyte puts it, responding to God's call is a process of living "half a shade braver."[17] To answer that call requires vulnerability and courage—though not the absence of fear. Stepping forward to live even half a shade braver does not mean fear is absent; rather, a little fear is good because it creates space for the Holy Spirit to enter our work.

We see this courage modeled in our Gospel reading today. In the fourth chapter of Matthew's Gospel, we encounter Jesus stepping boldly into His purpose. Following in the footsteps of John the Baptizer—whose message cost him dearly—Jesus proclaims, "Repent! Turn! Turn from the oppressive ways of the empire of Rome and turn toward the liberating ways of the kingdom of heaven that has come near. Turn and follow me." With these words, Jesus begins to build His movement of liberation and love.

Shortly after, Jesus meets Simon Peter and his brother Andrew, and then James and his brother John—fishermen mending their nets, the very tools that sustain their livelihood. Jesus calls them, *"Follow me, and I will make you fish for people."* With remarkable vulnerability and courage, these brothers immediately leave their nets, their boat, and even the comfort of family to follow Him.

In responding to the call to discipleship, these men embrace a new identity, a new way of living, and a transformative community. They step away from all they knew into a future that could be with Christ. "I will make you," Jesus tells them—He will make them into more than they could have ever asked, imagined, or dreamed on their own.

Now, I ask you: What might Jesus make of you if you say "yes" to God's call? What would happen if you answered that call—to become your best, most authentic, and joyful self, responding uniquely and faithfully to the needs of your community and culture? What safety nets must you be willing to drop to step freely into the joy of who God is calling you to be? What might Jesus create in you if you simply say "yes"?

I wonder if the openness and uniqueness of this question ever feel overwhelming, or if it triggers fear. Does it make you doubt yourself—thinking, "Who am I to do this or walk with Jesus?" Or perhaps, "I couldn't possibly do that ... I don't know what I'm doing ... everyone will see I'm a fraud the moment I speak on this issue."

I share this because many of us, myself included, struggle with what's commonly called impostor syndrome—the fear that our gifts, skills, education, and accomplishments aren't enough, and that soon everyone will discover we're a fraud.

Yet, the great news is that God does not call perfect, super-human experts. God calls all humans, all of us, and all parts of the human individual—gifts and growing edges included.

And thanks be to God for the example of the disciples living into this. Here, we get to see these imperfect people going and doing, wholeheartedly responding to God's call to be made into their fullest self. The disciples do not get caught up or stop themselves by saying, "Who am I to do this or walk with Jesus?"

They just go, immediately, without needing to be experts in building community or building movements or teaching, healing, and feeding. These were fisher folk working hard at the bottom of society, just trying to feed their families and make it by. They heard it in Jesus' words: "I've got bigger dreams for you than you have for yourself" and they moved bravely and boldly into step with Jesus.

And, with our hindsight, we know that things did not always go perfectly after this immediate self-offering. Here, Simon-Peter immediately steps in, but throughout the gospel stories, Simon-Peter is recorded as failing again and again. In misunderstanding Jesus' mission as he foreshadows his journey through the cross, Peter makes a hasty suggestion that results in Jesus calling him out as Satan. Then, his faltering faith causes him to sink when he steps out of the boat to go to Jesus on the water. When Jesus is at his death, Peter denies knowing him three times. Yet, throughout all of this, Peter models for us what it means to live half a shade braver.

When the work is this important and urgent, when the world needs to hear a message of liberation and hope so badly, it is always better to go ahead and bravely try to do it before perfecting the process or before figuring out all the right answers. By living half a shade braver, one accepts the inevitability of making a mistake and needing to ask for help down the road.

The promise and good news here, especially to anyone struggling to not feel like an imposter, is that God does not call the qualified; God qualifies the called. Jesus says, "I will make you into more than you can ask for or imagine." If you're struggling, trust that you matter, that you are worthy of your call and purpose in this world. Trust that as you follow, Jesus is making, equipping, protecting, and perfecting you. Know that God has made you with unique gifts and growing edges, and He is expanding those gifts as a beautiful offering to the world.

One thing I do know is that, reading the St. Margaret's Annual Report, it's clear we have an incredible community—filled with many gifts to offer to God and the world as we help build the Kingdom of Heaven here in and around west Little Rock.

I invite each of us to search and listen for the dream at the center of our hearts. What desire in you intersects with the world's need? What might Jesus make of you if you were to respond and say "yes"? And if you haven't yet found your dream in the world or in this community, how might you boldly step forward to help it come to be? How can we all respond to God's particular call and live half a shade braver?

# THE LIGHT OF RESURRECTION

The Rt. Rev. Larry R. Benfield
Fourth Sunday after the Epiphany – January 29, 2023

*Micah 6:1-8*
*Psalm 15*
*1 Corinthians 1:18-31*
*Matthew 5:1-12*

This diocese is currently searching for its next bishop. As the home office of the Episcopal Church strongly advised me, I have stayed away from the selection process, including the part when people are asked about what sort of bishop they want. You see, what we usually want is what we do not currently have. I noticed in the diocesan profile that our members want Jesus. Oh, well, I guess in part it means that people really want someone with more liturgical piety than I have: you know, all the stuff that some clerics do during church services, such as constantly crossing themselves and making a big deal about in what order the acolytes light the candles. You need to remember that the seminary from which I came historically would have none of that sort of stuff going on: wary of material things, so to speak. It was only in recent memory that the seminary put a cross and candles behind the altar. I think we were afraid that when you start down that pious path, there are all sorts of unintended consequences. In fact, my seminary's chapel burned down after I graduated when some hot charcoal was not disposed of properly as they tried to learn how to use incense.

But, burning incense aside, people want things that they can touch, see, and smell and that remain in sacred space long after they are gone. In the distant past, our Jewish ancestors in the faith were required to make an offering when they went to the Temple in Jerusalem. Jesus' parents made an offering when Jesus was brought to the Temple as a child—birds, which would have been appropriate for a poor family. It is why, in this secular age, people leave flowers and candles at the location of a tragic

82

death. Even today, there is something inside us that wants to go to a sacred place and leave something behind as a gift—and perhaps a bribe — to God, if only in the form of a lit votive candle.

Some churches make a big deal out of candles as offerings. I was once in a church in Philadelphia (not Episcopal, by the way) that had an electric votive candle stand. You put your quarter in the slot, and a flickering light bulb came on for thirty minutes. That is what I would call a real, cause-and-effect offering. The more coins you put in, the longer your gift to God lasted: great moneymaker but questionable theology.

Admittedly, I am conflicted about some devotional actions. They have the smell, not of burning beeswax, but of a transaction between God and me alone, by which I try to take care of my transgressions and hopes in a very private way. It reminds me of Micah in today's Old Testament lesson, when he says that God has a controversy with God's people, and they are wrong if they think that they are going to settle the issue with burnt offerings, rams, rivers of oil, or even human sacrifice. God will not be bought off.

Except for human sacrifice, the gifts I just mentioned were the religiously encouraged, even required, ways that the Hebrew people of the era expressed their thanks to God, the burnt offerings in particular. They were totally burned and thus became symbols of total dedication to God. In that sense they were very much like candles that burn in a church side aisle until the wick disappears: totally consumed, of no practical worth, but still a sacred symbol. I am not knocking symbols; symbols can indeed be important. We use them each week in the form of bread and wine and occasionally in the form of water poured on a forehead or hands laid on someone's head.

But like a good prophet, Micah is struggling to tell us something more about God than religious rites and ceremonies can ever evidence. Micah is focused on us remembering that God is the deliverer of people and how God takes us from death to life. In the early part of the lesson today, he tells his listeners what God has done. And what God has done is take an entire people from death in Egypt and march them across a sea into a new life. He tells his listeners to remember what once happened between Shittim and Gilgal, which are two points on either side of the River Jordan and the location where God led Joshua and the people of Israel, again through the water, into life in the Promised Land. Micah wants us to hear that God delivers entire groups of people, and our response to such deliverance is not individual religiosity.

Instead, Micah says that what God wants in response to such deliverance is for us to be agents of deliverance as well. What Micah says in the last sentence of today's lesson is what the biblical scholar Philip King calls the perfect summary of prophetic teaching on true religion. What God really wants is for us to do justice, to love kindness, and to walk humbly.

These are not the actions of a person in isolation from others, like someone who can walk into a church and walk out feeling justified because he left something for God. Justice, kindness, and humility are, by their very nature, communal and relational. If we are now the hands and feet of God in the world, as I think we are because we are the body of Christ, then we are called to deliver people just as God delivered the Israelites. We do it through bringing about justice in this society; don't forget that responsibility as our state legislature meets. We do it through kindness to those around us; don't forget it when you are in the grocery store checkout line. We do it through humility in the presence of others; don't forget it when tempted to one-up everyone else about the latest purchases we have made. These all-too-human tendencies are symbols as well. Micah is not happy with such tendencies.

Micah may indeed be frightening because of his insistence on justice, kindness, and humility. But remember that first and foremost, he brings good news: God delivers people from death to life. When you and I get into the deadly situations in which we often find ourselves, we may be scared to death by the rising waters on either side of us, but death-dealing waters don't have to have the last word. The biblical witness of Micah is precisely that.

People can be delivered every day from hurts, both small and great. In this age, as in any other, people are given new life, not by resuscitating dead loved ones or time travel so that we can go back and undo what was earlier done that ultimately caused death, but by looking at someone else in the here and now and offering kindness. Or seeing to it that justice is finally done so that another person is no longer dragged down. Or acting with humility so that others do not feel inferior any longer.

If we have ever been the recipient of justice, kindness, or humility, then we've been raised from the dead. And if we trust that we are part of God's body in this generation, then we have the power to be just, kind, and humble with everyone we meet so that God (or should I say God's hands and feet) can be seen yet one more time bringing people from death to life. These sorts of experiences, this sort of reaching out, keep any church alive and the doors to our buildings open.

It is through such experiences that we enter sacred space, and what I mean by sacred space is not limited to a building. Sacred space is any life-giving relationship with other human beings. As I said earlier, there is something in us that wants to go to a sacred space and leave something there. What we can leave in our lives as an offering is to make life more just for someone else and change them forever, show them kindness and lift their spirit, and act with humility and make them feel that they are beloved in God's eyes.

The light of resurrection will shine through us and our lives. If we trust that truth, then it makes no difference what our liturgical piety might be. What I am confident of is that people will continue to see the light of resurrection in one way or another through the witness that is made in local congregations, in the lives of everyday Christians. That is as good an offering as anyone can make, the kind of offering of which even stern old Micah would be proud.

# YOU ARE SALT

THE REV. MICHAELENE MILLER
Fifth Sunday after the Epiphany – February 5, 2023

*Isaiah 58:1-9a, [9b-12]*
*Psalm 112:1-9, (10)*
*1 Corinthians 2:1-12, [13-16]*
*Matthew 5:13-20*

Good morning! Today's gospel reading from Matthew continues Jesus' famous Sermon on the Mount, the first of five teaching discourses in the Gospel of Matthew. Jesus speaks to the inner circle of his disciples and the surrounding crowd, made up of the sick, the afflicted, and their care-takers, who are all listening in.

Jesus begins with the Beatitudes, which we heard last week. In these pronouncements, he paints a radically unexpected picture of blessedness. He doesn't uplift those who are easy to identify as well-off—the rich, the happy, the strong, the safe, or the well-liked. Instead, Jesus declares that the truly blessed are the poor, the mourning, the gentle, the hungry, the merciful, the pure in heart, the peacemakers, the persecuted, and those who are reviled. These—these unexpected and unseen people, the very ones who have gathered around Jesus, desperate for healing and consola-tion—are named as blessed. By naming them, Jesus isn't simply enacting a blessing upon them. Rather, in naming them, Jesus is reminding them of what they already are.

In today's gospel, Jesus continues to tell the crowd who they are. "You are the salt of the earth. You are the light of the world." This is not a call to become like salt or light, nor is it an instruction. Jesus isn't saying, "Do what salt does, and God will reward you." No, Jesus' language here is indicative—it is descriptive and factual.

Salt. Light. Jesus is identifying the created essence of those gathered around him. He's making a statement of their identity. As Jesus clarifies who they are and who God has created and blessed them to be, their pur-pose as a blessing to the world also becomes clearer. As disciples and members of the Body of Christ gather today, this is our identity. We are salt. We are light. And not just here in this one place of West Little Rock, but we are the salt of the earth. We are the light of the world.

But we must ask—why salt and light? For us today, the meaning isn't immediately clear. We often miss the blessing and consolation in this naming of us as salt and light. So, we miss the opportunity and don't know how to respond and live out the purpose of this identity.

Today, both salt and light are common household items. Salt is cheap and easily accessible, and light can be summoned with the flick of a switch. (This morning, when I arrived at church, I pushed ONE button on that back wall, and all the lights came on instantly!) In our American culture of instant access, we take salt and light for granted.

But in the time and culture when Jesus spoke these words, light was time-dependent, and a luxury only for those who could afford oil. Salt was a sought-after commodity with many uses, and its preciousness would have been deeply felt. Especially by that crowd of followers who had flocked to Jesus—outcast and forgotten people who were hungry, sick, crippled, and frightened. You, Jesus tells them, are the salt of the earth. You are the light of the world.

By naming them, Jesus reminds them that they are precious, essential, and powerful in their ability to affect the world and everyone they encounter. And they are created to encounter. Salt and light are relational in nature. They are not meant to be kept in isolation. Through this naming, Jesus commissions them. Jesus reminds them of their identity and purpose. And Jesus tells us the same today.

Being named salt and light, Jesus compels us to act like it. He reminds us of our purpose. Like salt and light, we are relational and effectual in our being as people of God and followers of the Word.

Light, in its very nature, illuminates and attracts. It highlights, reveals, and illuminates so that a hidden thing can be seen and known.

Salt, too, affects whatever it encounters, whether intentionally or not. Salt can enhance or embitter, soothe or irritate, melt or sting, preserve or ruin. This means that, like salt, we impact the world we live in, whether we intend to or not.

When practiced with humility and discernment, Christianity, like salt in proper proportion, enhances the world rather than dominating it. Christianity, practiced with intention, seeks out and aligns with God's will, illuminating and enhancing where God is already present and active in the world as a force for righteousness, blessing, and healing. This often happens in the most unlikely places and with the most unexpected people.

Without this intentional discernment, however, Christianity can become a domineering force, blinding others, driven by the whims of a few seeking to legislate power over others.

We see such injustices in today's Old Testament reading, where the prophet Isaiah calls out the people for their blind, hollow religious practices. They fasted with little intention or reason, beyond their individual desire to appear holy. Like a trumpet, Isaiah shouts, alerting them to more faithful practices—practices that align with God's will.

Isaiah witnesses the people living their faith as a fast that serves their own interests, rather than God's. They seem to have believed that proximity to a holy place like Jerusalem or performing a holy act like fasting made them holy. But this is a faith out of balance. Human interests here are misaligned with God's will and what is truly just.

Isaiah calls the people to a new way of living—one that loosens the bonds of injustice, undoes the yoke of oppression, and lets the oppressed go free. He urges them to fast from injustice and to adopt a lifestyle of relationship. Share your bread with the hungry, bring the homeless poor into your house, cover the naked, and don't hide from your kin. Be in relationship. Isaiah's prescriptions show that the work of revealing God's Kingdom can begin with one person reaching out in care to another.

Isaiah calls the crowds into a relational lifestyle and, in doing so, into the righteousness of God—the power of God at work in the world to redeem, sustain, protect, and bless.[18] This shows us that a full relationship with God requires just relationships with each other.

In the Gospel of Matthew, Jesus, perhaps echoing the prophetic words of Isaiah, tells the crowd that their identity compels them to do the same. Be who you are. In doing so, you will live out and reveal the heart of God's law. God created us to be in relationship. God created us to be effectual in our being. God blessed us to be a blessing to the world.

We can't hide under a basket or keep our salt to ourselves. We are salty people called to be in relationship—not sarcastic or full of shade, as the hip kids might mean by "salty" today, but full of light, with the ability to enhance and bless others. We are called to interact in ways that illuminate God's will and point others toward God's presence in the world so that they might recognize God.

This is who we are. We are salt. We are light. As the salt of the earth, where in your daily life can you preserve, soothe, and enhance the lives of others? As the light of the world, how might you reveal and illuminate God's love around you? God has blessed us with gifts that can bless the world. Jesus calls us to claim these gifts and be who we are—a salty and luminous people. A preserve and beacon of God's care, healing, and blessing. May it be so.

# TATTOOED ON OUR VERY HEARTS

THE REV. MARY VANO
Sixth Sunday after Epiphany – February 12, 2023

*Deuteronomy 30:15-20*
*Psalm 119:1-81*
*Corinthians 3:1-9*
*Matthew 5:21-37*

Today, we continue from last week in the middle of Jesus' famous Sermon on the Mount. While most people recognize the Beatitudes—the "blessed are you" sayings—few know that there's much more to this sermon. For the record, Jesus' sermons were longer than mine!

The sermon starts with the Beatitudes, where Jesus tells the crowds that they are blessed and loved by God. He then continues with last week's reading, where he reminds them that they are the salt of the earth and the light of the world, urging them to let their light shine so that others may give glory to God. Last week's passage also included a key transition, where Jesus says that he came not to abolish the law but to fulfill it, and that their righteousness must exceed that of the scribes and Pharisees.

This brings us to today's reading, which includes the first four of six sayings following a familiar formula: "You have heard it said... but I say to you."

- *"You have heard it said, 'You shall not murder.' But I say to you that if you are angry with a brother or sister, you will be liable to judgment."*
- *"You have heard it said, 'You shall not commit adultery.' But I say to you that if you treat another person as an object of lust, you've already committed adultery in your heart."*
- *"You have heard it said that if you divorce, you should do so legally, but don't pretend to be righteous just because you follow the law."*
- *"And you have heard it said, 'Do not swear falsely,' but I say don't swear at all. No more empty promises."*

After hearing these statements, surely no one can feel innocent. But what exactly is Jesus' point? After telling the crowd that they are blessed, loved by God, and that the world needs them, is he now saying they are walking a tightrope, and if they slip in even the slightest way, they will fall into oblivion? That doesn't seem to fit.

Rather, I believe Jesus is telling them that people have misunderstood the law. The scribes and Pharisees followed it like a checklist of personal righteousness, then used it to condemn others. But that misses the point entirely. The law, according to Jesus, is not a pedestal for some and a weapon for others; it's meant to teach us how to love one another, even when that's difficult. It's not just about avoiding murder; it's about not letting our anger harm others. It's not just about avoiding adultery; it's about being deeply faithful to our spouses, treating no one as an object for our own satisfaction. Even in the case of divorce, Jesus challenges us to love each other as God loves us. And we are called to be honest with one another—saying yes to what we will do, and no to what we won't. The heart of the law is all about relationships.

Unless the law is written on our hearts, we are missing it entirely.

In the book of Jeremiah, God promises future restoration to the Israelites in exile. God says through the prophet, "*I will put my law within them, and I will write it on their hearts; and I will be their God, and they shall be my people.*" (Jeremiah 31:33) I will write it on their hearts. Perhaps this is what Jesus is doing in the Sermon on the Mount—not just teaching what we should do, but inscribing the law on our hearts.

The older I get, the more preoccupied I am with my heart health. Our hearts are amazing muscles. I've read that the heart beats about 2.5 billion times over the course of an average lifespan. Its relentless job is to carry oxygen, fuel, and nutrients throughout our bodies. For this to happen most effectively, the heart needs to be both strong and flexible. As much as I struggle to keep up with the discipline, the basics of heart health are not hard to understand: diet and exercise. Doctors preach this all the time—more fruits, vegetables, and whole grains; less salt and fat. It's about fueling our bodies well and using that fuel to build strength—regular exercise to keep the heart working efficiently.

It's interesting to me that, although modern medicine didn't exist in biblical times, both Jesus and Moses seemed to understand that our lives depend on the health of our hearts. Physical and spiritual health may not be so different after all. Moses, in today's reading from Deuteronomy, presents a choice between life and death. "See, I have set before you life and prosperity, death and adversity." Choosing life is about following God's law, but it goes deeper than diet or behavior. Moses says, *"If your heart turns away and you do not hear ... and bow down to other gods, I declare to you today that you shall perish."* As the people prepare to enter the Promised Land, Moses implores them to choose life and let the law be written on their hearts.

Our hearts—our souls—need quality fuel and regular exercise. So, we must watch what we consume: is it junk that will calcify our hearts with anger, pride, or hatred? Or is it the good stuff that nourishes wisdom, compassion, peace, and patience? Are we only using our hearts in easy relationships with people we like, or are we stretching our hearts to love the different and even the difficult?

The heart of the law is about relationships. Unless God's love is written on our hearts, we're missing the point.

Now, lest you think all this sounds nice but not urgent, let me remind you of the state of the world right now. Many of us are so entrenched in our divisions that we no longer make any sense. On any given day, I can find people arguing for life—whether that's about abortion rights, refugees, or the environment—while, in the very next breath, condemning those who disagree with them to death or hell.

As followers of Jesus Christ, we must be better than this, because our lives—our souls—are at stake. We have things worth fighting for, but unless we fight with love and for love, love will not win. It's up to all of us to rise up in righteousness, with God's love tattooed on our hearts, so that with each of our 2.5 billion heartbeats, the love of God may bring life to the world.

Jesus loves us so much that he challenges us to this righteousness. And he knows—as we know—that none of us is without anger, lust, or falsehood. Yet he still loves us so much that even when we fail, he shows us the way—giving his life for us on the cross and hoping only that our hearts will beat with the love that has been entrusted to us.

# THRESHOLD MOMENTS

THE REV. MICHAELENE MILLER
Last Sunday after the Epiphany – February 19, 2023

*Exodus 24:12-18*
*Psalm 2*
*2 Peter 1:16-21*
*Matthew 17:1-9*

In his *Blessing for the Interim Time*, the Irish priest and poet John O'Donohue wrote:

> "You are in this time of the interim
> Where everything seems withheld.
> The path you took to get here has washed out;
> The way forward is still concealed from you.
> The old is not old enough to have died away;
> The new is still too young to be born."[19]

This Sunday, we find ourselves somewhere in the middle, at a threshold moment, in the midst of an interim time—where the old is fading, and the new hasn't yet emerged. We stand at the cusp, at a peak of sorts, with threshold moments all around us.

For one, in terms of our shared experience walking through the pandemic, I'm reminded by our lectionary cycle that three years ago, when we last encountered this reading of Jesus' dazzling Transfiguration from the Gospel of Matthew, we were blissfully unaware of how the world was about to change. We were enjoying one of the last "normal" Sundays before COVID-19 hit like a ton of bricks, transforming everything we once knew.

Now, while we are deep into the pandemic experience, we still can't clearly see where we'll land as a society and as a Church. It's clear that COVID changed all our lives, and its ripples continue to alter how we "do church" and how we are to be the Church in the world. Yet, it's still unclear where the path ahead leads.

Today also brings us to a liturgical threshold. We are nearing the pivot point, passing from the season after Epiphany into the season of Lent— a season of wilderness walking and journeying with Jesus to the cross. A season that, for some, might feel like we never really left 2020.

Finally, in our gospel story, we enter yet another threshold experience. In Matthew 17, Peter, James, and John join Jesus on an epic hike to the top of a mountain, where Jesus reveals his divinity in full, dazzling display. Everything they once knew about their teacher and expected from their friend is brought into question. Their path ahead is now entirely unclear.

A fellow preacher, Aaron Rogers, put it simply, saying that in this moment, "Jesus becomes Trans ... figured. His clothes look different. His face changes. And suddenly, the He in this story becomes a They. Jesus, in his glory, is no longer by himself but is in conversation with a chorus of divine identities, confirming his imminent departure from his current manifestation to his divine destiny. It is the ultimate coming out. The ultimate epiphany."

Jesus was transformed before Peter, James, and John in a way they could never have predicted. At this moment, Jesus was fully the teacher, healer, and friend they knew, but he was also revealed as much more— his divine identity shining brightly. Even more, he was conversing with Moses and Elijah, prophets thought to be long dead.

In this threshold moment of transfiguration, everything that Peter, James, and John thought they knew about their ministry with Jesus slipped away. And as we've come to know from our own experience living through this pandemic, there is grief in losing our comprehension of how the world works.

Alongside Jesus' transfiguration, their lives and understanding of their own identities were also transformed. If John O'Donohue were to describe their experience, he might say: "The path they took to get here has washed out; the way forward is still concealed from them."

In the next moments, Peter gives us a mirror of our human tendencies when faced with change and transformation. The Common English

Bible translation puts it plainly: Peter, overwhelmed by what he witnessed, said to Jesus, *"Lord, it's good that we're here. If you want, I'll make three shrines: one for you, one for Moses, and one for Elijah."*

Peter's reaction is an attempt to control the moment. Instead of pausing to absorb the weight of the revelation, Peter impulsively seeks to freeze this experience in time, suggesting that the best thing they could do is build walls to capture and preserve it. This is a very human response: the desire to cling to security in the face of discomfort.

Threshold moments of transformation are often scary, uncomfortable, and feel overwhelming. Like Peter, we tend to want to retreat to the safety of what we knew before—even if it meant living in ignorance. Rather than sitting with the discomfort of the new revelation, Peter rushes to turn it into something he can understand, like a monument to preserve the moment.

Yet often, when we feel discomfort like Peter's, it's because we've encountered a hidden truth that shifts our understanding, and we can't un-see what we've just witnessed. Our sense of order is upended.

In the next verse, we see a better way to approach such moments of revelation. While Peter was still speaking, suddenly a bright cloud overshadowed them, and from the cloud, a voice said, *"This is my Son, the Beloved; with him I am well pleased; listen to him!"*

In this moment, Peter and the other disciples are reoriented by God's voice. While they don't yet fully comprehend what they've witnessed, they do begin the journey back down the mountain with some clarity. God's message to them is clear: open yourselves to new revelation, a new way of life, and listen to Jesus' teachings.

Jesus adds to this instruction: *"Get up and don't be afraid."*

As we stand at this threshold moment in the Church year and in our collective journey, how do we get up and bravely continue onward toward Lent? We can take a note from what Jesus is doing in this passage. Here, Jesus gathers with Elijah and Moses for mentorship and encouragement as he prepares for his own threshold—his turn toward Jerusalem and the cross.

We, too, can look to a modern-day prophet for mentorship on how to walk through our own threshold moments. For the last few years, around this time of year, on the feast day of Absalom Jones, I've helped facilitate a virtual weekend retreat for young adults in the Episcopal Service Corps network, where we journey with the Rev. Dr. Pauli Murray.

One hundred seventy-two years after Absalom Jones became the first black person ordained a priest in the Episcopal Church, Saint Pauli Murray became the first black person assigned female at birth to be ordained as a priest in the Episcopal Church at the age of 62 on January 8, 1977. It was 46 years ago, around this time of year, on Feb. 13th, that Rev. Murray celebrated the Eucharist for the first time—the first person assigned female at birth to do so in the state of North Carolina.

The Rev. Dr. Murray lived through a great threshold time in American society and change in the Episcopal Church. They were born into the segregated south and raised in Durham, NC, by their Aunt Pauline and Grandmother Cornelia, who was a direct descendant of both an enslaved person and an enslaver.

Throughout their life, Dr. Murray learned how to hold together within them diverging and conflicting identities. Saint Murray once reflected, "It had taken me almost a lifetime to discover that true emancipation lies in the acceptance of the whole past, in deriving strength from all of my roots, in facing up to the degradation as well as the dignity of my ancestors."

Perhaps it was this, their journey towards the full integration of their self, their perspective of seeing a fuller, whole truth, that enabled them to courageously get up and work tirelessly down in the valley for God's Beloved Community. Murray was unrelenting in their work to reveal the right relationships of God's kingdom, and they fought for an entirely new way of living together in the world than what they saw unfolding around them.

Dr. Murray called themself "America's Problem Child" and later in life referred to themself as a "pixie priest" as they often got up into people's hair and raised people's blood pressure in their struggle to make "America [and the Episcopal Church] be who she *says* she is."

So, I ask: What epiphany is God revealing to you in this threshold moment? What invitation to transformation are you receiving? While the path behind us may have washed out and the way forward still concealed, how can we listen more intently to Jesus' call to walk the way of love? To get up and not be afraid?

# MOMENTO MORI – DO NOT BE AFRAID

THE REV. MARY VANC
Ash Wednesday – February 22, 2023

*Joel 2:1-2,12-17*
*Psalm 103*
*2 Corinthians 5:20b-6:10*
*Matthew 6:1-6,16-21*

"Memento mori" is not just the title of Depeche Mode's upcoming album—it is an ancient philosophical practice. *Memento mori* translates from the Latin as "Remember that you are mortal" or "Remember that you must die." In ancient Rome, after a major military victory, there was a tradition of parading the victorious general through the streets. The people would cheer, celebrate, and praise him, but—according to legend—there would be a slave standing behind the general, speaking into his ear, saying, "Look behind. Remember that you are mortal. Remember that you must die."[20]

Socrates once said that the proper practice of philosophy is "nothing else but dying and being dead." The Roman emperor Marcus Aurelius wrote, "Your days are numbered. Use them to throw open the windows of your soul to the sun. If you do not, the sun will soon set, and you with it."[21] We can see this contemplation of mortality across time, cultures, and religions because death is, after all, a universal human experience.

Yet, as humans are prone to extremes, these philosophies often go one of two ways:

- Remember that you are mortal. Tomorrow is not guaranteed. So have fun!
- Remember that you are mortal. Tomorrow is not guaranteed. So be good!

Of course, there's a false dichotomy here, suggesting that one can't be both good and have fun, but the deeper problem is that both paths are rooted in fear:

- Have fun while you can, because you're running out of time to enjoy life!
- Be good while you can, because you're running out of time to earn your passage into heaven.

No wonder so many of us would rather not think about it. It's scary. And though many preachers have used Ash Wednesday to scare people into repentance, I find that I can't reconcile this with the last words of Jesus we heard this past Sunday: "Get up, and do not be afraid." This is one of the most common directives in Scripture.

- Like in Deuteronomy, when God told Joshua, *"Do not be afraid ... for the Lord your God will go with you."* (Deut. 31:6)
- Or the Psalmist, who says, *"The Lord is my light and my salvation; whom shall I fear? The Lord is the strength of my life; of whom then shall I be afraid?"* (Psalm 27:1)
- Every time an angel appears in the Bible—whether to Mary at the Annunciation, to the shepherds at Christ's birth, or to the women at the tomb on Easter morning—the angel's first words are always, *"Do not be afraid."*
- Jesus taught his followers not to worry. In Matthew, he says, *"Are not two sparrows sold for a penny? Yet not one of them will fall to the ground outside your Father's care. And even the very hairs of your head are all numbered. So, don't be afraid; you are worth more than many sparrows."* (Matthew 10:29-31) In the Gospel of John, at the Last Supper, he says, *"Do not let your hearts be troubled. Believe in God; believe also in me."* (John 14:1)
- And in 1 John, we hear, *"There is no fear in love, but perfect love casts out fear."* (1 John 4:18)

I haven't counted them myself, but I've read that there are 365 verses of Scripture that essentially say, "Do not fear." We need this reminder every day.

Ash Wednesday is no exception.

So, when you come to the altar tonight, you will be marked with ash on your forehead in the sign of the cross—the same mark that was placed

100

on your head at your baptism. You will hear the words spoken to you: "*Remember that you are dust, and to dust you shall return.*"[22] It is a reminder of your mortality, yes, but also of your creation. In Genesis, God formed humanity from the dust of the earth and breathed life into them. We are dust, breath, and love. Our bodies may be fleeting, but our souls are not.

On this Ash Wednesday, do not fear your sin, but confess it. Receive God's mercy, that you may extend it.

Do not fear the passage of time, but let time carry you onward. Take each new day as a gift and an opportunity to love.

Do not fear your mortality, but embrace it. God made you for a good purpose. Put your life to good use.

Do not fear death, but respect the life God has given you, and take to heart the words of St. Paul in his letter to the Romans: "*If we live, we live to the Lord; and if we die, we die to the Lord; so then, whether we live or whether we die, we are the Lord's.*" (Romans 14:8)

Dear People of God: do not be afraid.

# OUR FORTY-DAY JOURNEY

THE REV. MARY VANO
First Sunday in Lent – February 26, 2023

*Genesis 2:15-17; 3:1-7*
*Psalm 32*
*Romans 5:12-19*
*Matthew 4:1-11*

One man faced a life-changing storm, so destructive that he made it through with only his family intact, losing his home and friends in the process. When the sun finally broke through, everything he had known before was gone, but he found a patch of green grass upon which to re-build his life.

In another time and place, a group of people bravely left behind the life they had known, hoping for something better. Though they had suffered oppression and abuse, at times, they wondered if they had made the right choice—at least they had known what to expect before. For years, they felt lost, unable to see what even the next day would bring. They doubted their leader and frequently rebelled against what they knew was right. But they held onto hope, because it was the only thing they had. By God's grace, they had what they needed, and by God's leading, they eventually found their way. When they reached their destination, they were a new people.

Many years later, a descendant of these same people reached a pivotal moment in his life, ready to give himself over to his calling. He had accepted God's mission and knew where he was headed, yet before he could reach it, he faced obstacles in the wilderness. Every piece of his identity was challenged. He knew he must rely completely on God, yet when hunger struck, he was tempted to use his power for his own needs. He had given himself to God's will, but he was tempted not to trust it. He knew whom he would serve, yet faced the temptation to serve another. By mastering these temptations, he emerged from the wilderness stronger, ready to do what he was born to do.

The first man was Noah, who spent forty days sheltered in the ark from the storm that God had instructed him to build. He survived the storm to rebuild the world.

The group of people was the Israelites—men, women, and children—who spent forty years in the desert, leaving behind oppression and learning to trust and follow God. They became the Chosen People, a light to the nations.

And their descendant was Jesus, who spent forty days in the wilderness after his baptism, facing temptations that challenged his very identity and his trust in God's plan When he emerged, he was ready to guide us through our own wilderness.

Just as Noah spent forty days in the storm, the Israelites wandered forty years in the desert, and Jesus faced forty days in the wilderness, we, too, spend forty days each year preparing for transformation. That's what forty is for: a sufficient period of time to transition and develop into who God has made us to be. The number doesn't matter; what matters is that forty is enough to bring about meaningful change.

This Lenten journey of forty days will take us somewhere—but unlike the unexpected trials that come suddenly in life, in Lent, we have some say in the journey we choose.

Perhaps your journey this year will be like Noah's. Your task might be to build a boat—strong and large enough to endure the storms that will come. But building such a boat requires more than just good carpentry; it requires radical obedience. Noah had to listen to God even when he didn't understand the plan, and he had to remain faithful, even when others criticized him. His obedience enabled him to survive the storm and to restore God's creation.

Or perhaps your Lenten journey will be more like the Israelites'. Their journey toward freedom was far from easy. Though they had been enslaved by abusive masters, they often looked back, unsure if they had made the right decision. Their journey was about learning to let go of the old and embrace the new. They had to trust God, who was now their master instead of their former oppressors. It took them years to learn that trust, but in doing so, they found true freedom.

Or your Lenten journey may echo Jesus' experience. After hearing God's love proclaimed at his baptism, Jesus entered the wilderness where his love for God was tested. In the wilderness, he had to become who he was called to be—not by remaining in a safe place, but by venturing into the world full of obstacles. Having mastered his temptations, Jesus was prepared to meet us where we are—in our own wildernesses.

So, maybe your Lenten journey is to learn to be obedient so that you can weather the storms ahead, or to let go of past suffering and embrace God's love, or to embrace the calling you've received and take it into the world. Whatever your journey, by the time we reach Easter, you will be changed. That's what Easter is about: resurrection to a new life that begins when we invite God into this one.

Let's go there. May your forty days be truly holy.

# OUR FAITH JOURNEY WITH NIC AT NIGHT

The Rev. Michaelene Miller
Second Sunday in Lent – March 5, 2023

*Genesis 12:1-4a*
*Psalm 121*
*Romans 4:1-5, 13-17*
*John 3:1-17*

It was night. I pedaled my red Schwinn bike down Clifton Street, turned right on Hairston, and left on Mitchell. At night, Conway, Arkansas, is quiet—especially ten blocks from Hendrix College on a Sunday evening. The air was still, the summer heat and humidity beginning to subside. It was late fall, during my freshman year of college.

I had recently left the Episcopal Collegiate School I had grown up in for Hendrix College, a liberal arts school known for its emphasis on reason and philosophy. It didn't take long to realize that I had left the religious environment of my high school years behind—a marinade of faith I had taken for granted. At Hendrix, a campus largely identified as the "Religious Nones," the name of Jesus rarely came up, and I was forced to wrestle with and define my faith in new ways.

One Sunday evening, I found myself at St. Peter's Episcopal Church, returning to gather with a few other young adults for Compline, or Night Prayer. We gathered on the floor of the sanctuary at the foot of the altar. I came as Nicodemus did—alone, in the dark. Under the cover of night, away from the eyes of my peers. At that age, many of my classmates were running away from the religion of their parents, and I, too, was questioning and seeking.

I came to ask Jesus questions. What does it mean to follow you in this world? What does it mean to have faith? To live a life of discipleship? These questions felt all the more urgent in the post-Christian world of Hendrix College, a microcosm of society where Christianity had been rejected, forgotten, or, worse, distorted to align with societal power and security.

Today, the lectionary shifts from the Gospel of Matthew to the Gospel of John for the remainder of this Lenten season. We will explore themes of discipleship and faith, and like Nicodemus, we may find ourselves questioning and seeking answers.

Oftentimes, we lift up stories of disciples who immediately respond in faith when God calls them. Take, for example, Abram in our reading from Genesis 12. The Lord says to Abram, "Go," and "Abram went." This is a beautiful example of faithful obedience—a story that I often turn to for encouragement in my own journey of struggling with faith and God's call.

But more often than not, our journey with God is not that clear-cut. It is a road full of risks, doubts, and twists, leading us to places of bewilderment and confusion. Our faith journeys can often be long and winding, full of potholes and rough patches. And today, we meet Nicodemus in just such a place of uncertainty and struggle.

Nicodemus, a Pharisee and leader of the Jewish community, comes to Jesus by night. Vulnerable, curious, and uncertain, he seeks Jesus out. "*Rabbi,*" he says, "*We know you are a teacher who has come from God, for no one can do these signs that you do apart from the presence of God.*"

In the Gospel of John, seeking Jesus marks the first step of discipleship. But Nicodemus comes at night, in the dark—a symbol of separation from the full presence and understanding of God. We might wonder, is Nicodemus hiding from the risks of his confession? Or is he simply not ready to confront the full weight of his faith struggles in the harsh light of day?

Whatever the case, Jesus is willing to meet him, offering love while speaking the hard truth. He tells Nicodemus that true discipleship requires much more than signs and miracles. It is a radical transformation: "*Very truly, I tell you, no one can see the kingdom of God without being born from above.*"

Jesus calls Nicodemus to move beyond a faith based solely on signs and miracles, to a deeper, more transformative relationship with God. Nicodemus, who has come to Jesus seeking signs, misses the deeper truth:

that knowing God goes beyond intellectual assent; it is about experiencing God's love and entering into a deeper relationship.

"*Very truly, I tell you,*" Jesus continues, "*no one can see the kingdom of God without being born from above.*" This new life of faith is not about understanding everything logically. It's a life of imagination, mystery, and transformation—one that calls us out of the confines of human knowledge and control.

Nicodemus, not yet ready for this radical shift, protests. "*How can anyone be born after having grown old? Can one enter a second time into the mother's womb and be born?*" He clings to his literal understanding, unable to grasp the new life Jesus is offering.

But Jesus gently continues to explain. There will be a physical birth, through water, and a spiritual birth, through the Spirit—who moves as it wills. The new life of a disciple will be shaped by the cross, a life that constantly challenges us to move beyond our certainties and embrace the unknown.

This life of faith, this journey with God, is full of risks. It calls us beyond what we can imagine, especially when it comes to our capacity for love and grace. This life asks more of us than we might be ready for, and at times it feels offensive or demanding. It calls us to trust in the Spirit, who blows where it wills, and to journey with God through times of confusion and uncertainty.

Nicodemus fades from the passage here, not yet ready to leave the safety of his questions and misunderstandings. But we come to know him well—often through our own struggles, our own midnight questions, our own hesitant seeking. We journey with him as we walk through our own times of uncertainty and doubt, seeking God in the darkness and waiting for the light to shine.

Through this encounter, we are reminded that we are called to be a community of faith that welcomes one another, challenges one another, and journeys together. As we move through the wilderness of Lent, we are called to accompany one another in love, helping each other navigate our questions and struggles.

And through all of this, we come to know God more fully—the God revealed in Jesus, whose mercy has no bounds. This is the God who calls us, time and again, to walk through the wilderness, trusting that God is with us, shaping us, and calling us to live out God's kingdom in this world.

# COME AND SEE

THE REV. MARY VANO
Third Sunday in Lent – March 12, 2023

*Exodus 17:1-7*
*Psalm 95*
*Romans 5:1-11*
*John 4:5-42*

Journalist Robert Krulwich once wrote an article for NPR in which he pondered the remarkable Australian lyrebird, calling it "Nature's Living Tape Recorders." These birds are incredible mimics, capable of imitating almost any sound they hear. One story particularly caught my attention: In 1969, an Australian park ranger named Neville Fenton recorded a lyrebird singing a tune that sounded like a flute being played by a human. After some investigation, Fenton discovered that 30 years earlier, a farmer who played the flute for his pet lyrebird had unintentionally passed the songs down to the wild population. The lyrebird had "downloaded" the music, and those tunes became part of the birds' songbook passed on from one generation to the next. A scholar named Norman Robinson figured out that the songs the wild lyrebirds were singing in 1969 were modified versions of two popular tunes from the 1930s, "The Keel Row" and "Mosquito's Dance."[23]

I don't know these songs, but they must have been catchy tunes. It all started with a man playing his songs for a bird.

We pick up today in the Gospel of John, almost exactly where we left off last week, after Jesus' conversation with Nicodemus. If you found yourself scratching your head after reading the third chapter of John, you're certainly not alone. Nicodemus, too, had difficulty understanding Jesus' words about the spirit, the flesh, and being born from above. Yet, the message becomes clear when Jesus says, *"For God so loved the world that he gave his only Son, so that everyone who believes in him may not perish but may have eternal life."* (John 3:16) In this simple yet profound statement, Jesus bridges the divide between flesh and spirit, between earth and heaven. *"For God so loved the world."*

God loved the world so much that he sent his Son, and after speaking to Nicodemus, Jesus set out to show his disciples the very world that God loves. But Jesus doesn't take the easy path; he goes into the risky territory of Samaria to meet a lonely woman at a well, all by herself, in the heat of the day. And there, he sings his song for her.

She was thirsty. Normally, women would go together to fetch water in the cooler parts of the day—morning or evening. But this woman came alone at midday, in the sweltering heat, a sign of her isolation and need. Jesus was thirsty, too, having sent his disciples to buy food. And so, crossing not only gender boundaries but also the long-standing enmity between Jews and Samaritans, he speaks to her. He offers her something far greater than a simple drink of water.

He says to her, *"Everyone who drinks this water will be thirsty again, but those who drink the water that I will give them will never be thirsty. The water that I will give will become in them a spring of water gushing up to eternal life."*

We don't know much about this woman—her name is never given. But we do know that love has not worked out well for her. She has had five husbands and has known loss, abandonment, and perhaps shame. Yet, Jesus does not judge her; he does not condemn her. Instead, he meets her where she is. He knows her story and offers her living water that will quench her thirst forever. She is unafraid to challenge Jesus and to ask him questions. And we know she is the first person to whom Jesus reveals his full identity. She has met the Messiah, and she is transformed by this encounter.

No longer is she thirsty. She becomes like a spring herself, gushing forth with wonder and love. She came to the well alone, perhaps seeking solitude, but she leaves in haste, eager to share what she's found. She becomes a witness, an evangelist, a conduit of God's grace. With a simple invitation, "Could this be the Messiah? Come and see," she spreads the news. She didn't need to convince anyone; she only had to share her story and offer the invitation. God did the rest. And though the Gospel doesn't tell us more about her, I believe her encounter with Jesus changed her life completely. She was no longer the nameless woman coming to fetch water; she was a woman filled to the brim with living water, ready to share it with others.

Our context today may look very different from the world of John's Gospel, but it's no less dry. We live in a desert of broken relationships, and often we are too afraid to work for healing. The rise of social media in the 21st century has given us more frequent contact with others, but it has done little to satisfy our thirst for true, authentic relationship. We also live in a desert of sin—guilt, shame, and fear—that we often try to hide. We can't trust that others will love us despite our failings, so we close ourselves off from those we love most.

Part of our Lenten journey is to discover these dry, barren places within ourselves. Sometimes we become so accustomed to our spiritual thirst that we don't even notice it anymore. But there are parts of our souls that are longing for the Living Water that only Jesus can give. We must allow these areas to be exposed—open to God's healing touch. When we do this, we align ourselves with God's saving purpose, joining God in extending love and grace to others. This is what Christ thirsts for when he asks the woman at the well for a drink. And he still thirsts. A few weeks from now, we will hear him cry out from the cross, "I thirst."

He thirsts for us, and we thirst for him. And just like the lyrebird that echoes a song from generation to generation, the invitation rings out for us: "Come and see." Come and drink. Quench your thirst, and in doing so, you, too, will sing. Your song may sound different, but don't doubt that it is beautiful—and someone needs to hear it from you. Think of the people who have sung that song of salvation for you. Think of how others have invited you to come and see and how they have given you a taste of that thirst-quenching water. Consider how Jesus has known and loved you. This is your song to sing. And I hope you will. I hope that together, we will fill the world with music.

# HEARING AND MOVING WITH JESUS

The Rev. Michaelene Miller
Fourth Sunday in Lent – March 19, 2023

*1 Samuel 16:1-13*
*Psalm 23*
*Ephesians 5:8-14*
*John 9:1-41*

Phew! Take a seat! Today, we take another big bite from the Gospel of John, and just a heads up—next week is an even longer passage! But hang in there. After all, we're on a Lenten journey, a pilgrimage through the Gospel of John. If our ancestors could wander the desert for 40 years, we can surely persist for a few more weeks through this Lenten time set apart for us to deepen our understanding and relationship with God.

So, let's buckle up and continue our pilgrimage, exploring themes of discipleship and faith. Today, we begin to glimpse how the new thing God is doing in Jesus will ultimately lead him to the cross.

In today's long passage, we witness how Jesus encounters and re-stores a man born blind. We also navigate the confusion and interrogation that follow—first from his neighbors, then his parents, and finally his re-ligious leaders.

The restoration of the man's sight—often called the healing of the man born blind—is the sixth out of seven major signs in John's Gospel. While the actual moment of healing occurs in only two of the 41 verses in this story, much of the remaining dialogue can distract us from the heart of the message.

So, I want us to focus on the margins. Let's pay attention to the parts of the story at the beginning and the end—the spaces between the main events. I believe there's a vital message in those margins.

Right at the start, before the dialogue and confusion take over, we meet Jesus. As we heard, *"As Jesus walked along, he saw a man."* Jesus sees this man and moves toward him.

And it doesn't take long before confusion erupts. The disciples are distracted—perhaps even distracting us—with a theological question about sin and blame. But Jesus cuts through the noise, declaring that neither this man nor his parents sinned. Instead, he refocuses the disciples—and us—on the mission, saying, "We must work the works of God." This is what's important now.

From the very beginning, Jesus sees this man—not just as a beggar, but as a person with a need to be seen, recognized, and restored. In Jesus' time, being blind meant being socially excluded. This man was seen only as a beggar, forced to depend on others' charity. But Jesus sees him differently. He moves to restore him, not only physically, but to reintroduce him into the community.

Jesus spits on the ground, makes mud, and spreads it on the man's eyes, telling him to wash in the pool of Siloam. The man obeys, and when he returns, he can see.

Yet, instead of rejoicing, the community questions him relentlessly. The man, once blind but now healed, is still only seen as a beggar by his neighbors, recognizable only when he is in his place begging on his corner. We come to see how he is kept pigeonholed even by the disciples and other religious leaders as a poor man destined only to suffer the consequences of someone's sin.

Questions about both Jesus' and this man's identity pour forth so profusely that the opportunity for connection that Jesus created in the restoration of this man's sight, which should have been a cause for celebration, only leads to the man, once again, being rejected! Again, *they drove him out,* his healing overshadowed by these interrogations.

But Jesus hasn't gone far. He hears that the man has been cast out and immediately goes to find him. Jesus seeks him out, going to the margins, to restore not just his sight but his place in the community.

And then, Jesus invites him beyond the physical healing to a deeper, fuller restoration—inviting him into a new relationship as a disciple, as part of a new community. He says, *"You have seen [the Son of Man], and the one speaking with you is he."* The man responds, *"Lord, I believe,"* and worships Jesus.

From the start, Jesus sees this man—not just as a beggar, but as a potential witness, someone who could see and know God's work through Jesus. Jesus calls him to be a disciple.

The man's journey of recognizing who Jesus is gradual. First, he hears Jesus' call and obeys. We are reminded that, just as God's voice commanded on Transfiguration Sunday, *"This is my Son, the Beloved; with him, I am well pleased; listen to him!"* The path of discipleship, as the Gospel of John teaches us, is one of listening and following—hearing and obeying.

As the man's understanding of Jesus deepens, so does his testimony. Through questioning and confrontation, he comes to recognize Jesus for who he truly is: Lord. And he worships him.

So, what is the message of the margins? In the margins, outside and beyond all the debate and on either end of the interrogation, we notice Jesus moving. Here in the margins of this story is the Jesus movement!

Jesus is constantly in motion. In the Gospel of John, he is constantly moving out to the Judean countryside, all across Galilee, and up and down from Jerusalem, constantly gathering and caring for those who are lost, or considered sinners, or those scattered and forced by society to roam at the margins.

Like a shepherd looking for the lost sheep, Jesus moves. Here, in the margins, we see the *Jesus movement!* Jesus is always in motion, always moving to those who are lost, rejected, and cast out. He is constantly gathering the scattered and showing love to those pushed to the margins of society.

This movement isn't just physical. Jesus' heart is moved with compassion for those he sees. After this healing, Jesus explains that he is the good shepherd who has come to bring abundant life to those who are lost, disinherited, or cast aside. His sheep follow him because they know his voice, and they live in full relationship with him.

The way of Jesus, the Jesus movement, is a way of love. As Presiding Bishop Michael Curry puts it, it is "a way of love that seeks the good and well-being of the other before the self's own unenlightened interest; a way of love that is not self-centered, but other-directed; a way of love that is grounded in compassion, goodness, justice, and forgiveness."[24] Bishop Curry goes on to describe this way of Jesus as one that is "loving, liberating, and life-giving" and that a community joins in this movement of Jesus when it commits to living this way of love and commits to going out into the world to help this world transform into one that is loving, liberating, and life-giving.

Bishop Curry describes this way of love as one that invites us to commit to living it out, going into the world to transform it into a place that reflects these values.

I've heard it said that our lives may be the only gospel some people ever read by our neighbor.[25] I know that I've mentioned this once in a sermon already, but it is something that scares me, so it is usually on my mind. And while this scares me, because it reminds me of the real responsibility we take on in our baptism—it also invites the Holy Spirit into my fear. It's a reminder that we must constantly pray. We must pray that we are moved with compassion, that we notice our neighbor, and that we can help bring about reconciliation in a broken world.

We must pray for the eyes to see clearly so that we can continuously join the work of reconciliation in an ever-evolving world. We must pray for ears to hear God's voice, and for the strength to be part of the work of gathering, not scattering. We come to this place to be nourished by the teachings of Jesus and the body of Christ, and bite by bite of the Eucharist, so that we may be replenished in our work. We find the strength for the journey.

And we can trust that we are not alone in this work. We are part of the Episcopal branch of the Jesus Movement, and we do all of this *not for God but with God's help.*

# HOPE IN THE WILDERNESS

THE REV. MARY VANO
Fifth Sunday in Lent – March 26, 2023

*Ezekiel 37:1-14*
*Psalm 130*
*Romans 8:6-11*
*John 11:1-45*

*"Out of the depths have I called to you, O Lord; Lord, hear my voice."* Our psalm today sets the stage. It is still Lent, and we are still in the wilderness. It is still Lent, and we are still reflecting on the sin and death in our own souls. Yet today is all about hope!

It is about hope, even in the midst of exile. The story of the Israelite people is one of liberation, failure, and restoration. God brought them out of slavery to the Promised Land, only for them to squander that gift. They worshiped false idols and did evil, becoming enslaved by their own sin. Their faithlessness divided them, and eventually, they were conquered, exiled, and once again subject to the powers of the world.

The Israelites had been forcibly removed from their land into exile, far from home and their accustomed ways, compelled to toil for a conquering nation. Though alive, they felt dead—like a nation of dry bones. They cried out in their misery, as all enslaved people do.

And so Ezekiel prophesies. In his vision, Ezekiel is taken to a valley filled with dry bones—the remains of long-dead humans. God asks Ezekiel, *"Mortal, can these bones live?"* Ezekiel replies, *"O Lord God, you know."* Then God commands Ezekiel to prophesy to the bones, and as he does, the bones come together and take on flesh. God then tells Ezekiel to prophesy to the breath, so these bodies may live again. They will live, and they will know that God is the source of life, who will not only give them life again but bring them out of exile and back home.

Today is about hope—hope that when we are in exile, we may be returned, and hope that when we feel powerless, Christ will enliven and empower us. In Romans, Paul writes, *"To set the mind on the flesh is death, but to set the mind on the Spirit is life and peace.*" Paul argues that we cannot save ourselves. No matter how much we try to follow the law or separate ourselves from those we deem unrighteous, we will find that we are the unrighteous. We have no power to save ourselves.

But, Paul says, "*If the Spirit of him who raised Jesus from the dead dwells in you, he who raised Christ from the dead will give life to your mortal bodies also.*" We cannot save ourselves, but we can give our lives to the one who gives us life. Without this offering, we remain in death. But when we set our hearts to God, we can have life, peace, and hope.

Today is about hope—even in the face of death. Mary and Martha, sisters, lost their brother Lazarus. It was heartbreaking. They loved him, relied on him, and as followers of Jesus, they hoped Jesus would come and save him. When Jesus arrives on the fourth day after Lazarus' death, the sisters greet him with the same words: "*Lord, if you had been here, my brother would not have died.*" Both an accusation and a statement of faith.

Jesus weeps—salty tears of grief, disappointment, and sympathy. Yet, even as he grieves, he raises Lazarus to reveal that in God, death will not destroy us. "*I am the resurrection and the life,*" he says. All must die, but death cannot destroy the life we have in God through faith in Christ.

Like the ancient Israelites, we exile ourselves with wandering hearts. Like the first-century Romans, we think if we follow the right rules, we won't need to rely on God's mercy. And like Mary and Martha, we know death comes for us all, but when death touches our beloved, it shakes us.

But the constant message of our faith is that, despite the wilderness, God still acts. Even when the covenant people fail to uphold their end, God upholds the promises. Despite sin, God forgives. Despite blindness, God gives sight. Despite being outsiders, God reaches out. Despite despair, God brings hope. Despite death, God *will* bring life.

As we wait in the midst of the season of Lent, we remember the wilderness seasons in our own lives. These are times for repentance and return, because no matter how thick the trees or how dry the desert, God is calling to us to bring us what we need most: *hope.*

# A PROTEST TO SAVE US

The Rev. Michaelene Miller
Sunday of the Passion: Palm Sunday – April 2, 2023

*Matthew 21:1-11*
*Psalm 118:1-2, 19-29*
*Isaiah 50:4-9a*
*Psalm 31:9-16*
*Philippians 2:5-11*
*Matthew 26:14- 27:66*

This day is referred to in the Book of Common Prayer as "The Sunday of the Passion: Palm Sunday." As you can hear, this service carries two titles, each pointing to a different liturgical element: the dramatic reading of the passion we'll soon experience and the joyous waving of palms we just remembered.

These events are held in tension, brought together in one day by the simple punctuation of a colon. Today's liturgy stretches our emotional capacity, taking us on a journey from the emotional high of hope to the lowest depths of despair and disappointment. This service invites us into the extremes, pivoting from one gospel passage to another, both marking the beginning of Holy Week.

We began this morning by recalling the triumphant procession of disciples, shouting praises of blessing upon Jesus, who they recognized as their king, the Son of David. We join our voices to theirs in our liturgy, calling out, *"Blessed is he who comes in the name of the Lord,"* and responding, *"Hosanna in the highest!"* With palms raised, we join the celebration of Jesus' entry into Jerusalem.

And then, in a nearly whiplash-like moment, we will leave in silence after crying out, *"Let him be crucified, let him be crucified!"* We leave Jesus brutalized and sealed in a tomb.

After another long season of Lent, where we've wandered and reflected on the dry, life-suppressing deserts between us and liberation, I both welcome and hesitate at stepping into Holy Week. This liturgy, and

118

the ones that follow, "hold within it the fullness of the human journey," containing all the complexities and emotional ranges: from hope to despair, from courage in community to fear in isolation.

It's a journey we've all experienced with unique intensity in recent years. But it is also within the context of our world today, where we have all walked closer to the reality of death and destruction—where young adults hesitate to plan families due to concerns about the earth's capacity, where bodies—trans bodies, children's bodies—face legislative attack, where schools too easily turn into battlegrounds, and where the false sense of a post-segregation America has vanished. Here, in a city reeling from a catastrophic storm, we should be able to hear, in our very bones, the crowd's shouts of *"Hosanna!"*

Instead of a joyous shout of praise, I now hear the deeper, desperate cry of the original crowd, their plea: *"Hosanna!"*

It is curious that we don't translate this word from its original Hebrew in our Bibles or in our liturgy. If we did, we might be able to feel and better understand the weight of the crowd's desperation and need. Hosanna! We join the people's cry. "Hosanna! Save us!" *"Save now"* is what we pray when we echo the multitude's cry of *Hosanna.*

It is in this context that I now understand Jesus' actions in this story better than ever before. Rather than the parade I once imagined, I can now see more clearly the intentional, strategic protest Jesus leads into Jerusalem and the protest in the temple that follows immediately after in Matthew's Gospel.

Before entering the city to commemorate the Passover, Jesus sends two disciples to find a donkey and colt, which he has arranged to use. *"Go into the village ahead of you, and immediately you will find a donkey tied and a colt with her; untie them and bring them to me."* Jesus leads a protest march into the city in a strategic, intentional protest. And after this procession, in the temple, Jesus disrupts the status quo by driving out those who were exploiting the faithful, turning the Lord's house of prayer into a den of robbers. He overturns tables, clearing the space for a teach-in about the Kingdom of God.

After clearing the temple of the merchants, the blind and lame immediately come to him, and Jesus continues his ministry of healing. These actions—Jesus' protest and his healing ministry—set the stage for his eventual arrest. His public demonstrations of disruption and his teaching about another way of living led directly to his criminalization by the authorities. The chief priests and elders conspired to arrest Jesus and kill him, seeing him as a threat to the false peace of the Pax Romana.

In today's gospel passage, we should note that Jesus' march into Jerusalem parallels the procession of the Roman governor of Judea, who would also enter Jerusalem for the Passover. Pilate, dressed in armor and surrounded by armed troops, represented the power of Rome. But Jesus enters from the east—on donkeys, unarmed and vulnerable—challenging the very symbols of power and control.

The people gathered around Jesus expected a king who would overthrow Pilate, but instead of a majestic warhorse, Jesus arrives on donkeys. And as the crowd lays their cloaks on the road, they unknowingly express their misunderstanding: they believe Jesus is entering Jerusalem to take a throne, to rise above the messiness of the world. Yet Jesus' entrance and his entire life show that his mission is not to rise above, but to enter into the mess of the world. He does not ascend to a throne; he is lifted up on the cross.

On the cross, Jesus exposes the messiness of the world—sin, injustice, and oppression—for all to see. As Christians, we are called to look at the cross and recognize the truth about the world and our participation in these systems. In the cross, we find the one who stands in solidarity with the oppressed, who offers God's sustaining Word to the weary and vulnerable. This is where salvation begins.

I wonder if you've experienced this protest tradition we've inherited from Jesus. Have you joined protests, walked with your neighbors, or prayed with your feet in demonstrations for justice? If you were unable to be there physically, did you spiritually join in lament, praying for justice and against oppression?

Next to participating in the Eucharist, I've found that community gatherings in protest against injustice are some of the most incarnational expressions of God's love and restorative hope. Just last night at our church's community dinner, one of our youngest members made a welcome sign that read, "Love and care and praise is the only thing that can save us." Hosanna, we pray—save now.

Our gospel passages today leave us in the streets—from a triumphal protest to a state-sanctioned execution. I wonder where you find yourself in the streets today. Are you there celebrating, rejoicing in community? Are you there protesting and praying with your feet? Are you there judging and criminalizing? We all inhabit these spaces, and we are all capable of being in all of them. Where do you find yourself today?

# KEEP WATCH

THE REV. MARY VANO
Maundy Thursday – April 7, 2023

*Exodus 12:1-4, (5-10), 11-14*
*Psalm 116:1, 10-17*
*1 Corinthians 11:23-26*
*John 13:1-17, 31b-35*

> Keep watch, dear Lord, with those who work, or watch, or weep this night, and give your angels charge over those who sleep. Tend the sick, Lord Christ; give rest to the weary, bless the dying, soothe the suffering, pity the afflicted, shield the joyous; and all for your love's sake.

This is one of my favorite prayers from the Book of Common Prayer. I say it before I go to sleep each night, and, especially over the past week, I feel as though I'm inviting God's loving presence to meet each soul where they are—whether in peace or chaos, joy or grief. *"Keep watch,"* we pray, with the restless and weary, the anxious parents, the lonely widows, and those whose lives seem to be slipping away. And keep watch, dear Lord, as storms roll in and leave destruction in their wake. Keep watch with emergency responders, insurance adjusters, line workers, and all those working to restore us in our times of need.

And when I pray, I sense God's invitation to me to keep watch as well. So, like many of you, last week I did everything I could to help those affected by the tornado. In the immediate aftermath, I tried to stay out of areas where my presence might do more harm than good. But finally, on Sunday, my brother invited me to visit his neighborhood in North Little Rock—to simply witness. He was still waiting for professional help with trees, power, and roof damage, but what he asked of me was simply to come and see.

And so, I did. What struck me among all the destruction was the mark left on each home by the emergency responders: the X-Code. It's a bright orange X, with additional symbols to indicate that the home had been checked for injuries or deaths. At first, it was jarring to see. But at the same time, I found comfort knowing that others were keeping watch. The tornado left its own mark, but the X-Codes were a sign to me that God was watching over us, too. Helping hands were everywhere.

Last year, a friend here at St. Margaret's gave me a book by Tish Harrison Warren called *Prayer in the Night*, an exposition of that favorite prayer of mine for those who work, watch, or weep. In the chapter on keeping watch, the author introduced me to the way nautical flags communicate between ships at sea. When radios fail, flags can be raised to send out warnings or requests for assistance. There are forty flags in a complete set of international maritime signal flags, one for each letter of the alphabet, one for each number, and four special flags for unique operations. Raised by themselves or in different combinations, these flags send various messages.

One flag—a white flag with a red X—signals, "I require assistance." A particular combination of flags might signal in response, "I will keep close to you during the night."

Where we meet Jesus tonight, at the Last Supper with his disciples, in the final hours before his betrayal, arrest, and trial, Jesus signals to his disciples how he will be with them. He removes his outer robe, ties a towel around his waist, and fills a basin with water. These actions clearly signal that he is preparing to wash his disciples' feet. This was a common ritual in the first century: before paved roads and shoes, guests would remove their sandals, and the feet would be washed—a sign of hospitality and preparation. But this was a servant's task, not one for a respected teacher or leader.

But Jesus' signal was clear. As their teacher, their leader, he would take off his robe, tie a towel, and wash their feet. Peter, representing the stunned disciples, objects: *"Lord, are you going to wash my feet?"* Peter understands the role being played, but he objects to the implication—he respects and admires Jesus too much to let him tend to his feet. Like Peter, I think we much prefer to look up to our leaders, not see the tops of their heads as they wash the dirt and stink off our bodies.

But this is what love looks like. The time will come for the disciples to look up to Jesus, but to understand the cross, the disciples first need to understand the foot-washing. They need to recognize the signs of Jesus' presence. With attention given to their needs, they will know that Jesus is keeping watch. In the work of hospitality, they will feel God's recognition and appreciation. In acts of service, they will understand the leader whose example they must follow. In these tender acts of compassion, they will know how Jesus loves us. *"Love one another,"* Jesus said, *"as I have loved you."*

In our darkest and stormiest moments, when we silently raise a white flag with a red X, wordlessly crying out for help, Jesus signals back to us, "I will keep close to you during the night." This is the hope God offers us. As Warren writes in her book, "*[God]* will keep close to us, even in darkness, *in* doubt, *in* fear and vulnerability. *[God]* does not promise to keep bad things from happening. *[God]* does not promise that night will not come, or that it will not be terrifying, or that we will immediately be tugged to shore. [God] promises that we will not be left alone. *He* will keep watch with us in the night.*"*

The Gospel of Matthew tells us that after the Last Supper, Jesus took a few disciples to pray. He asked them to keep watch with him—remain with him, stay awake. In his hour of need, Jesus asked for prayer, for presence, for vigilance. He asked that they not leave him alone. This is what we can do for Jesus, and it's what we can do for each other. We can love one another as Jesus has loved us: by being attentive to needs, by welcoming and caring for one another, by serving each other, and by showing the tender compassion that God has shown to us in the love of Jesus Christ.

*"Keep watch,"* therefore, with those who work, or watch, or weep this night. Tend the sick, give rest to the weary, bless the dying, soothe the suffering, pity the afflicted, shield the joyous. For the sake of his love, *"keep watch."*

# IT IS FINISHED – IT IS JUST BEGINNING

THE REV. CINDY FRIBOURGH
Good Friday – April 7, 2023

*Isaiah 52:13-53:12*
*Psalm 22*
*Hebrews 10:16-25*
*John 18:1-19:42*

>*Jesus "breathed his last." "It is finished."*

Before his arrest, Jesus prayed in the Garden of Gethsemane: *"Father, the hour has come; glorify your Son so that the Son may glorify you ... I glorified you on earth by finishing the work that you gave me to do."* Finished. Jesus completed the work of seeking and saving the lost, atoning for humanity's sins, and reconciling our sinful selves to God.

He preached the good news: *"Blessed are the poor in spirit, those who mourn, the meek, merciful, pure in heart, and the peacemakers. Blessed are those who are persecuted for righteousness' sake. When people revile you and persecute you and utter all kinds of evil against you falsely on my account. You are the salt of the earth, the light of the world."*

And he taught us—both in word and example—the greatest of all commandments: *"Love the Lord your God with all your heart, with all your soul, with all your mind, and with all your strength. And secondly: 'You shall love your neighbor as yourself.'"*

Jesus showed us what that love looks like: feeding the hungry, standing up for the powerless, touching the untouchable, and giving hope to the hopeless. Pray without ceasing.

*It is finished.* Completed. Fulfilled.

Hanging on the cross, giving up his spirit, Jesus fulfilled the ancient Messianic prophecies. The 39 books of the Old Testament—from Genesis to Malachi—contain more than 300 prophecies about the coming of the Anointed One: the *seed* who would crush the serpent's head in Genesis, Isaiah's Suffering Servant, and the prediction of the virgin birth. *"The one who is more powerful than I is coming after me; I am not worthy to stoop down and untie the strap of his sandals. I have baptized you with water, but he will baptize you with the Holy Spirit,"* declares John, the "messenger" of the Lord.

Psalm 22 poignantly expresses the agony endured by humankind's Savior, and we remember it today:

*My God, my God, why have you forsaken me?*

*Why are you so far from helping me, from the words of my groaning?*

*O my God, I cry by day, but you do not answer;*

*And by night, but find no rest.*

*"It is finished."* For the Roman soldiers and the Jewish leaders, this cry likely meant something very different—a cry of defeat.

When Jesus was growing up, Judea was in chaos. The people were split into hostile factions, and itinerant preachers and prophets roamed the countryside, some drawing large crowds. After his baptism by John, Jesus began to draw his own enormous crowds with a message of love and hope. There was a kingdom greater than Rome, and God would provide for the poor and helpless.

His followers claimed he was the Son of God, a king. Jesus became an increasing threat to the Roman authorities and to social and religious traditions. He had to go.

Literally thousands of revolutionaries opposing the Roman Empire were executed in the first three centuries of the Common Era. To the Roman soldiers and religious leaders, Jesus was just one more to deal with. *Crucify him!* They believed Jesus, his ideas, claims, and movement, were dead along with him.

But *ha! It is finished.* In reality, though, it had just begun: the work of Christ's mission.

*"As the Father has sent me, even so, I am sending you,"* Jesus says in the Gospel of John. *"Whoever receives the one I send receives me, and whoever receives me receives the one who sent me."*

From the first-century disciples to ourselves, the Christian mission is to bring the good news of Jesus Christ to all persons. To bear witness, to carry on Christ's work of reconciliation in the world. To pray, responding to God by thought and deed, with or without words. To live with confidence in the newness and fullness of life. To await the coming of Christ in glory and the completion of God's purpose in the world. And then, say with Jesus Christ victoriously, *"It is finished."*

# DARK NIGHTS

THE REV. MICHAELENE MILLER
Easter Vigil – April 8, 2023

*Romans 6:3-11*
*Psalm 114*
*Matthew 28:1-10*

We began this most holy night like Mary Magdalene and the other Mary—quietly and in near darkness, looking to encounter the risen Lord.

Having walked with the Living Word of God through his life, having supported and provided for him as he traveled and gathered great multitudes, healing and teaching, these women had stayed with Jesus. While he was hanged upon a cross, they remained, though from a distance. When he was dead and sealed away, they sat in waiting, opposite the tomb. Now, having stepped away for the sabbath rest, their story culminates in the dark, just before the dawn: Mary Magdalene and the other Mary went to see the tomb.

These women remained close through all that had just unfolded, while other disciples deserted in fear and confusion, and Peter denied knowing Jesus three times. And as the darkness was just beginning to pass into light, they went in wonder to take a closer look, to contemplate the tomb, and to try to understand whatever was to be found.

As the women approached the tomb, their world was shaken once again. Suddenly, there was another great earthquake, and an angel of the Lord appeared, like lightning, rolling back the stone and saying, *"Do not be afraid; I know that you are looking for Jesus who was crucified. He is not here, for he has been raised, as he said."*

Jesus had told them. Three times in the Gospel of Matthew, Jesus attempted to prepare his disciples and tell them the kind of death he was to die and how he would rise. The disciples had been prepared, but when confronted by the trauma of the cross, their responses were still confusion, denial, and wonder.

128

While the first disciples witnessed Jesus' miracles and teachings with their own eyes and ears, they had also constructed their own ideas of who Jesus was and what he would do. This is only human—to allow thoughts and dreams about the future to flourish. They constructed expectations of a victorious Messiah and an earthly king. However, all these hopes and cultivated expectations seemed to die with Jesus upon the cross.

And yet, in this moment of lingering darkness, something different—something entirely new—was happening. As the angel reported, the tomb was empty. *He is not here, for he has been raised.* The entire world—not just their hopes and dreams, but what the disciples knew about the world, the rules of life and death—all of it was brought into question.

In the midst of this lingering darkness, the disciples—both the absent ones hiding in confusion and denial, and the women present in their wonder—reveal how transformation and resurrection can be a disorienting experience that brings on the darkness of not knowing before the light of truth is found and understood. In resurrection, there is a passage through death before new life, and into darkness before light.

Many have written about experiences of deep spiritual transformation that occur beneath a veil of disorienting darkness. This experience of spiritual darkness happens when previous ways of relating to or knowing God fall away, and the new, emerging pull toward a deeper relationship with God is not yet understood. Among spiritual writers, this is known as the "dark night of the soul."

Author Sue Monk Kidd reflects on her own experience of a dark night in her book *When the Heart Waits*. She describes the transformation as a "process that involves undoing ego patterns, recasting the old story we created for ourselves to live in, and unraveling illusions not only about ourselves but about God."

It's too easy to get distracted by what we expect or want God to be. In these moments, we need the experience of the dark night to help us let go and let the new thing emerge. The women went to the tomb to see—to see what was needed. To see whatever was to be found. Would there be a body? If so, did they need their spices to complete the burial rituals for their dear friend? If not, then what was next? They teetered at the edge of the old, familiar story of how the world worked, yet they dared to look.

It helped that God had sent a messenger. *"Do not be afraid,"* the angel said, as he reminded the women of who Jesus was and helped them interpret what was unfolding before them in the empty tomb. They needed guidance on what to do next. The angel was clear about that, too. *"Come, see the empty tomb. Then go quickly and tell the others!"*

This need for reminding, interpretation, and guidance makes sense. We need reminding, too. Every year at the Easter Vigil, as we gather in the darkness of night around the new fire, we become pilgrims in search of remembering. All of the readings we hear on this night remind us of God's faithful and loving power to create order out of chaos, liberation out of oppression, abundant nourishment out of dry places, hope out of despair, and life out of death. These are the stories of God's saving acts throughout history.

It is fitting that we gather in the darkness of night to remember this. These stories help to reorient us to the truth of God's identity and our own identity as God's people—a resurrection people. As we remember this truth, it works on our lives. Just as the world was transformed in the moment when Jesus was resurrected in that dark tomb, resurrection changes us, too.

Sue Monk Kidd, reflecting on how necessary the experience of darkness is in the process of transformation, offers this insight: "Everything incubates in darkness ... whether it's the caterpillar in the chrysalis, the seed in the ground, the child in the womb, or the True Self in the soul, there's always a time of waiting in the dark."

Matthew's account of the empty tomb and what follows in the story, after the women go and tell, reminds us that Easter joy does not unfold quickly or easily. Faith is a process that will see us through many bright days and dark nights. Faith is a relationship with God that takes time and effort to look closely in contemplation to understand, because it often calls us beyond what we know to be possible.

Transformation, renewal, and remembering demand time to incubate. As we leave here and return to the still darkness of the night, my prayer is that we all allow time for this resurrection hope to incubate within us. Let it expand and take hold of your imagination. It has the power to transform us. It has the power to transform the world. And then, don't be afraid—go and tell about it! *Alleluia! Christ is risen. The Lord is risen indeed. Alleluia!*

# MEMENTO VIVERE – GARDENING

THE REV. MARY VANO
Easter Day – April 9, 2023

*Acts 10:34-43*
*Psalm 118:1-2, 14-24*
*Colossians 3:1-4*
*John 20:1-18*

Suppose you can remember just a little over forty days ago. In that case, you'll recall how we began our Lenten season of preparation on Ash Wednesday: with the mark of ashes on our foreheads and the statement, *"Remember that you are dust and to dust you shall return."* In my sermon that night, I related this statement to the ancient philosophical tradition, the *memento mori*. The Latin phrase translates to *"Remember that you will die."* That night, I asked you, Christians, not to shape your lives around a fear of death but to trust that in both life and death, we belong to God.

So now we have arrived at Easter—the day of resurrection—and today I want to tell you that the *memento mori* has a companion philosophy: *memento vivere. "Remember to live."*

For some, "remembering to live" means throwing all caution to the wind: going to all the parties, drinking all the wine, eating all the good food, spending every penny—just wringing all the pleasures out of life. This path, though thrilling, if taken to the extreme, can lead not to life but likely to more suffering.

Yet Jesus came so that we may have life and have it abundantly! If the abundant life into which we are invited on this day of Resurrection isn't found down a path of consumption, where will we find it? Like the age-old quest for the fountain of youth, the search for abundant life seems elusive. Will I have an abundant life when I've achieved a successful career? Or in a never-anything-but-blissful marriage? Can my dream home fill me with abundant life? Perfect children? Retirement? When will I be able to look around me and declare, *"This is the life!"*?

Let us look to Easter for the clue. On the day of Resurrection, the Gospel of John includes a moment when we realize that Mary Magdalene isn't just in a cemetery; she is in a garden. Her tears were flowing outside the empty tomb of her beloved Jesus—exhausted and confused—when a man appeared beside her, asking why she was weeping. She assumes he is the gardener.

After all, isn't that what we do with cemeteries? We turn them from death by filling the grounds with living things—things that will grow, clean the air, delight the eye, and produce food for more living things. That empty tomb opened out into a garden, where Mary Magdalene first laid eyes on the Resurrected Jesus and mistook him for the gardener. The new resurrected life begins—as Genesis did—in a garden.

The garden is where all life begins. It is the home of God's creative work, where God first blessed humanity, walking alongside them, having given them both a place to thrive and the meaningful work of tending it. The abundant Easter life to which we are now called is a life of gardening.

It begins with planting. What are the good things you hope will grow in the world? What can nourish the souls around you and bring life to yourself and others? What do you think God hopes for? I believe that God hopes for gardeners to prepare the earth and plant those tiny seeds of faith, hope, and love.

Of course, gardening isn't only about planting. It's also about cultivating. The good things that we hope to see grow in the world need our attention and are worthy of our efforts. If we want a healthier planet, we'll need to care for the earth. If we want less hate in the world, we need to give more attention to love and nurture it wherever we find it. If we want friendlier neighborhoods, let that begin with you meeting your neighbors. How can we better support our teachers if we want children to thrive through quality education? Anything we want to grow will need the right environment, regular nutrition, and just the right amount of light. Gardeners are required, so let us cultivate the life-giving Spirit among us.

Pruning is another aspect of our work as gardeners. The season of Lent is especially focused on this work, but pruning can happen at any time when we learn to let go of those dying and dead things that prevent our thriving. Gardeners also know that it's not just the dead branches that need pruning but also those living parts that distract and take up energy that would otherwise go toward bearing fruit.

The work of pruning is about focusing on the life to which we are called, putting our energy toward growing and thriving, and removing everything else. What needs to be removed from your garden so that you may live more fully?

Planting, cultivating, and pruning all move us toward the primary goal: to bear fruit. This is God's good purpose for us—to feed one another, nurture the world, and provide for others those things we all need to thrive. There is such a beautiful variety of good things that work together to nourish us. What you provide will have its own unique flavor. Together, and allowing God to work through us, we can provide the rich feast for all people foretold by the prophet Isaiah.

So, on the Day of Resurrection, when Mary heard her name and realized that the gardener was indeed Jesus, she reached out to touch him. He told her not to hold on to him—not for the sake of some sense of purity or propriety, but because she had work to do. *"Go,"* he told her. *"Tell them."* Go and use those hands to plant a garden.

Tend to God's garden with the love that I have given you and spread your faith over all the earth so that all may flourish, all may enjoy the astounding beauty of God's creation, all may be free to breathe, and all may thrive.

This is the life. This is the life for which we have been made—gardening. Planting, cultivating, pruning, and bearing fruit. This is the path of our flourishing and the hope to which we are called. This is the Easter life. So, *memento vivere*: Remember to live it.

# RESURRECTION IMPLICATIONS

THE REV. MICHAELENE MILLER
Second Sunday of Easter – April 16, 2023

*Acts 2:14a,22-32*
*Psalm 16*
*1 Peter 1:3-9*
*John 20:19-31*

Our gospel passage for today tells us that when it was evening on that day, the first day of the week, and the doors of the house where the disciples had met were locked for fear of the [Jewish authorities], Jesus came and stood among them and said, *"Peace be with you."* After he said this, he showed them his hands and his side.

In this appearance, on the same evening that Mary discovered the empty tomb and proclaimed for the first time the good news of the resurrected Lord, Jesus interrupts the disciples' paralyzed wonderings, where they are hiding in fear, with his body. With his entire, bodily presence before them—scarred flesh and rigid bone—Jesus reminds the disciples of his identity and his earthly ministry, which is now their own as he commissions them as his followers.

Jesus comes to the disciples in their fear, gives them peace, and reminds them of the work now entrusted to them as witnesses of his life, death, and resurrection. He says, *"Just as the Father has sent me, so I send you."* When he had said this, he breathed on them and said, *"Receive the Holy Spirit. If you forgive the sins of any, they are forgiven them; if you retain the sins of any, they are retained."*

Empowered by the breath of God and the gift of the Holy Spirit, the disciples can no longer stay behind locked doors. They can no longer expect Jesus alone to perform the miracles and do the work. They can no longer stay quiet about what they believe. Here, just as in the Genesis Creation story, the breath of God is creating something new.

In the Gospel of John, the resurrection of Jesus Christ is intimately linked with the moment of Pentecost—the birth of the Church. The disciples are breathed upon, empowered by the gift of the Holy Spirit, and reminded that they are to continue Jesus' work of declaring a gospel of forgiveness to the world.

The disciples, as witnesses of the resurrected Lord, are commissioned in their ministry to testify, to proclaim repentance and forgiveness of sins, and to continue Jesus' ministry of reconciliation to all bodies. This work of reconciliation, now the mission of the Church, is defined in the Book of Common Prayer as "the work of restoring all people to unity with God and each other in Christ."

Today, as we begin to experience the effects of the climate crisis, we might consider expanding this statement. The Church's responsibility is not only to restore all people to unity with God but also to restore all of creation to its intended unity with God.

In his own body, Jesus breathes upon the disciples, reminding them of their work to reconcile the bodies of creation—bodies of humans, land, water, and animals—to each other and to God. The disciples are moved from the security of locked doors into a ministry of witness, presence, relationship, and reconciliation.

Accepting the ministry of Jesus and what it means to be a disciple, to follow in the way of Christ and continue his mission of reconciliation, must be fueled by great faith. So, where does this great faith develop? Our series of gospel stories this Easter season tells us that faith comes from personal encounters with the risen Lord.

The location of the disciples, fearfully locked away in a room, shows us that the empty tomb is not enough to produce Easter faith. Resurrection faith is born from post-resurrection appearances—from personal encounters with the risen Lord. In these intimate, personal encounters, the disciples are changed. Their life purpose has changed.

When Jesus appears to the disciples and later to Thomas, they are immediately transformed from eyewitnesses of Jesus' life to ministers of the Living Word who are sent to testify and share the Good News of the

Easter story. As the disciples first experience the risen Lord, they rejoice and then tell their brother Thomas, *"We have seen the risen Lord."* Later, when Thomas encounters Jesus, he is moved to confess, *"My Lord and my God!"* With this new faith, they are commanded to go out and share the story and live in a way that others might come to know the risen Lord.

After these encounters, they each become living reminders of a risen Christ. Henri Nouwen, the late professor and practitioner of Christian spirituality, writes, *"In a world so torn apart by rivalry, anger, and hatred, we have the privileged vocation to be living signs of a love that can bridge all divisions and heal all wounds."*

It is a privileged vocation to be living signs of the reconciling love of Jesus Christ! And we are all capable of this work—the work of loving as Jesus has loved. We must continue to be these living signs of love in the world today, each in our unique way.

As for seeking our own encounters and personal relationship with God, we have many options. While we can't join Thomas as he reaches out his hand to touch Jesus' wounded body, we can encounter Jesus as we share our own and graciously receive another's story of faith. We can encounter Jesus as we read and study the Gospel stories and all scriptures that record God's saving acts throughout history. We can find glimpses of God reflected in creation when we reconnect to and reconcile with nature.

As Episcopalians, we also turn to the liturgy of our worship. In the Liturgy of the Table, as a gathered community at the altar, we encounter the risen Lord in the sharing of the cup and the breaking of the bread. This is why, at the fraction, a moment of silence is held. After we pray the Eucharistic prayer, asking the Holy Spirit to bless and sanctify the bread and wine, we have a moment to pause. Something great, something faith-producing, something faith-sustaining, is happening here. A mystery is unfolding.

If you have a Book of Common Prayer nearby or on your phone, I invite you to turn to page 834. There is a prayer I want you to know about—it's one of the prayers for personal use before receiving communion: "Be present, be present, O Jesus, our great High Priest, as you were present with your disciples, and be known to us in the breaking of bread; who live and reign with the Father and the Holy Spirit, now and forever."

Our repeated encounter with Christ in the Eucharist sustains and nourishes our faith, so that we can continue to go out and be ministers of reconciliation to all the beloved bodies of creation we encounter.

Take time today to recall the personal encounters that have changed you. In these encounters, the big issues of our day—the "hot topics" and "buzzwords"—become incarnate in the lived, bodily experience of others. In these encounters, the other's truth becomes tangible, so that we can reach out, touch, and embrace their lived reality. In these incarnational and relational encounters, the other becomes part of and marks our own life. In these markings, we witness and see the other in the relationship. We are changed—our purpose in life changes.

I find Lent and Holy Week easier. It's easier for me to linger in and be present in Christ's suffering on the walk toward the cross. Easter is more difficult. The resurrection is a mystery with implications—real implications that change us. One commentary succinctly stated, "The uniqueness of the Easter message invariably changes the lives of those who find themselves touched by it."

We are called to be a crazy, counter-cultural people, marked by our personal relationships with God and God's creation—the bodies of our human neighbors, the bodies of animals, the bodies of land, and the bodies of water. These markings change us.

They change our life purpose in this world. By the breath of God and the gift of the Holy Spirit, our hands, our feet, and our bodies become qualified and commissioned through Christ to reach out, seek, and learn to better love anyone. In this work, we continue to remember, testify, and make incarnate the good news of Easter: *"Alleluia, Christ is risen!" (The Lord is risen indeed, Alleluia!)*

# DID NOT OUR HEARTS BURN WITHIN US?

THE REV. MARY VANO
Third Sunday of Easter – April 23, 2023

*Acts 2:14a,36-41*
*Psalm 116:1-3, 10-17*
*1 Peter 1:17-23*
*Luke 24:13-35*

Think of it. Two disciples of Jesus leaving town on the day of Resurrection. *"Why are they leaving?"* we might ask. Surely, Jerusalem would be the place to be on this first Easter. But no, these two are leaving—maybe not literally running away, but still headed out of town.

Luke doesn't tell us why they are going to Emmaus, but we can imagine some reasons for their choice. Their friend, their leader, has died. Along with him, the vision of what they believed they were working for is gone. He was the glue that held all the disciples together. Now, their friendships are falling apart, their mission and purpose have been buried in the tomb, and the grief in their hearts is just too great a burden. The Gospels tell us that others of their group stayed in Jerusalem, but their grief and fear were just as gripping. They locked themselves away. Yes, they've heard what the women said about the empty tomb, but in their hearts, they do not yet really believe in the Resurrection. So, our two disciples leave the others behind and start out toward Emmaus.

This is precisely where Christ meets them. He goes to them on their way out of town, right in the middle of all their pain, grief, frustration, and fear, and walks beside them.

It's interesting that Cleopas and his companion don't immediately recognize Jesus. Much has been written about what we can learn from this about Jesus' resurrection: He is resurrected in flesh, but somehow different—a transformed and mysterious kind of life. But the disciples' inability to recognize a man with whom they had shared countless meals and endless hours also reveals what happens to us when we are grieving. Loss and fear cloud our vision. Grief makes it difficult to see beyond ourselves, so we might miss the divine hand that guides, protects, comforts, and heals us.

Yet this is exactly what Easter assures us of—Christ is risen indeed, and he is with us, whether we recognize it or not. This is the hope of the Resurrection—that in believing, we too shall be transformed—restored and made whole, even beyond the pain that life offers.

So, out on that road to Emmaus, even though the disciples cannot see what is right in front of them, Jesus opens their hearts and minds to understand what he had been trying to teach all along. Everything is different in the light of the Resurrection. The Risen Christ helps them not only make sense of recent events in light of the scriptures, but also to make sense of all of scripture in light of God's ongoing redemptive work. In the light of the Resurrection, they see that Christ's death did not defeat God's plan but made its fulfillment possible. They also see how they, too, are subject to God's mercy. No wonder their hearts were burning within them.

It is at this point in the story when the three companions share a meal. Their hearts and minds have been opened, and now, at the table, as Jesus blesses and breaks the bread, their eyes are finally opened to see Christ with them. In the breaking of the bread, they see the Feeding of the Multitudes—the miracle of abundance. In that bread, they see the shared experiences of being broken and the nourishment that sustains them. Most of all, in that broken bread, they see the power of Christ's love—his life broken and offered to all. They see all of this, and then, suddenly, they don't see him anymore. But their eyes, hearts, and minds remain open, and now they don't need to see him to know that he is there.

This profound experience changes the journey for these two disciples. Not only do they change directions and head back to Jerusalem, but we can imagine that the path before them is forever altered. They are no longer running away, but are now headed to share the Good News that they have received. Once again, they have a community, and with that community, they have a purpose and a mission. Their leader is the Risen

Christ, who sends them out to heal the sick, comfort the afflicted, bring sight to the blind, and proclaim Good News to the poor.

Does your heart burn within you now? If so, hopefully, it's not from this morning's brunch! No ... our hearts burn because most of us, at one time or another, have traveled the road out of town. We have sought escape from grief, pain, and fear. We've locked the doors of our hearts to protect us from whatever threats we imagine are out there. Wherever you are on that journey, this is where Christ meets you.

Today's story should sound familiar, not only because you've heard it before, but because this is what we do as a community of Christians.

It is our weekly pattern to invite Christ to walk with us on our journeys, to listen to the holy words of scripture and open our minds and hearts to them, and then to break bread together, encountering the Risen Christ in our lives so that we may then follow him out the door and into the world.

You are invited to the same journey and the same table. You're invited to join the meal and share the hope for transformation it embodies and pours out upon us. Together, we will live by the light of the Resurrection.

# THE GATE AND WAY OF LOVE

The Rev. Michaelene Miller
Fourth Sunday of Easter – April 30, 2023

*Acts 2:42-47*
*Psalm 23*
*1 Peter 2:19-25*
*John 10:1-10*

The Fourth Sunday of Easter is commonly known as Good Shepherd Sunday. You may have been reminded of this by our collect for the day as we prayed, "O God, whose Son Jesus is the good shepherd of your people: Grant that when we hear his voice, we may know him who calls us each by name, and follow where he leads."

Or perhaps you picked up on this theme throughout our lectionary readings, which get lifted up each year on this Sunday.

And this is good. Year after year, we need the reminder to listen closely for Jesus' voice. We need to be reminded that Jesus knows each of us by name and that God holds us tightly. Psalm 23 reminds us that even in the valley of death and under the shadow of life-consuming empires, God is with us, protecting and guiding.

Year after year, we need the reminder of what the shepherd's pasture of abundant life looks like. Acts 2 tells us about life in the earliest Christian community and reminds us that following the Good Shepherd leads us to cultivate the abundant pasture where what people need to survive is held in common and provided so that all are sustained and cared for.

Year after year, we need these reminders, especially during the Easter season. Easter is a season of continuously processing, integrating, and re-calibrating our lives around the truth of the resurrected Jesus.

- That this loving, liberating, life-giving Christ overcame death and the powers of oppression.
- That this loving, liberating, life-giving Christ constantly gathered and cared for those who were lost, scattered, or forced by society to roam at the margins.

- And that this loving, liberating, life-giving Christ calls us to do the same today as the Church, the Body of Christ—his hands, feet, and heart—at work in the world today.

This, at least, is what Jesus was beginning to explain to his original audience in our passage for today. This passage, found at the start of chapter 10 in the Gospel of John, records Jesus' attempt to explain what he had just done in chapter 9 and what it meant for the world.

Right before our reading today, there is the story of Jesus healing a man born blind. You might remember it from a few weeks ago when we encountered it during Lent In this story, Jesus sees a man who has been separated and cast out from his community. Because of his blindness, he is forced to the edges of society to beg and depend on the charity of others.

In the end, Jesus sees this man and invites him into complete restoration, into relationship in a new community as his own disciple, into a pasture of abundant life as a sheep of his fold. And the man responds to Jesus' call; he comes to know Jesus more fully—he comes to know, in his very being, the promise of salvation and abundant life that Jesus offers to the world.

Following this story of healing in Chapter 9, we land here, in our passage for today. Jesus is still trying to bring his original audience—his disciples and the other religious leaders in the Jewish community—to a greater understanding of who he is and what he is called by God to do in the world.

Jesus explains why he did all that he had just done for the man born blind. He clarifies how these actions embody his mission of restoration. He shares that he is the shepherd who calls *the sheep by name*—especially the disinherited, the cast out, and the rejected. He explains how the sheep follow him because they know his voice and how they are in a whole, mutual relationship. He shares that he is the gate, the way leading to new, abundant life in a pasture of sanctuary in community.

These identities of Jesus are important for us to know and understand, because these identities of who and what Jesus is for the world

143

inform and determine what our identity is and what we, as a community centered around Christ, are called to do out in the world.

As a life incarnate, fully God and fully human, Jesus is our gate, our point of access to God. Jesus is our way, our very doorway for knowing God. As Jesus acted in the world, he was revealing God's dream for creation. In this way, Jesus is our revelation—the fullest disclosure of the way and nature of God. Through the life, death, and resurrection of Jesus Christ, we know that God is a God of love, always reaching out and calling us into relationship, especially those who are scattered and cast out.

This gate to abundant life and the call of the leading, guiding shepherd is always there, and it is there for all. This passage does not record Jesus saying, *my sheep*, but that he is *the gate for the sheep*, and further on in verse 16, Jesus says, *"I have other sheep that do not belong to this fold. I must bring them also."*

Too often, the way of the shepherd through this gate is overtaken in the name of hate and judgment. Too often, this gate to the loving salvation of God is policed and built as a wall that divides the "insiders from outsiders," tribe from tribe, the "saved from the misled," those "normal enough" to pass under the status quo of the dominant society from those who are not, who look "different," love "different," or are differently abled.

This voice of hate, shrouded under and claiming the Christian identity, is loud. It constructs the open gate into a wall that surrounds the shepherd, making Jesus' voice strange. Nowadays, many are running from Christianity because they do not know the voice of Jesus—because his voice has been made as strange as a stranger.

The gate of Jesus, though, is wide and open to all. And the way of Jesus is a way of love that leads out of isolation and marginalization into relationship and community. And Jesus calls us to follow him and live in this way of love, to echo his love louder than the voices of hate and judgment.

Luckily, our Presiding Bishop Michael Curry and the wonderful staff of the National Episcopal Church have created a path of practices to help us along in walking Jesus' Way of Love. Our Compass Groups, the small groups that St. Margaret's invites people to form each Lent, explored these seven Way of Love practices throughout the season and into this Easter season as they aimed to form lives centered around Jesus. The practices are: Turn, Learn, Pray, Worship, Bless, Go, and Rest.

In the practice of TURN, Bishop Curry and the curriculum authors explain that we must choose to orient our lives around following Jesus every day. Every day, we must decide to turn from the powers of sin, hatred, fear, and injustice and towards the way of God's love, peace, hope, and liberation.

In the practice of LEARN, we choose to draw near to God's Word daily, opening our hearts and minds to scripture, wrestling with it so that we can develop eyes to read God's story and activity in everyday life.

In the practice of PRAY, we choose to dwell daily in the loving presence of God, offering our grief and gratitude or simply listening for God's still, small voice in our lives and in the world.

In the practice of WORSHIP, we gather with others weekly to dwell with God and to hear the Good News of Jesus Christ; to give thanks, confess, and offer the brokenness of the world to God. As we break bread, our eyes are opened to the presence of Christ in our midst. By the power of the Holy Spirit, we are made one body, the body of Christ, sent forth to live the Way of Love.

In the practice of BLESS, we choose to live as a blessing, unselfishly giving and serving others with generosity, hope, and compassion.

In the practice of GO, we choose to cross boundaries and travel beyond our circles of comfort to listen with humility, to join God in healing a hurting world, and to help build a Beloved Community—a people reconciled in love with God and one another.

Finally, in the practice of REST, we turn over our labor to God in trust, receive the gift of God's grace, and experience restoration and wholeness—within our bodies, minds, souls, and within our communities and institutions—before we begin again anew.

Turn, Learn, Pray, Worship, Bless, Go, and Rest—Bishop Curry explains that these are "words that point to practices to train up the spirit to follow in the way of Jesus, to train up the spirit to look something like Jesus in this world."

Which of these practices are you already living in your daily life? Which practice might be missing? Reflect on these practices—identify where they are present or missing in your daily and weekly rhythms. Then, choose them and keep choosing them, so we can answer Jesus' call to be his loving, liberating, life-giving hands, feet, and heart in the world today.

# TROUBLED HEARTS

THE REV. MARY VANC
Fifth Sunday of Easter – May 7, 2023

*Acts 7:55-60*
*Psalm 31:1-5, 15-16*
*1 Peter 2:2-10*
*John 14:1-14*

Has your phone ever rung in the middle of the night? For me, when the phone rings in the small hours, it's never good news. Before I'm fully awake, my body tenses, bracing for what I'll hear. Maybe someone has relapsed. Or there's been an emergency and someone's at the hospital. Or worse, maybe someone has died.

Sometimes, I don't even need a phone call to wake up in fear. There have been times when I've laid awake in the middle of the night, troubled by things that don't seem as pressing during the day. I find myself worrying about the challenges we face—challenges I know you face as well. I worry about myself too. Am I on the right track? Am I making the right decisions? What's ahead? Am I prepared for what's to come?

I'm guessing I'm not the only one here who's had these sleepless nights.

Not long ago, during one of these restless mornings, I decided to get out of bed and find an alternative to my anxiety. I made a cup of tea, sat down in a comfy chair, and wrapped myself in a blanket. I opened my Bible to John 14, and read the words: "*Do not let your hearts be troubled. Believe in God, believe also in me.*" These were Jesus' words to his disciples on the night before he died. They spoke to my heart, and they speak to ours today.

"*Do not let your hearts be troubled. Believe in God, believe also in me.*"

This was a frightening night for those disciples. They had followed Jesus and witnessed his mighty works. He had given them such hope that they left their homes and families to be with him. But now, on this dark night in a small room, Jesus tells them goodbye. He's washed their feet and called them to follow his example of love. He's warned that one among them would betray him. And to Peter, who swears he will die for Jesus, Jesus predicts his denial. I imagine the pain on Peter's face as he hears this.

Yet, Jesus, in the very next breath, reassures them, saying, *"Do not let your hearts be troubled. Believe in God, believe also in me."*

In this moment of darkness, Jesus tells his disciples that he's going to prepare a place for them in God's house—where there's plenty of room for all. Still, they're afraid. Thomas protests, *"We don't know how to get there, Lord!"*

Jesus reassures them again, saying, "Of course, you know how to get there. You know me." *"I am the way, the truth, and the life."* Jesus is giving them the comfort that though he's leaving, he will remain with them, showing them the way. He assures them: *"No one comes to the Father except through me."*

Today, we too find ourselves in a world of uncertainty. With an increasingly diverse society and so many unknowns, there are many who fear they will lose their way. We, like the disciples, wonder: "Will we find the way to life?" But our question, often, is not theirs. The disciples asked, "Is there a way?" We often ask, "Which way is the right way?"

This passage is sometimes quoted to answer the question, "Which way is the right way?" But I believe that's not the real question we should be asking. We tend to quote Jesus, "I am the way, the truth, and the life," without considering his larger context—the verses before and after, where Jesus speaks of many dwelling places in God's house and points to the good works of those around him. Often, we extract these words to claim exclusivity, to say that "my way is the only way." But that misses the point of Jesus' message.

Instead of asking, "Which way is the right way?" we should be asking, "Is there a way?" Like Peter, we wonder if we can find our way back when we fall short, when we fail to live up to God's love. Is there a way for us to return? Like Thomas, we yearn for truth that transcends our own limited perspectives, something bigger than the prejudices that surround us.

Is there truth we can rely on? Like all of them, we face the fear of death—the death of our dreams, our relationships, our loved ones. Is there life beyond this fear? Can we hope for life that defeats the power of death?

These are the questions we ask. When we falter, when we lose our way, we must ask, "Is there a way for us?" Jesus answers, "I am the way." When the world fills us with confusion, when we're unable to discern truth, Jesus says, "I am the truth." And when we face death and fear, when we wonder if life will have the final word, Jesus assures us, "I am the life."

The question is not about which religion is the "right" one, as often posed. God is big enough to love and to provide a way for all. The question is, in the darkest times, in the moments when we are afraid or uncertain, who do we believe in? Who will guide us to make the right decisions, to help us face our fears, and to show us the path to life?

Jesus steps into this darkness and says, "Do not let your hearts be troubled. Believe in God; believe also in me. I am the way, the truth, and the life."

In that moment, we are given the light of hope that guides us toward the truth, toward life. And one day, when the morning light comes, we will say, "Alleluia, Christ is risen!"

# A LOVE LIKE JESUS'

THE REV. MICHAELENE MILLER
Sixth Sunday of Easter – May 14, 2023

*Acts 17:22-31*
*Psalm 66:7-18*
*1 Peter 3:13-22*
*John 14:15-21*

If you were here at St. Margaret's for worship last Sunday, you would have noticed that I was missing. Fortunately, I wasn't out sick or feeling unwell, nor was I away on an early summer vacation. As I am most Sundays, I was gathered with others around the Lord's table, participating in the breaking of the bread and the prayers. But last Sunday, I had the privilege of doing this at Camp Mitchell on Petit Jean Mountain, where I joined others for the Mountain Lights program to pray over and kick off Camp Mitchell's summer camp season.

While I was there leading worship, I knew that many of you were gathered here at St. Margaret's, around this outpost of the Lord's Table, joining me—as many other Episcopal Churches in Arkansas did that day—in special prayers for Camp Mitchell's Mountain Lights. We prayed for the campers, staff, and volunteers who will spend time at camp this summer, and who will return to their communities renewed with flames burning bright.

While I was at Camp Mitchell, its Executive Director, Rebecca Roetzel, shared a quote in her homily from Brené Brown, a research professor at the University of Houston known for her work on shame, vulnerability, and leadership. Rebecca lifted up a few words from Brené Brown's book, *Dare to Lead*, which read:

> "We must be guardians of a space that allows students to
> breathe, be curious, explore the world, and be who they are
> without suffocation. They deserve one place where they can
> rumble with vulnerability and their hearts can exhale. What I
> know from the research is that we should never underestimate

the benefit to a child of having a place to belong—even one—where they can take off their armor. It can and often does change the trajectory of their life."

Rebecca lifted up these words as her prayer for what the summer at Camp Mitchell would be for all the Mountain Lights: the campers, volunteers, and staff members planning to arrive in the coming months. Those present joined her in this prayer, and personally, my heart rejoiced because I knew it to be possible.

This is what Camp Mitchell was for me, summer after summer in my late teen and early adult years. It was the place where I learned to rumble with joy and vulnerability, taking off my armor and coming to accept myself—flawed and gifted as I am. It was the place where I could be curious, explore, and be myself freely. To this day, it's where my heart exhales.

I bring these words and reflections to you today because they were still floating in my heart when I first received Matthew Echols' and Clem Fortune's Senior Letters to St. Margaret's in my email box. As I read each of these letters, Brené Brown's words were echoed louder.

Today is Senior Sunday at St. Margaret's. At both the 9 and 11 o'clock services, we celebrate and pray over our graduates as they prepare for significant life changes: leaving home, even the state, to continue their studies and take on new roles in the world. As the seniors stood here on the precipice of change, two were willing to share reflections and write letters to the congregation. You can read Matthew and Clem's words in a special edition of the *Celebrations eNewsletter* that went out just yesterday.

To give you a glimpse of their words, Matthew mentioned how, as he grew up, he realized that he had something that many other kids didn't have: a second home. He wrote about a sense of belonging that he found at church, especially in youth group. Matt made a particular point that it wasn't just that he was made to feel he belonged, but that he came to *know* that he did. (Matthew, thank you!) What a powerful witness and gift of reflection.

And Clem, in his letter, shared how some of his earliest and fondest memories were from St. Margaret's. He mentioned rolling down the hills before and after youth group. I don't know about you, but that sounds like exhaling to me. It sounds like the rumble of vulnerability—the joy and freedom of letting go. Clem shared that he knows he has a place and community here that would welcome him with open arms at any time. (Clem, thank you!) Again, what a powerful witness and gift of reflection.

When these letters first arrived in my inbox, I sat back in full gratitude—for the gift of reflection *and* for the larger community of St. Margaret's. This past week, I replied to Matthew and Clem, joining them in giving thanks to God that they had experienced a place of belonging here.

Because this—this sense of belonging and the deep knowing that you are beloved and valued—is what Jesus called his disciples to and calls us to continue cultivating in the world.

We hear this call at the very beginning of our passage for today. Jesus says, *"If you love me, you will keep my commandments."* Following right after our passage from last week, Jesus again speaks to us from that upper room, where he is with his disciples for the Passover supper. He has just washed their feet, and in explaining what he did, he said, *"I give you a new commandment, that you love one another. Just as I have loved you, you also should love one another."*

It is Maundy Thursday, and Jesus is talking with his disciples, who are also on the brink of significant change. He is in the midst of his Farewell Discourse, his last teachings before his arrest and crucifixion. He is trying to prepare them, sharing with them what the life work of a Christian is. He says, *"If you love me, you will keep my commandments."* Put back into this context, we know that Jesus is again asking them to love as he has loved them. Marked by this love, the world will know that they are his disciples.

He calls them to love in a way that allows others to have abundant life and the freedom to become who they were created to be. He calls them to love in a way that will enable others to exhale in liberation and roll down hills with joyful abandon. He is calling them to love in a way that others may find a home away from home—where they are welcomed and reassured of belonging.

This love sounds great, and when we find it, it feels great. But the reality is that this love is not exactly simple. A love like Jesus' is not the love of sentimentality that we find in romantic movies. It is not the love of a fleeting, bubbling emotion. A love like Jesus' moves us to a depth of compassion and a sense of urgency that, at times, is impossible to fathom. A love like Jesus' moves us well beyond our affinity circles and comfort zones. A love like Jesus' reorients our hearts and moves us to empathize with and respond to the world's pain. To love like Jesus is to love others. *All* others.

And for us on our own, it's an impossible love. But the good news is that Jesus does not stop his teaching here. Going back to our gospel text for today, we see that we don't do this work of love alone. For the first time in the Farewell Discourse, Jesus makes a promise and explains how the Spirit of Truth is coming. He says, *"I will ask the Father, and he will give you another Advocate to be with you forever. This is the Spirit of truth ... You know him because he abides with you and will be in you. I will not leave you orphaned."*

Jesus is pointing to another Advocate who will remain in his place and continue the work of God that he was unfolding in the world. The Spirit—the Paraclete in Greek, meaning the one who is called to be alongside us—is sent to be and do whatever is needed in the situation to prompt us toward the love that is like Jesus'. The Spirit is here to be the Advocate, the Comforter, the Helper, or the Intercessor—to guide, nudge, or even push us toward love.

And again, hear the good news and the truth: we are never alone. Even in those moments when we feel lonely, we are never alone. Even when we feel depleted, the truth is that the Spirit's resources are inexhaustible. Even when the love like Jesus' seems impossible and beyond our imagination, we can quiet our focus, turn inward, and align with the Spirit who moves through us to make it possible.

This quieting to focus and turning inward to connect with the Spirit is the work of spiritual practices, and these can look like many things. For some, quieting down and turning inward may look like gardening or running. It might look like sitting still with centering prayer or another quiet practice. For others, it might look like singing, writing poetry, painting, knitting, or birdwatching. It could even look like going to youth group or rolling down hills.

However our spiritual practices might look, let us always seek to develop them, so we can continuously turn inward, seek the Spirit, and connect to this wellspring of unending love. In doing so, we can keep the commandments, cultivate belonging, and always offer a love like Jesus' to the world.

# RETIREMENT – HISTORY / FUTURE

THE REV. CINDY FRIBOURGH
Seventh Sunday of Easter – May 21, 2023

*Acts 1:6-14*
*Psalm 68:1-10, 33-36*
*1 Peter 4:12-14; 5:6-11*
*John 17:1-11*

October 30, 2000: Kneeling before Bishop Larry Maze at Trinity Cathedral. He lays his hands on my head. *"Give your Holy Spirit to Cindy, fill her with grace and power, and make her a deacon in your church."*

I knew it wouldn't, but I still kind of hoped this would be a sensational spiritual moment like the one in our passage from Acts today. The apostles gathered with the resurrected Christ. They asked him, *"Lord, is this the time when you will restore the kingdom to Israel?"*

Jesus responds, *"You will receive power when the Holy Spirit has come upon you."* A cloud appeared, and Jesus ascended into heaven.

While ordination that day in late October, not quite 23 years ago, was a profoundly spiritual and joyous occasion in my life, it was somewhat less spectacular. *"Give your Holy Spirit to Cindy ..."*

No cloud.

What was spectacular was the many ways the Holy Spirit has been present in my life in and through ministry with St. Margaret's, and the many ways the Holy Spirit has been at work in our lives together as the gathered body of Christ.

Let's begin at the beginning of this journey.

St. Margaret's held its first service on November 3, 1991, under the leadership of the Rev. Dr. Chris Keller, our founding vicar. I'd been raised in the Episcopal Church, but at that time, I was somewhat less than faithful in weekly attendance. I'd been feeling drawn back to the church but hadn't decided where to go.

Then, I literally ran into Rick Keech playing indoor soccer. I'd known Rick since high school camp at Camp Mitchell. He greeted me warmly,

155

even though I had completely plowed into him, and he told me that our mutual friend from camp, Chris Keller, had started a new Episcopal church a couple of months ago in west Little Rock. St. Margaret's was meeting at the Market Street Bargain Cinema, and I should come. The Holy Spirit at work.

I showed up, and I kept showing up, becoming more and more engaged with the people and work of St. Margaret's. My son JJ loved that he was baptized at the Market Street Bargain Cinema. The congregation grew, and we moved to the Breckenridge Cinema. Having church in a movie theater was interesting in so many ways.

St. Margaret's was a close-knit community of Christians, and where we worshiped was secondary. Everything we needed for worship and Sunday school was stored in a trailer. Each Sunday we set up for prayer and worship, then packed it all up before the first feature film of the afternoon. One week, we found ourselves locked out. So, we had church in the parking lot. The Holy Spirit at work, again—a little playfully.

We experienced extraordinary growth. A capital campaign raised the funding needed to build on this land, given by the Diocese for our church home. Dr. Keller and I released a pair of doves at the groundbreaking ceremony, a symbol of the Holy Spirit embodied in our congregation. My husband Richard was baptized in 1996 at the first Easter Vigil in this building. Both he and JJ were confirmed here.

As I became more and more engaged, I found myself nudged toward ordained ministry as a deacon. I explored that call in community with the vicar and bishop, several of my St. Margaret's brothers and sisters, and the Commission on Ministry, a diocesan committee of about a dozen people who met with me six or seven times over the next three years. Even though they were welcoming and friendly, these people terrified me. They advised the bishop and held my fate in their hands. They affirmed the call to diaconal service, and I could breathe again.

There was an extensive formation program through the Diocese, and I found myself at the Cathedral being presented to Bishop Larry Maze for ordination. I was pleased and excited, though a little stunned. The call of a deacon is beautifully outlined in the ordination liturgy: *"God now calls you to a special ministry of servanthood directly under your bishop. In the name of Jesus Christ, you are to serve all people, particularly the poor, the weak, the sick, and the lonely."*

The liturgy continues: *"You are to make Christ and his redemptive love known by your word and example, to those among whom you live, work, and worship."* You are to interpret to the Church the needs, concerns, and hopes of the world. You are to assist the bishop and priests in public worship and in the ministration of God's Word and Sacraments. My favorite part: *"You are to carry out other duties assigned to you from time to time."* Hmmmm.

I believe I have lived into that, with God's help, during the 22 years and 7 months since that day. It has been an extraordinary Spirit-filled path, and I am so grateful that you have walked it alongside me.

Celebrations! The joy of weddings, new babies, baptisms! Holy Week and Easter, Thanksgiving, Christmas, and Pentecost! Building this building, the Arkansas House of Prayer, the Bosmyer Education Wing, and the recent placement of our beautiful cross on Chenal Parkway.

The list of ways we have taken the Holy Spirit into the world is long and broad: meals with our friends at St. Francis House, feeding the hungry through the backpack program and the Little Free Food Pantry, Women2Women, Hope Sacks, and the Institute for Theological Studies at St. Margaret's. These lectures served the community and incubated the Interfaith Center and SUMMA Theological Debate Society, a week-long summer camp for high school students, now nested within the seminary of the University of the South in Sewanee, TN. I served as Program Director for SUMMA until two years ago, working alongside Dr. Keller to build a nationwide program. Our incredible ministry resettling a family displaced from Afghanistan is one of our largest outreach efforts. Zoom church, classes, and Mary's podcasts—just a few ways we've taken the light of Christ into our world.

St. Margaret's has experienced the Holy Spirit in more unusual moments, too. The beautiful, controlled chaos in the 9:00 service. It's absolutely wonderful, and I hope it never ends. The not-so-well-controlled chaos of kids running up and down the aisles of the movie theaters, crawling around searching sticky floors for gummy bears dropped on the floor. Finding ourselves locked out of the Breckenridge Cinema. The Christmas Eve when the fire alarm went off during a lovely, quiet moment of the liturgy. Mary remained in her seat, serene amidst the shrill alarm and flashing lights. Everyone followed her lead, sitting quietly, nervously stealing glances at one another. Should we reverently run like the wind? Turned out it was just the smoke from incense used in the service, stashed in the stairwell. The fire department wasn't particularly amused, but we were ... later.

The comfort of the Holy Spirit has been especially present as we've held each other up during tragedy, illness, Covid, and deep sadness. The death of our beloved vicar, Peggy Bosmyer, and so many members of our community. I felt this extraordinary love and support when our son JJ died three years ago, especially from you, Mary. I cannot express how meaningful this was for Richard and me.

We've all experienced the devastating loss of beloved members of our church, as a family or extended family, and the quiet, profound, comforting presence of the Holy Spirit in the outpouring of love from our community.

And now, I stand at the edge of retirement—from St. Margaret's altar. I intentionally chose the Day of Pentecost for this transition. The Holy Spirit will be in the midst of our celebration of that holy day and the baptism of a new Christian. That seemed so appropriate. Afterward, we'll have a big picnic—what fun! And I like red.

Please know that I am not leaving St. Margaret's. I will worship sometimes with dear friends at other Episcopal churches in Arkansas and new friends at churches I don't even know about yet, during my travels. And you will find me in the place I began my journey as a deacon: here in the congregation with you, as well as alongside you, as our work continues—taking the good news of the resurrected Christ into the world, energized by the life-giving presence of the Holy Spirit.

# YOU ARE GIFTED

THE REV. MARY VANC
Day of Pentecost – May 28, 2023

*Acts 2:1-21*
*Psalm 104:25-35, 37*
*1 Corinthians 12:3b-13*
*John 20:19-23*

(This is a transcript of a sermon for which children were invited to listen and participate.)

Today is the Feast of Pentecost, sometimes known as the birthday of the church. And what happens when it's your birthday?

> [Kids:]
> We celebrate!
> We eat cake!
> We get presents!

Yes, there are gifts involved! And that's what Pentecost is all about. It's about the gift that God has for all of us—the gift that was Jesus' own first gift for all those he loved. Do you know what the gift is? What is the gift of Pentecost?

> [Haley:] The Holy Spirit.

Yes! Haley's got it. The gift is the Holy Spirit. Now, depending on which Gospel you're reading, this gift happens at different times. In the Gospel of John, the gift is given on Easter Day, the first day of the Resurrection. The disciples are still struggling to understand what's going on when Jesus appears to them behind locked doors. He breathes on them, gives them the gift of the Holy Spirit, and says, *"Peace be with you."* The gift of the Holy Spirit through Jesus' peace empowers the disciples, he says, to go out and forgive. Isn't that an interesting gift? The power to forgive.

In the Gospel of Luke, which continues in the Book of Acts, the gift of the Holy Spirit comes on Pentecost—today, 50 days after Easter, and 50 days after Passover. For the Jews, this was a harvest festival—the first fruits of the harvest. When the disciples were gathered together, the Holy

Spirit descended upon them and gave them another gift—the gift of speaking in different languages. This empowered them to proclaim the Good News of God's love across cultures, across languages, and across barriers of nation and race. They could share God's love and heal their divisions. What a gift!

In the Church, we recognize the gift of the Holy Spirit given to each of us individually at baptism. Like today, when we will mark Easton's baptism, saying, *"sealed by the Holy Spirit in baptism and marked as Christ's own forever."* And the gifts just keep coming—from our baptism to confirmation, to marriage, to ordination. We continue to receive the gift of the Holy Spirit—empowering us to forgive, giving us peace, sending us to proclaim God's love, to heal divisions, and empowering each of us uniquely with our own gifts.

In Paul's letter to the Corinthians, we hear how each one in the community has their own unique gifts—gifts of ministry, gifts of healing, gifts of mercy, gifts of discernment, prophecy, miracles, and teaching. All of these individual gifts are empowered uniquely in each of us for ONE purpose: the common good.

That's what the Holy Spirit does for us—the Spirit empowers us to build community, share the Good News, heal our divisions, and bring peace to the world. And each and every single one of you is gifted.

But I hope you won't leave those gifts on the table, because they're there for you. It's hard sometimes to accept the gifts of the Holy Spirit. I'm reminded of the prophet Isaiah, who knew he wasn't worthy when God called him to speak to the people of Israel. He was reluctant, thinking, *"I'm a man of unclean lips. How dare I speak God's good news?"* But in his vision, the angels purified him and empowered him to speak. Isaiah responded to God's call: *"Here am I, send me."*

Today, we are celebrating Deacon Cindy's ministry. She has been a deacon for 23 years in the Episcopal Church—most of those here at St. Margaret's. Twenty-three years ago, she said, *"Here am I, send me."* The call to be a deacon is a call to serve—it's a call to work without pay, but with pure-hearted love, leadership, and service. For 23 years, Cindy has been here to proclaim the Gospel, ensuring that all hear the Good News of God's love. She's set the table so that all can be nourished by that love. And for 23 years, she's stood in the back, sending us out to go into the world to love and serve the Lord—recognizing that our call is to go out and serve too.

Thanks be to God that Cindy said, *"Here am I, send me."* Thanks be to God!

And thanks be to God that the Holy Spirit hasn't stopped giving yet. This room is full of gifted people! Full of people who have the gift of pastoral care, to be there in times of need. Will you say, *"Here am I, send me?"* In this room, there are people with gifts of administration, gifts to organize, and gifts to bring those things together for the sake of the community. Will you, too, say, *"Here am I, send me?"* Here we have gifts for caring for the altar, for making this place a holy place that gives glory to God. We have gifts for going out into the world, for taking care of creation, and for growing food. We have gifts for caring for animals, for bringing justice, for serving those in need—so many gifts! Will you leave them on the table, or will you say, *"Here am I, send me?"*

I know some of you are asking, *"Who is going to be our next deacon?"* Who are the leaders we need in the world? Who are the leaders we need in the Church? Who will teach Sunday school? Who will serve at the altar? Who will fill up the Little Free Food Pantry? For all those questions, look no further than yourselves. Consider the gifts God has given you, and then stand up and say, *"Here am I, send me."*

I was thinking about what to wear today (red for Pentecost) (I don't know why, but the brain is a funny thing!) I thought of an old episode of the *Oprah Winfrey* show. I know that some of you are too young to remember the Oprah Winfrey show, but she had a talk show. And it was common for Oprah to have a studio audience and to give a gift—like a door prize. Someone in the audience would win something special to take home. One day, in 2004, the audience was told that someone would win a car that day. Now, reading about this story, apparently, the producers of the show went through a great deal of trouble to make sure that everyone in the audience that day was someone who could really use a car. They didn't want to give away the surprise, so they did a survey and asked people questions like, how do you get to work? And how old is the vehicle that you are driving? And from those surveys, they selected 276 people for the studio audience—all of whom could really use a new car. Those people were probably delighted when they came to the studio and were told that someone would win a car that day. Everyone was then given a gift-wrapped white box with a red bow on it, and they were told that they were going to get to open their box, and the person who had a set of keys inside their box was going to win a car. And, of course, every single one of them knows that they would really like to win a car, and so they're all getting excited, and then they're given permission to open their box, and someone exclaims, "I've got a key!" But they're not the only ones. Someone nearby shouts, "I've got a key, too!" It goes on and on, and they realize that every single person in the audience has a set of keys for a new car. And Oprah was up there—it's iconic, you can find the meme—shouting, "You get a car! And you get a car! Everyone gets a car!!!"

Well... none of you get a car today! But you are all gifted. Even more powerfully. You are gifted to transform the world! With your heart, with your service, with your Good News, you are gifted. Those are powerful gifts.

You know what? After that Oprah show, there were people who were kind of mad. People who won cars—because there were taxes. As generous as Oprah was, the government, not so much! People were upset about that. But isn't that the truth? The gifts that the Holy Spirit has for you will not be without cost. There are sacrifices involved. Always, there is something that we must give up in order to fully receive the gifts that God gives us—the gifts that give us the opportunity to go out and make a difference in this world.

Is it worth it, Cindy?

[Cindy:] *Absolutely.*

162

It's absolutely worth it! The sacrifices we make—our time, energy, effort, and the things we give up so we can give—they are absolutely worth it.

Cindy, we are so grateful for you. Thank you for saying, *"Here am I, send me."*

Today, I ask all of you to consider your gifts. Know that you are fully gifted by the Holy Spirit. And be brave enough to say, *"Here am I, send me."*

# A DAY OF MIXED EMOTIONS

THE REV. MICHAELENE MILLER
Trinity Sunday – June 4, 2023

*Genesis 1:1-2:4a*
*Psalm 8*
*2 Corinthians 13:11-13*
*Matthew 28:16-20*

Good morning, Trinitarians, and happy Trinity Sunday! Trinity Sunday is a day of leaning into the mystery and theological doctrine of the Triune God. It's a chance for us to intentionally reflect on one of our most important (and challenging!) beliefs. As such, Trinity Sunday is also a day of mixed emotions ... head-scratching and staring off into space for hours on end as we try to grasp the mystery of God! But ultimately, Trinity Sunday is about looking closely at whose we are so that we can know who we are and, thus, how we are to be out in the world.

Trinity Sunday, as a day of leaning into the deep end of theology, is about celebrating the eternal Trinity of Persons: God the Father, God the Son, and God the Holy Spirit, AND confessing belief in the Unity of Substance and Oneness of God. This ancient doctrine of the Trinity developed over time, as all doctrines do, through many conversations among followers who wanted to express their experience of transformation through a relationship with God.

The doctrine arose from early Christians reflecting together on scripture, their encounters with Jesus, and their experiences of the Holy Spirit. And so, over time, the church's doctrine of the Trinity emerged: the idea that God is rightly conceived as both Three in One and One in Three.

But ultimately, this day of celebration is not meant to create further distance between us and God. Celebrating the doctrine of the Trinity is not meant to cause our eyes to glaze over or lead to jokes about how Christians are bad at math, adding 1+1+1 to equal 1. Leaning into the Trinity is meant to bring God close—so, so close. Close to us in our origin, close to us in the present day, and close to us until the end of the age. The doctrine of the Trinity casts a vision of God as eternally present and constantly in relationship with Creation.

Rather than reinforcing the obscure notion that God is far away, somewhere "up there," the doctrine of the Trinity helps us grasp the practical and impactful truth that God is "up there, down here, and everywhere," always in relationship with us, dancing within a relationship within God's self: constantly creating, redeeming, and sustaining creation in every moment. The doctrine helps us understand that the world is awash with God's divine presence. We heard this truth echoed in the reading from Acts a few weeks ago: that it is in God "in whom we live, move, and have our being" (Acts 17:28).

Thus, Trinity Sunday is a day for us to turn to God, stepping in close to God, who is always near, as we seek to know God more clearly. If we take this doctrine and our scripture seriously, we also come to know ourselves and our purpose more clearly. In today's Old Testament reading from Genesis, we're reminded that we reflect this relational mark of the Trinity in our very being.

On the sixth day of creation, God said, *"Let us make humankind in our image, according to our likeness."* Here we have the original echo of the Triune relationship in the plurality of God's self-reference (Let *US* make in *OUR* image ...), and we also have humanity's origin story, emerging from and forever rooted in the goodness of this relational likeness. The doctrine of the Trinity points us to the reality that we are created by a God of relationship to be a people of relationship.

This is challenging and good news in an age marked by loneliness and societal divisions. Bearing this mark, this image of God, our purpose is to be in relationship with God and with each other. Relationships aren't just something we "do." Relationships are who we are and how we are to be in the world. Our reference can never be "I, me, or my" but must always be reoriented around "we, us, and ours." Good and challenging news, indeed!

And still, if you find yourself full of emotions—whether confusion as you try to grasp the vast expansiveness of God or gratitude for the many ways that God interacts with creation—or some mixture of joy and doubt, please know that you are in very good company. Included in that company are the disciples from our gospel reading today.

We find them trudging up a mountain in Galilee to look for Jesus, who had just been murdered on a cross. And when they finally make it to the mountaintop—a place of sacred revelation in Matthew's gospel—they see him. They see a resurrected Jesus, and as we read, mixed emotions abound! *"When they saw him, they worshiped him; but some doubted."* This might even be better translated to read, *"They worshiped him while doubting."*

This is so real and honest. It's the reality of living as people of faith in a hurting world. Worship, awe, praise, wonder, and yet doubt, worry, fear, and anxiety. It all goes together.

And in this moment, in the midst of the disciples' mixed emotions and mixed states of readiness, Jesus calls them, all of them, and passes on his work that is now theirs to do. He doesn't rebuke or kick anyone out. He commissions them all to his way and work of love. Jesus calls them, as they are, to go forth—not with perfect faith or understanding—but with love and, in relationship with God, to build more relationships of love in the world.

Just as Jesus called the disciples in their mixed emotions and mixed readiness, he calls us when we are ready and when we are not. God calls all of us to the Way and the work of love. God does not expect us to be perfect or without worry and doubt.

This is good news because I know there are mixed emotions and different states of readiness here today. As many of you have read in the most recent update about the bishop search, our beloved Rector, Mary Vano, has been selected to be on the initial slate of candidates for our next bishop. I know we rejoice with her, and I also know there are doubts and fears.

As I said before, the reality of life—especially as a person of faith—is often mixed emotions. Grief in the midst of gratitude. Gratitude in the midst of grief. The hope of resurrection and new beginnings in the midst of endings. We rejoice with Rev. Mary and celebrate this recognition of her gifts as a leader, and yet we feel doubts and fears about the changes ahead.

This is where we are, and we are here together on this Trinity Sunday—a day of mixed emotions. It's a day when we need each other, our different emotions, states of readiness, and various gifts in the work and Way of Love. In relationship, we help remind each other who we are and whose we are.

And we are here with God, who is always with us, now until the end of time. So, as we have been, let us continue to pray for our diocese and those in discernment to answer the call to become our next bishop. Through all the changes and chances of life, let us also give thanks to God that we have a God who is wildly creative.

Thanks be to God that amid confusing times and constant change, we have a God who is loving, liberating, and life-giving. Thanks be to God that as we face a wide-open, uncertain future as a community, we have a God who is always seeking to come alongside us and is near to guide us and prompt us toward the most beautiful Way of Love.

Thanks be to God that we are in God's hands.

# FOLLOWING JESUS WITH OUR WHOLE SELF

THE REV. MICHAELENE MILLER
Proper 5 – June 11, 2023

*Genesis 12:1-9*
*Psalm 33:1-12*
*Romans 4:13-25*
*Matthew 9:9-13, 18-26*

To start my sermon, let me make a confession. I, for one, don't have it all together. I don't have all the answers. I mess up. I make mistakes. I am pretty clumsy. I sometimes ... err, I frequently need help. Surprise! But is it really? Probably not, haha. But why does it come as such a surprise when individuals bare their weaknesses, scars, or stories of messing up?

Why is it so easy for us to assume that other people have it all figured out? Why is it such a shock when we hear a close friend or family member, a teacher or preacher, or a community leader admit that they need help, that they aren't perfect, that they aren't whole but have a growing edge? Similarly, why can it feel so uncomfortable to be and remain for long in the presence of someone in the midst of a struggle?

Well, in today's gospel passage, we find a series of encounters where Jesus reveals growing edges and pleas for help as sacred, not shameful. Here, Jesus not only remains present in the midst of another's struggle but models following alongside, turning towards, and reaching out to the one in need. He calls them into relationship.

I will start with Jairus, the leader of the synagogue, who is not named here but is in other gospel versions of this same story. He goes to Jesus, bold in his request for help on behalf of his daughter, who has just died. He says, *"Come and lay your hand on her, and she will live."* This moment leaves Jairus exposed and vulnerable. And, seemingly without question or surprise at witnessing this important and influential synagogue leader profess his fear and deepest need, Jesus got up and followed Jairus. Jesus did not shy away from another person's pain; instead, he saw this man for what he is—a human in need. Jesus enters into relationship with Jairus to walk together through his pain; however, they are interrupted.

Another encounter happens with an unnamed woman, who is said to have been suffering from hemorrhages for twelve years. We know from other gospel tellings of this story that she had suffered, endured much, and spent all that she had in her attempts to be healed so that she could enter back into society. This woman's illness, her unceasing hemorrhaging, would have left her alone, seen as broken, and cast out from society. Her bleeding makes her unclean and untouchable. However, like Jairus, she is also desperate to have a life restored to health.

Unlike Jairus, she is not a powerful leader. She does not have a place to fall from because she is already at the bottom of existence. Her desperation makes her bold. She has very little to lose. So desperately, she secretly comes up behind [Jesus] and touches the fringe of his cloak.

Yet Jesus notices. He notices a human has changed on account of his power to heal, and he refuses to let a miracle transpire without a proper exchange or a true relationship. He turns, wanting to see this person face to face. Seeing her, Jesus assures her that she is made well. I imagine that Jesus saw her vulnerability, her honesty about how she was, and her openness to change and be transformed. He saw her faith.

Jesus calls us all into true relationship with him and each other. And Jesus is clear. We hear him say, *"I have come to call not the righteous but sinners."* He calls us not in our perfection on our best days. He calls us just as we are in all our broken humanity. No one is left out of this invitation to be known and healed, to enter into full relationship with him.

We see this in the first encounter of our gospel passage. There, we see Jesus approach a tax collector named Matthew, who calls him to join his movement as his 12th disciple. It is interesting that Jesus pursued this man. Matthew would have likely worked as a collector of taxes or tolls upon goods going out to market, goods like fish. He would have likely been widely unpopular, not only because the taxes were burdensome and they funded the Roman Empire—but also because tax collectors were often tempted to charge more than required and pocketed the difference.

Calling Matthew into relationship would have made Jesus' message very clear, not only to those watching him from the outside but also to his immediate followers—the other 11 disciples, the ones who were previously fishermen and likely overtaxed and exploited, possibly even by this very man. No one is disqualified from the invitation to be part of the Jesus movement, especially those who need help.

In their own ways, each individual of our gospel encounters entered into a true relationship with Jesus. True relationship goes deeper than what our culture typically allows. Our Presiding Bishop, Michael Curry, once said in a Sunday School class:

*"It is easy to follow [Jesus' call] because [he calls us to] become our true selves and who we were meant to be—yet it is profoundly difficult because we live in [our] false selves. We are of the world."*

We exist in a culture that values power and perfection, competition over true connection. This true relationship that Jesus cultivates goes deeper than the surface highlights of our lives that we present to each other most days or on social media. Our moments are so often painted or edited to appear perfect and show how successful we are at navigating through this mysterious world, but Jesus wants more. Jesus calls the leaders, the sick, the religious, the lost, the hopeless, the perfectionists. He calls everyone into this right relationship of being truly known and of deeply knowing the other. As Bishop Curry put it, "he calls us to become our true selves."

And it's not easy. When I first worked at St. Margaret's as a youth minister nine years ago, I was also engaged in my clinical pastoral education as a hospital chaplain at UAMS, and it was in that program that I came to terms with the fact that I'm a perfectionist. I fear losing control, fear being "too much," and fear messing up. Every morning in the program, the intern group would do a "check-in." I came to understand that it was only in sharing and actually participating in the "check-in" that allowed others to know me and for me to know myself.

At one point in the program, my supervisor told me that chaplains do not "leave their baggage at the door." Instead, she said that the bags are brought into the room, slowly unpacked, and each item held up for inspection in front of everyone before lovingly packing everything away again. The baggage is allowed and processed instead of anxiously avoided. I am continuing to learn how to embrace my baggage and my dirty laundry because it is my story, and I would not be who I am today without it.

In the book *Searching for Sunday*, the beloved and greatly missed author Rachel Held Evans focused one chapter on the subject of "Dirty Laundry." It opened with a quote from Walter Brueggemann: "Churches should be the most honest place in town, not the happiest place in town." Evans went on to propose that church, at its highest capacity, should function like an Alcoholics Anonymous group.

She explained that these recovery groups have achieved the "kind of intimate fellowship" that many Christian groups fail to achieve. She hoped church could be a place where "a bunch of struggling, imperfect people come together to speak difficult truths to one another." Evans longed for the day when Christians didn't feel the need to hide our dirty laundry every time we entered into our church communities. "Churches should be the most honest place in town, not the happiest place in town."

I don't have all the answers—so I thank God for Google and the existence of the phrase "I don't know." I need help often—so I thank God for those in my communities that are willing and able to answer my plea. I mess up, I make mistakes—so I thank God for Grace. I'm a recovering perfectionist ... and today, I bring my baggage with me, and I encourage you to do the same.

Jesus calls us—not on our perfect days—but in all our humanity, with our many bags full of dirty laundry, into true relationship with him and each other. Thanks be to God for that.

# STEADFAST LOVE

THE REV. MARY VANO
Proper 6 – June 18, 2023

*Genesis 18:1-15, (21:1-7)*
*Psalm 116:1, 10-17*
*Romans 5:1-8*
*Matthew 9:35-10:8(9-23)*

Every Sunday, when we gather for worship, we begin with a prayer called the "collect of the day." There is a collect appointed for every Sunday and every special occasion throughout the church year. This opening prayer is meant to catch our attention and direct us toward the special themes of the day, and today, this prayer particularly caught my attention.

> Keep, O Lord, your household, the Church in your steadfast
> faith and love, that through your grace we may proclaim your
> truth with boldness and minister your justice with compassion
> for the sake of our Savior Jesus Christ, who lives and reigns with
> you and the Holy Spirit, one God, now and forever. Amen.

It was the first phrase that really got me ... "Keep, O Lord, your household the Church in your steadfast faith and love." Steadfast faith and love. There is a claim being made here, and it is about who God is—it is about a particular quality of God's love, and of God's faith. The prayer reminds us that God's love is steadfast.

Behind this prayer is an idea taken from the Hebrew scriptures. When the people of Israel pondered the mystery of God, they consistently described God this way: *"compassionate and gracious, slow to anger, overflowing with steadfast love and faithfulness"* (Exodus 34:6). That fourth descriptor—"steadfast love"—is the Hebrew word *chesed*. *Chesed* is a little difficult to translate because the concept covers several ideas in our own language. It combines love, generosity, and enduring commitment. Motivated by a deep and personal care, *chesed* suggests a promise-keeping loyalty. This steadfast love is a part of God's character independent of anything we do or fail to do. It

172

is one of the most common words used to describe who God is in all of the scriptures.

We don't have time to review all the ways that God exhibits *chesed* in the scriptures, but consider today's readings:

- In our reading from Genesis, the Lord meets Abraham by the oaks of Mamre and sends three messengers, who assure him that his wife Sarah will have a son. The idea was laughable because they were old. But God had promised to make Abraham with Sarah, the father of multitudes. No matter how old they are, God loves them, and God wants Abraham and Sarah to be a blessing to the whole world that God loves, and God will fulfill the promise. This is *chesed*.

- In Paul's letter to the Romans, he writes about the steadfast love shown by God in Jesus—"for while we were still weak, Christ died for the ungodly." God's steadfast and self-giving love did not rely on our faithfulness. God gave himself to us and for us even when we did not deserve it because this is who God is. *Chesed* is God's character.

- Our Gospel reading today tells us that Jesus saw that the crowds were harassed and helpless, like sheep without a shepherd, and he had compassion for them. He does not decide that all those people are just too messy and probably aren't worth the effort; instead, his whole purpose is to love them. Generous and committed compassion. *Chesed*.

*Steadfast love* is who God is, independent of who we are, but it does not leave us as we are. God's steadfast love—if we let it—will transform us. Paul, who taught us that love is patient and kind, never arrogant or boastful, and does not insist on its own way (1 Corinthians 13), also taught us that this same love has a way of working on us. When we discover God's heart, it will shape our own—and not just our hearts, but our thoughts and deeds too ... our whole lives. In Paul's letter to the Romans, he says that the process of transformation begins in suffering.

- *Suffering*—Let's take a little care with this idea because Paul is not directly talking about illness or injustice. He is not saying that we should celebrate our cancer or accept without challenge a difficult situation. Instead, Paul is talking about the suffering that we experience because we have seen the glory of God but have not yet experienced its perfection. This is suffering as a result of our faith —the sorrow that we experience when we can see the distance between the world as it is and the world as God intends it to be.

- Such faithful suffering builds our endurance, exercising those muscles of love and compassion as we work against hate, against apathy, and against destruction. The more we practice compassion in the face of contempt, and the more we take down the bricks of the walls between us that others continuously try to build, the more endurance we have to walk this way of love.

- The more we build the endurance to stay on that path, the more God's character becomes ours, too. *Chesed*. Our character becomes a reflection of God's when we love, not just when the circumstances make that easy, but all the time, because love is who we are, independent of what others do or don't do.

- Our own steadfast love will bear fruit in hope. Justice is slow, and we have to wait and work for it—but we never have to wait for God's *Chesed*. God's steadfast love is with us now and will take us where we need to go. Healing may be slow and come in ways that are unexpected or not what we wanted, but we can always rely on God's steadfast love to get us there. Hope will never disappoint when we trust in God's *chesed*.

- Our response to God's steadfast faith and love is to develop and practice loyal love because, as Paul wrote, *"suffering produces endurance, and endurance produces character, and character produces hope, and hope does not disappoint us, because God's love has been poured into our hearts through the Holy Spirit that has been given to us."*

God continues to give God's self to us and to give us to one another. As you know, I'm just returning from a family vacation, for which I am very grateful to you. We traveled to New York City and to Boston. Stephen, Drew, Matthew, and I saw a Broadway show and some live music, went to museums and gorgeous old churches, and even connected with some old friends. Most of all, it was just a good time to work on building those bonds of loyal love. Truly, it was a great vacation, but also, I want you to know that it was not a picture postcard of one. Like every community, our family comes with unexpected stressors, complicated interpersonal dynamics, hunger and exhaustion and general grumpiness sometimes, balanced out with laughter, good meals, and exciting discoveries and learning opportunities. But that intentional time away is mostly about being together. It's a way for us to practice and secure our steadfast love for one another. And we need that. We all need that.

Because change happens. We never know exactly what life will bring, but if we have steadfast love, we don't have to worry too much about what changes may come. Because of God's steadfast love, we can be confident that we are in good hands. If we, too, have steadfast love, love will direct our path as we go. This is why we pray that God will keep his Church in his own steadfast faith and love—because the world is full of harassed and helpless people. It's full of sheep who have no shepherd. By God's own love, we are called to the same love—to proclaim truth with boldness, and minister justice with compassion. My prayer for us, St. Margaret's, is that we will remain in steadfast love for God and for one another. My prayer, O Lord, is that you will keep your household, the Church, in your steadfast faith and love.

# THE PEACE OF CHRIST

The Rev. Michaelene Miller
Proper 7 – June 25, 2023

*Genesis 21:8-21*
*Psalm 86:1-10, 16-17*
*Romans 6:1b-11*
*Matthew 10:24-39*

I have recently spent a lot of time at summer camp, which is one of my favorite markers of summertime life and routine. This past Wednesday, I spent the day with the Sr. High campers at Camp Mitchell, our diocesan summer camp. I led morning prayer and taught at the morning chapel session.

The previous week, I spent Monday-Friday at Saint Christopher Camp, the Episcopal summer camp in the Diocese of Lower South Carolina. I went because the current Camp Director and interim Executive Directors are dear friends, and when friends call me to summer camp, especially when it is a camp on the beach, it is really hard for me to resist. So, I went and was the camp chaplain leading worship and the Christian formation for the entire week for over 100 third through fifth graders.

Now it had been a while since I had been fully immersed in the summer camp setting, but it didn't take long for me to remember how, with a group of that size—over a hundred nine-through-eleven-year-olds—that even their whispering, inside voices can sound like a roar that is impossible to talk over, even with a microphone.

Luckily, it also did not take me long to remember the old attention-getters and call-and-responses that I had employed multiple times a day as a counselor and camp director years ago. The muscle memory all came back. Do you know what I'm talking about? Do you remember any of those call and responses?

For example, one that we said often when I was a counselor went like this: "Hey Camp Mitchell, how do you feel?"—and the crowd would respond, "We feel good! Oh, we feel so good, HUH!" And it didn't take me long to learn Camp Christopher's tradition of calling out, "What are all these kids doing here?" and letting them all respond together in one voice, "Camp, baby, camp!" before they quieted down and waited for my next instruction.

In my time as a counselor and camp director, I have always loved these calls and responses. Something about the nature of these shared words and their familiar rhythm sort of reminded me of our worship liturgies. Personally, I definitely look back and think of those moments of learning how to get beyond my own shyness to stand in front of all those campers and shout out these calls and responses—I think of those moments as part of my formation as a priest and worship leader. Because of those moments, they are not far out of my ordinary weekly routine as a worship leader here at St. Margaret's. Every Sunday, moments of call and response are a regular part of our liturgy. These are moments where the worship leader gathers the voices and attention of the people to prepare for a shared prayer or important moment in the liturgy. In a very similar way, it is important for the call and response at camp to be relevant to the lived, shared moment of the group. The calls help the large group to focus their attention on the shared task or lesson that is ahead of them.

So, it wasn't long into the week at St. Christopher Camp when I started falling back into our liturgy for other examples to use in the midst of chapel time because, again, even when the campers were whispering quietly in the chapel—100 quiet voices are still 100 voices against my one voice—so, for a call specifically relevant to my teaching in chapel, I would shout out "God is with you!" And then, knowingly and automatically, these 100 campers would reply, "And also with you!" I would thank them for that sweet reminder of our reality that we do live, move, and have our being in God, and then I would continue with my teaching. I found it important that my call in chapel was relevant to what I was teaching because even on its own, that call and response was a tool in my teaching. Those words shaped those campers as they listened to me telling them that God was with them, and then they would affirm that truth by replying and telling me the same. And also with you!

The call and response was a tool that shaped and formed my campers that week, and I knew there was also the chance that out of everything I said that week, those words might be the only thing that stuck, and I went home with them.

Our liturgy every Sunday is full of words and phrases that shape and form our faith in God and the priorities that determine how we live our faith in this world. In our shared liturgy every Sunday, a familiar one of these calls and responses is when the celebrant calls out, "The peace of the Lord be always with you," and the congregation replies, "And also with you."

These familiar and common words that we say every week shape our belief and make it easy to think that we, as Christians, are a people of peace. We are to pass the peace to those in the pews and others in the world. That peace is of the Lord and that we, as followers of Jesus—the Prince of Peace, are to make peace, love peace, and keep the peace.

And, yes, that is an easy takeaway from that moment in our liturgy, but then we get our gospel passage for this week, and it shakes us; it confuses and troubles this easy truth. This week, we read Jesus telling his disciples, *"Do not think that I have come to bring peace to the earth; I have not come to bring peace, but a sword."*

Maybe these words jarred you as much as they did me when I first sat down for my sermon prep this week. "It's a weird scripture passage," I said to a friend. These words of Jesus jar us from our assumptions about peace and jolt us from our comfortable lull and automatic recitation of our liturgy. These words make us look with eyes wide open to see the whole picture, not just the nice, comfortable part that goes so well on a tee shirt.

With eyes wide open, we see the larger context. In our liturgy, the peace comes after the confession and absolution of our sins. It is only after telling the truth and naming our sins—those things that separate us from God and from each other—and participate in the act of turning those things over to God that we are able to rejoice in and come together in the peace of Christ.

With eyes wide, we see the details. In our liturgy, it is not just peace that we pass but the *peace of Christ* that we are called to pass and live out in the world when we come back into full relationship with God and each other. This peace is not the stagnant, passive peace in our culture that seeks conformity and niceness and enforces the status quo. The peace of Christ is an active peace that seeks to transform, even as it may first cut away and divide in the long process of shaping the world into the Kingdom of God.

These are the details we find when we look with eyes wide to see the larger context of our scripture passage, too. Our gospel reading for today is part of the Missionary Discourse—Jesus' second out of five teaching discourses in Matthew's Gospel—and in this block of teaching, Jesus is specifically talking to his disciples and teaching them about what discipleship really is and what it will cost them.

Our passage for today follows right after last week's gospel reading. There, Jesus commissions his disciples to do what he is doing—He prepares to send them out to cure the sick, raise the dead, cleanse the lepers, cast out demons and proclaim the good news that 'The kingdom of heaven has come near.'

In Jesus' first block of teaching in Matthew—the sermon on the Mount—Jesus teaches what the kingdom of heaven was like. Then he lives it and models the ways of God's Kingdom—he loves, liberates, and gives life. And then here, he teaches his disciples as he commissions them to do the same that it won't be easy.

He warns them, if you are to do what I do, if you become like your teacher if you prioritize and live out God's kingdom in the here and now amongst the empires of this world, this path will not immediately lead you to a life of peace but rather division.

Jesus makes it clear—the Peace of Christ is a sword that breaks in order to heal; it cuts down the proud from their thrones as it levels and lifts up the lowly; it divides and severs those relationships that block and prevent the liberation and love of God.

Following Jesus in his work of building another world is risky as well as life changing. And it is all too easy to lose perspective on the long view of where this struggle will lead. It is all too easy to pick and choose the parts that we would like to hear, to choose a peace that denies the reality that following Christ is difficult.

So, how can we faithfully listen for and respond to Jesus's call upon our lives? And are we willing to accept the risk?

How do we keep our eyes wide open:

- to see those blocks of love within ourselves and outside in the larger community?
- to see those things within and around us that we might need to let go of or help dismantle in order for God's Kingdom to emerge?

And in the meantime, as we consider this call, let us participate in and allow our liturgy to shape us, to break us open, and prepare us to go and live the peace of Christ, loving and serving the Lord. (Thanks be to God.)

# WARM HEARTS! COOL WATER!

THE REV. MARY VANO
Proper 8 – July 2, 2023

*Genesis 22:1-14*
*Psalm 13*
*Romans 6:12-23*
*Matthew 10:40-4*

Last week, we heard Jesus say, *"What I say to you in the dark, tell in the light; and what you hear whispered, proclaim from the rooftops."* We've been reading from this section in Matthew's Gospel for the last two weeks. It's a full chapter of Jesus preparing his disciples to go out into the world, doing the ministry to which God calls them in Christ's name. So far, we've heard that Jesus prepared them for the hardship, rejection, and persecution they would likely face. But here, at the end of chapter 10, he whispers to them the secret of success. It's nothing grand. Nowhere does he mention great temples or overflowing pews. Instead, he points them to the simple yet profound gestures that transform lives. He says, *"Whoever welcomes you welcomes me, and whoever welcomes me welcomes the one who sent me."* And he continues, *"Whoever welcomes a prophet, whoever welcomes a righteous person, whoever gives even a cup of cold water."* This is the secret to success that we need to proclaim from the rooftops: Warm hearts! Cool water!

The most important words in this passage are repeated:

*Whoever* and *welcomes.*

"Whoever" is a wonderfully broad word. Jesus isn't picky. It can be anybody—rich or poor, educated or not. "Whoever" means that the color of their skin, their country of origin, or their native language does not matter in the mission of God. This is significant because prophets don't wear name badges to identify themselves as such, and there are no visible halos to help us spot the righteous among the unrighteous. We are all more complicated than that. So, Jesus prepares his disciples for their faithful mission by reminding them that they have no way of knowing who God intends for them to encounter. Stay open-minded. Keep your eyes and hearts open because whoever welcomes you is welcoming God. When you welcome others, you are welcoming divine love.

And to welcome can mean many things—it can mean inviting someone in or offering them refreshment. It can mean listening and finding common ground. It can mean receiving the gifts others have to offer and accepting people for who they are. To welcome is to invite, make space for, listen, receive, and accept—all of which can be contained in a small glass of cool water.

*Whoever welcomes*

As simple and wonderful as this sounds, it's actually quite countercultural. Instead of being open to "whoever," we often find ourselves guarded, regarding strangers with suspicion until they prove otherwise. Instead of welcoming others with openness and a cool cup of water, we show them where the hose is and close the door.

Stephen and I were laughing this week about a funny video we saw online. It showed a young adult questioning why Gen X-ers so often talk about drinking water from the hose when they were children. "Was the sink not available?!" they asked. Then a Gen X-er (from my generation) comes on the screen and says, "You don't understand; our parents didn't let us in the house during the day! They literally had a PSA that came on TV at night to remind them, 'Parents, it's 10 pm. Do you know where your kids are?' So, it's kind of funny now, but some of us were parented this way—'Don't come in the house. You kids can drink from the hose.'"

Parenting philosophies aside, I sometimes think this is how people treat one another in the world.

- We keep our doors closed and locked. We work to protect our territory and our power. Lord, have mercy.
- We silence and reject the voices and perspectives of others. We fail to listen and resist growth. Christ, have mercy.
- Instead of focusing on what others might offer and how, together, we might do something new and wonderful, we cling to a failing status quo. Lord, have mercy.

But Jesus calls us to a different way. It's not that we will always agree, and we shouldn't burden every newcomer with the expectation that they will save us, but we certainly don't need to regard those we don't know or those with whom we disagree as enemies. We don't need to show them the door and the hose. In another place, Jesus says, *"Whoever is not against us is for us."* (Mark 9:38-40) He flips the common thinking that if someone is not with us, they must be against us. Jesus' way is to draw the circle wider. To be generous and hospitable. We need to be prepared to accept the hospitality of whoever will offer it. And whoever comes our way, we need to be prepared to welcome them. This is the path of transformation.

This week, my son Drew—now 20 years old—spent a few days in Austin, Texas. He's preparing to move there. It feels like a lifetime ago that we came to Little Rock, but we used to live in Austin, and I've been amazed and grateful at how old friends are helping him now. I've been reflecting on how those relationships began—one friend met my husband in college when they stood in line to register for classes. From that small welcome began a lifelong friendship. Two of these friends came to church for Drew's baptism twenty years ago and promised, through their prayers and witness, to help him grow into the full stature of Christ. This week, they gave him a place to stay and played music with him. Another former colleague now works at the college Drew will attend and helped him complete his registration. A woman from our old neighborhood, whom we first met while watching our children play outside, helped us sell our house when we moved away and is now helping Drew find an apartment. From school, church, work, and neighborhoods, a lifetime of welcoming strangers with warm hearts and sharing cool cups of water has led to enduring and meaningful connections.

Warm hearts, cool water—this is how we build resiliency. Warm hearts, cool water—this is how we learn to care for each other. Warm hearts, cool water—this is the secret to success as we work with God to build the kingdom of heaven.

Today's passage reminds me of another in Scripture, from the first letter of John, which also uses the words "whoever" and "anyone." The author writes, *"Beloved, let us love one another, for whoever loves has been born of God and knows God. Anyone who does not love does not know God, because God is love."* (1 John 4:7-8)

It's a wide-open world out there, and it's not easily divided into categories of prophets and reprobates, or saints and sinners. As Jesus has warned his disciples throughout Matthew 10, they will be vulnerable in the world. They may face rejection and even threats to their safety. Yet, it all comes down to this: Love them. Trust in and rely on God. Do not fear. Move on from failure.

And then, understand what success looks like in this mission. It looks like learning to trust God above worldly goods. It looks like letting go of fear so we can live in love. It looks like welcoming all kinds of people with warm hearts and cool water.

Go, and proclaim it! Go, and do it.

# YOKED TO REST AND RESPONSE-ABILITY

The Rev. Michaelene Miller
Proper 9 – July 9, 2023

*Genesis 24:34-38, 42-49, 58-67*
*Psalm 45: 11-18*
*Romans 7:15-25a*
*Matthew 11:16-19, 25-30*

> *Come to me, all you that are weary and are carrying heavy burdens, and I will give you rest. Take my yoke upon you, and learn from me; for I am gentle and humble in heart, and you will find rest for your souls. For my yoke is easy, and my burden is light.*

These words of grace, this invitation to rest, are unique to Matthew's Gospel, but they are not unique to all of Scripture. Here, Jesus is interpreting Scripture and personally taking on the voice of wisdom personified. His invitation to rest and take on his gentle yoke is rooted in the wisdom literature of Sirach. In chapter 24, we read, *"Come to me, all who desire me, and be filled with my fruits."* And in chapter 51, *"Put your neck under her yoke, and let your souls receive instruction."*

Even in the face of frustrating circumstances and rejection, Jesus persists in revealing himself and inviting others into the grace of God. *"Come to me, all you that are weary and are carrying heavy burdens, and I will give you rest."*

Do you know this feeling of rest?

Likely not. Too many of us don't. In the United States, we live in a culture of hurry and rush, a culture that values productivity over process. Our capitalistic grind culture marks humans as machines—vehicles of labor to oppress and use, rather than beings who care and need to be cared for.

Our sense of urgency is an affliction of the dominant white supremacy culture—and it too often sacrifices human needs and care, particularly the interests of Black, Indigenous, and People of Color, in the pursuit of so-called "advancements" for society. Another tendency of this dominant culture is the belief that one must be "exceptional to be acceptable." This drives over-achiever, perfectionistic, and competitive patterns that separate people from one another in the relentless drive to succeed. In the end, this often leaves people feeling inadequate, disconnected, depleted, and isolated.

Do you know this feeling of rush, of depletion and disconnection?

Likely, yes. We are caught in systems of oppression and rushed to the point of being so depleted or distracted that we become unresponsive to the needs of others—and even unresponsive to God's presence in our midst.

I don't think we've come far from the crowd Jesus spoke to that day. Our gospel passage opens with Jesus comparing that generation to disconnected and unresponsive children crying out in misunderstanding. When there were wedding songs, no one danced, and when there were funeral dirges, no one mourned.

Jesus goes on to explain that when John the Baptist came with a grim message of repentance, no one responded but to say he had a demon. And when Jesus came eating, drinking, and sharing an invitation of hospitality and forgiveness for all to gather at the table of unconditional love, they called him a glutton and a drunkard. Oppressed by or caught up in the oppressive systems of the Roman Empire, the people of that generation missed John the Baptist and Jesus in their midst.

We are not much different today. Caught up in these systems of exploitation, either by choice or out of necessity to survive, we often remain depleted, distracted, and unresponsive. We regularly miss what matters, whether it's the invitation to dance or the moment to mourn. We reject the call to repent and remain unresponsive to those in need of care—and to the divine encounter right before us.

When encountering movements, policies, or leaders that point to ways of love and liberation that we can't even begin to imagine, our default is to remain unmoved by these revelations and say, "That is too much, too severe, too demanding, or too provocative."

For me, *The Nap Ministry* is one such movement that both catches my attention and stirs my resistance. These reactions, though, should be seen as invitations to get curious: What about this leads me to hesitate? What about this calls out something in me that makes me want to freeze?

The Nap Ministry is a movement founded by Tricia Hersey, a poet, theologian, community organizer, performance artist, and activist who advocates for the importance of rest as a racial and social justice issue. Hersey developed the "Rest is Resistance" framework in 2016 after experimenting with rest as a tool for her own liberation and healing starting in 2013. Hersey explains:

"It has always been about more than taking a full nap. My rest as a Black woman in America suffering from generational exhaustion and racial trauma was always a political refusal and social justice uprising within my body. I took to rest and naps and slowing down as a way to save my life, resist the systems telling me to do more, and as a remembrance to my Ancestors who had their DreamSpace stolen from them. This is about more than naps. It is not about fluffy pillows, expensive sheets, silk sleep masks, or any other external, frivolous, consumerist gimmick. It is about a deep unraveling from white supremacy and capitalism. These two systems are violent and evil. History tells us this, and our present living shows this. Rest pushes back and disrupts a system that views human bodies as tools for production and labor. It is a counter-narrative. We know that we are not machines."

For me, I think it's this movement's calling out of my own deep socialization to America's system of "Keep Going!" that causes me to freeze. This movement brings me to the edge and begs the question of whether I want to see myself clearly—as someone who can and has pushed beyond healthy limits in pursuit of perfectionism, and, in doing so, perpetuates those systems upon those most burdened to the bone. It brings me to the paralyzing oscillation between the shame and guilt of feeling lazy and unproductive and the honest, universal realization that I'm in need of healing and liberation too.

Jesus invites us: *"Come to me ... For my yoke is easy, and my burden is light."* In reality, St. Margaret's, like all those before us, we are all yoked to something. Whether we are yoked to the unending, unforgiving work and grind of the empires of the world, or we choose to yoke ourselves to the work of Christ and God's loving, liberating, and life-giving dream for creation that Jesus revealed.

As a tool in God's Kingdom, the yoke of Christ unites us and sets us on a path of turning and returning towards God in devotion. Christ's yoke directs us so that, with our whole hearts, we can follow Jesus' commandments to love God and our neighbor.

Even as Jesus invites us to a yoke of response-ability—of loving God and loving our neighbors as ourselves—Jesus makes it clear that this is an invitation to rest as well. It is only in regularly finding rest and liberation from the systems of oppression in which we exist that we will be able to truly and fully live into the response-ability of loving care and life-giving relationship. When we rest, we find the ability to respond to the needs of others and the revelation of God in our midst.

I'd like to close with a practice of rest—offering a poem by Mary Oliver, called *The Summer Day*. This poem is gentle in nature, both in setting and tone, yet it leaves us with two challenges. First, it suggests a revolution. Moving us beyond our cultural definition of a successful day marked by productivity, Oliver calls us to reconsider how a good day might instead be blessed by a sense of idleness and rest. Second, in the wake of this revolution, Oliver challenges us to answer what we "plan to do" with the rest of our "wild and precious" days. Please, as you are comfortable, close your eyes and let these words be a moment of rest for you on this day.

*The Summer Day* by Mary Oliver
> Who made the world?
> Who made the swan, and the black bear?
> Who made the grasshopper?
> This grasshopper, I mean—
> the one who has flung herself out of the grass,
> the one who is eating sugar out of my hand,
> who is moving her jaws back and forth instead of up and
> down—

who is gazing around with her enormous and complicated eyes.
Now, she lifts her pale forearms and thoroughly washes her face.
Now, she snaps her wings open and floats away.
I don't know exactly what a prayer is.
I do know how to pay attention, how to fall down
into the grass, how to kneel down in the grass,
how to be idle and blessed, how to stroll through the fields,
which is what I have been doing all day.
Tell me, what else should I have done?
Doesn't everything die at last, and too soon?
Tell me, what is it you plan to do
with your one wild and precious life?[26]

# LET EVERYONE WITH EARS LISTEN

THE REV. MARY VANO
Proper 10 – July 16, 2023

*Genesis 25:19-34*
*Psalm 119:105-112*
*Romans 8:1-11*
*Matthew 13:1-9,18-23*

"*Let anyone with ears listen!*" The thirteenth chapter of Matthew's Gospel contains a series of seven parables in which Jesus uses storytelling to teach the crowds about the reign of God and the kingdom of heaven. The parables employ simple, everyday subjects—concepts with which Jesus' audience would be very familiar—to help them understand the less familiar. In our Tuesday morning Bible study this week, we discussed why Jesus would use parables to teach. Wouldn't it be more direct to just give us a lecture—a PowerPoint presentation about who God is and what God desires for us? Well, yes, a lecture might be more direct and even more informative, but would it be as memorable? Probably not. Could it be as comprehensive? No. Would listeners engage deeply in the subject? Educators know that lectures can be efficient for providing information but not always effective for helping students gain understanding. And that's the goal.

Jesus teaches in parables because he wants disciples not just to hear, but also to understand—and that requires active listening. Parables invite people into conversation with one another. They require us to open our hearts and imaginations to see through the story to the deeper Truth that Jesus hopes to convey. Parables may not be straightforward, but they move us along a certain path.

I was thinking about this as Stephen and I took a road trip to Tennessee this week. I was in the passenger seat, managing my Waze app, which provides real-time traffic updates like hazards and speed traps. The app is crowd-sourced, so users share traffic information as they travel. It's handy technology. With parables on my mind, I wondered how Jesus

190

might weave a story in our fast-paced modern world. Could there be a "Parable of the Waze"?

"Our journey of faith is like a road trip across I-40. Some cars will break down along the way. Waze will say 'Watch out—vehicle on road.' There will be traffic jams, and Waze will suggest a safer route, but only some will choose to follow. At times, you might get going too quickly. Waze will warn you of a police officer up ahead. At the end of the journey, you'll arrive at a friend's home and be embraced by love. Let anyone with ears listen!"

Okay, that's not the best parable ever, but I bet you'll think about it later. And that's sort of the idea. We keep reflecting on it. We revisit it to uncover nuggets of wisdom that don't force us to believe anything but offer guidance if we choose to follow. Jesus told a story to a crowd 2,000 years ago, and we're still thinking about it today to see how it speaks to our lives now. So, listen again to the Parable of the Sower:

> *Listen! A sower went out to sow. And as he sowed, some seeds fell on the path, and the birds came and ate them up. Other seeds fell on rocky ground, where they did not have much soil, and they sprang up quickly, but when the sun rose, they were scorched; and since they had no root, they withered away. Other seeds fell among thorns, and the thorns grew up and choked them. Other seeds fell on good soil and brought forth grain, some a hundredfold, some sixty, some thirty. Let anyone with ears listen!*

The story begins and ends with an exhortation to listen. That's not just about turning up your hearing aids. Jesus wants us to focus. To set down distractions and pay attention. From his seat on the boat, he calls out to the crowds on the shore, asking them to go deeper.

Jennifer Kaalund, an Associate Professor of Religious Studies, writes about the listening required by parables. She says, "Deep listening is the idea that we listen with compassion. We listen to understand, and we listen with intention, specifically the intention to act." In other words, to open one's ears is to open one's heart. The Greek word *eisakouo* can be defined as to hear, to heed, or to obey.

Jesus means all three. Listen, Jesus says. Hear the story. Heed its lessons. Obey and follow where the story leads. When Jesus says "listen," he's asking us to hear, understand, and act. This little parable of the sower is more than just an interesting story or a teaching about the kingdom of heaven. It's an invitation to participate in the manifestation of God's kingdom.

So, are you listening? Like any parable, there's more than one way to read this one. Let me throw out a few ideas you might glean from it:

- This is a story about a sower, one who scatters seeds so they might grow. God is a God of life and creation. Growth is neither neat nor perfect, but that's who God is—a God of life and growth.
- The story acknowledges that the world is full of obstacles that challenge the life and growth God seeks. These obstacles include:

    - **Misunderstanding.** When people don't understand who God is or what God desires, there's no place for the seed to take root. Closed minds and hardened hearts can't bear fruit.

    - **Challenges to faith.** Like the rocky soil, life presents many challenges to our faith. Pressures can tempt us to abandon the love we've been given. The rocky soil is a hard place for lasting life.

    - **Worry and greed.** Jesus names these as obstacles born from shallow trust in God. Without deep trust, the demands of the world will choke out the growth God desires.

- The obstacles are both external and internal. This is not just the world in which we live, but also the landscape of our hearts.
- The life toward which the story points is both rooted and flourishing. We're invited into a deep relationship with God, where we're nourished and grounded, but also encouraged to branch out, flower, and produce fruit to share God's nourishment with those around us.

- This is a story of both caution and hope. Not every seed will grow, but every seed holds within it the full potential of the kingdom of heaven.

Let everyone with ears listen! What is Jesus inviting you to hear, heed, and obey today? How are you being asked to participate in the manifestation of God's kingdom? There's more than one way to respond to this story, but here are a couple of suggestions:

- As fellow disciples of Jesus, we need to value life, knowing that God is a God of life and growth. Listen with compassion, stretch your hearts wide open, and stand together on the side of life and growth.
- The story doesn't mention the larger work of farming, yet there's something here about cultivating the earth. Good soil doesn't just appear; it requires intention and effort. The more good soil there is, the more we all thrive.
- The story invites us to go to work for the Creator—scattering seeds of God's love not only in good soil but also in the hard places, the rocky places, and the weedy places. Life is unpredictable, and you never know where a seed might take root.

A parable may be an imprecise teaching method, but I believe it's the most effective way to learn what we need to manifest the kingdom of heaven. The kingdom of heaven isn't about everyone having the right ideas. If that were the case, a good, thorough lecture would've done the trick long ago. The kingdom of heaven isn't about everyone always doing the right thing all the time. If it were, a strict ethical code would suffice.

No, the kingdom of heaven is about living in right relationship. God's realm is manifest when we know and love God. We live under God's reign when we know and love one another. As Jesus said, "The kingdom of heaven has come near." Let anyone with ears listen.

# THE LORD IS IN THIS PLACE

THE REV. MARY VANO
Proper 11 – July 23, 2023

*Genesis 28:10-19a*
*Psalm 139: 1-11, 22-23*
*Romans 8:12-25*
*Matthew 13:24-30,36-43*

Today, we read another chapter in the life of our ancestor Jacob—a dreamer if there ever was one. Just to remind you, Jacob was the younger twin of Esau, the sons of Isaac and Rebekah. Though Jacob's mother thought he was special, everyone else preferred Esau. Esau was the firstborn in a world where that mattered a lot. He was his father's favorite, no doubt because he was good at hunting and loved the outdoors. Esau was the kid who was always the first chosen for the team. Jacob was none of this. And so, Jacob dreamed. He dreamed of the day when he would surpass his brother and rule the family. He dreamed of climbing the ladder to the top where others would admire and respect him. His mother assured him that God had chosen him for this, but that wasn't good enough—he was determined to make it happen.

We pick up Jacob's story today just after he and his mother have deceived his brother Esau out of the birthright. Jacob received his father's blessing, but as a result of his deceit, he is forced to flee for his life. His mother sends him away, not only to escape Esau's wrath but also to find a wife. Fleeing his home to save himself, he wanders out into the desert toward an uncertain destination. He probably never felt more alone. But, I imagine, the disappointment and disorientation he felt haunted him throughout his journey. The ladder he'd tried to climb had been kicked out from under him. The dream he worked so hard for had been shattered.

It's the kind of disappointment and disorientation that comes with seeking greener pastures only to find them dry—or achieving exactly what you thought you wanted, only to discover that it wasn't what you expected. Jacob wanted the birthright—the birthright was not about money; it was about leadership, about becoming the patriarch of the family and carrying God's blessing to the next generation. He got the birthright, but because he deceived his father and cheated his brother, he was effectively expelled from the family. He found himself in isolation. And though he may not have truly appreciated his family when he was with them, he likely never imagined what it would feel like to be without them. What good is a birthright without a family?

I imagine these thoughts ran through Jacob's mind as he sat alone in the desert and laid his head upon a hard stone. But in this moment, when he felt most alone, God came to Jacob. As his eyes closed to the night, his mind and heart opened. He dreamed as he had never dreamed before.

Some translations call it a ladder or a stairway; scholars debate the best translation of what Jacob saw in his dream. But, in any case, Jacob envisioned a place of access to God. It was not a ladder he had to climb. God was there, and the angels were ascending and descending freely between Jacob and God. And God reiterated the promise made to Jacob's grandfather, Abraham: *"All the families of the earth shall be blessed in you and in your offspring."* It's astounding, isn't it? Jacob was alone, and he deserved to be alone. But even in this isolation, God came to redeem him. God promises Jacob not only the gift of family but the privilege of participating in God's blessing.

And guess what? This isn't a dream Jacob had to strive for—it simply was. Jacob had tried to force the promise and, in doing so, had only made trouble for himself. But here, God reminds Jacob that his mother was right: he is special and loved, no matter what, and God has a blessing for him.

The next thing God says to Jacob is this: *"Know that I am with you and will keep you wherever you go, and will bring you back to this land; for I will not leave you until I have done what I have promised you."* Jacob still has quite a journey ahead of him—he must find a wife, return home, and reconcile with his family. He cannot stand still. But he cannot go far either. God has placed upon him a tether. In the story, this tether is represented as a holy place—Jacob says, *"Surely the Lord is in this place,"* and calls it Bethel. But the tether God places on Jacob is not so much to a place as to his source—that is, God. What Jacob stumbled upon in his desert dream was a place of being with God, and God reminds him that this is his home. No matter where he goes, his home is with him.

Jacob is our ancestor. Jacob is us. Don't we all have a twin—someone out there who seems just like us, but only better? More beautiful. Smarter. More successful. With a better personality. It doesn't matter who you are—there's always someone who seems better—and our own insecurities drive us to chase after dreams. To strive for things that can really only be received. Like Jacob, we sometimes find ourselves isolated by our own actions, because we've hurt someone in our blind quest to get what we want.

But Jacob also reminds us of the redemption that comes when we arrive at just the right place. He teaches us that the best dream we can have is God's dream for us—the dream that simply is there for us to receive. The love of friends and family, knowing that we have a purpose in life, and having companions, not competitors, on life's journey. We are reminded by Jacob that God intends for all of humanity to be blessed, and that we are not only the beneficiaries of the blessing but also conveyors of it. God calls us out of our own deserts to receive and pass on this love. And best of all, Jacob's dream assures us that we are never alone—a message echoed in the words of Jesus at the end of Matthew's Gospel: *"I am with you always, to the end of the age."* God is with us. Through Abraham, through Jacob, through Mary, and through Jesus, God has revealed this. Through you and me, God continues to reveal it: God loves us, and God promises to be with us. Surely, the Lord is in this place.

Jacob's ladder is not about climbing the corporate ladder or any ladder at all. Rather, it's about realizing that God is among us. Jacob may not have "gotten ahead" in life, but he found life when he learned this truth. We are offered the same—and I pray that we may all find the life through which God blesses us.

# SURPRISE, SURPRISE, SURPRISE!

THE REV. MARY VANO
Proper 12 – July 30, 2023

*Genesis 29:15-28*
*Psalm 105:1-11, 45b*
*Romans 8:26-39*
*Matthew 13:31-33,44-52*

There's a funny little debate that has emerged in recent generations due to advances in technology. When you're expecting a baby, do you choose to be surprised? Today, multiple ultrasounds are routine, and in most cases, an experienced ultrasound tech can easily determine the sex of the baby. So parents are given a choice: Do you want to know the sex of the child before birth, or would you prefer to wait and be surprised at the time of delivery? Everyone seems to have an opinion on this topic, and different reasons for their choice. I find it fascinating because the choice reveals a bit about a person's personality. Who wants more control over the situation? Who is more patient? Who is more traditional?

It's amusing to me because when it comes to the sex of the baby, the possibilities are rather limited, so how surprised are you actually going to be anyway?! If it tells you anything about us, Stephen and I chose not to be surprised both times. Both times, we were prepared for the boys we got. But what we weren't prepared for was the constant stream of surprises that followed!

In today's Gospel, Jesus gives us five little parables. Each one begins with the phrase, "*The kingdom of heaven is like ...*" If you like surprises, you should enjoy these!

We start with the mustard seed. Jesus points out that it is surprising that something so tiny can grow into something so large. But there's more to it than that. Mustard is not a seed most farmers would want to plant. It's nearly a weed—it grows on its own without any tending, and once it's there, it's hard to get rid of. Jesus makes sure to mention that it grows large enough for birds to take shelter in it. For his contemporary Jewish

197

audience, the birds are a subtle hint that the Gentiles, too, will find shelter in the kingdom.

Surprise! The kingdom of heaven grows large from something tiny, doesn't require human tending, may even be unwelcome at first, and even the Gentiles will find refuge in it.

Then there is the yeast: *"The kingdom of heaven is like yeast that a woman took and mixed in with three measures of flour until it was all leavened."* What's surprising here? First, yeast! Yeast is potentially harmful, but when mixed in just right with flour, it causes the dough to rise and creates beautiful, delicious bread. Yeast, used to make leavened bread, is also associated with everyday living, as opposed to the unleavened bread reserved for holy days. Oh, and let's not forget how much bread this woman is making—three measures of flour is roughly 50 pounds, more than enough for a grand feast.

Surprise! The kingdom of heaven is like this tiny fungus that, when mixed in just right, can create a feast for the whole world!

Next, Jesus says, *"The kingdom of heaven is like a treasure hidden in a field, which someone found and hid; and in his joy he goes and sells all that he has and buys the field."* This sounds a little sketchy, doesn't it? Shouldn't the worker have told the owner about the treasure? But that misses Jesus' point. He's asking us to notice this ordinary person who gives up everything for the one thing that truly matters.

Surprise! The kingdom of heaven is a treasure waiting to be found, and when you discover it, you'll give everything for it—and it will be worth it!

Again, *"The kingdom of heaven is like a merchant in search of fine pearls; on finding one pearl of great value, he went and sold all that he had and bought it."* That doesn't sound like the best business decision, does it? A seasoned merchant finds a single pearl that moves him so much, he sells everything to obtain it.

Surprise! Even when you think you've seen it all, the kingdom of heaven can still capture your heart.

Finally, *"The kingdom of heaven is like a net that was thrown into the sea and caught fish of every kind."* This one I'm familiar with. If you drag a net from your boat, you're likely to catch more than one type of fish. The net doesn't discriminate—it brings in everything, the living and the dead, the edible and the inedible, the dangerous and the harmless, even the litter left behind by humans. Everything gets gathered in. It all needs to be sorted out.

Surprise! The kingdom of heaven is a net that will gather all kinds of people.

In each of these short parables, Jesus challenges the way we see the world. He calls us to stretch our imaginations, because we need to see what the world will look like when it is reconciled with God's good will. In the kingdom of heaven, a tiny bit of faith can grow beyond our imagination. In the kingdom of heaven, God's grace blesses and feeds us all. In the kingdom of heaven, the love of God is worth giving up everything, and all we get in return is joy. And this kingdom is for all of us.

So, grab your magnifying glass. Come prepared with your shovel. Be ready to cast your net far and wide, because the kingdom of heaven is here for us to discover, if we're willing to look. The biggest surprise of all is that the kingdom of heaven doesn't have to be a distant dream. It begins now, within us, when we seek out the grace of God and allow it to transform us.

If you think it's an adventure to wait until birth to be surprised by the sex of your child, just wait! For one thing is certain—the love of God exceeds our imagination. Everything else is a surprise!

# BLESSED TO ENDURE

THE REV. MICHAELENE MILLER
Proper 13 – August 6, 2023

*Genesis 32:22-31*
*Psalm 17:1-7,16*
*Romans 9:1-5*
*Matthew 14:13-21*

Good morning! Some weeks, there are lectionary texts that preachers simply have to work with. We dig in, going line by line, word by word, in search of something to latch onto—a message to share. And then, there are other texts that latch onto the preacher or reader, demanding attention, calling us to engage with every word, every line.

Today, the Hebrew Scripture from Genesis is one of those texts for me. This short, cryptic story of Jacob's wrestling match with the unidentified man has drawn me in, and I haven't been able to let go. As I meditated and prayed with these scriptures, I returned to this story again and again.

As Jacob holds on and refuses to let go of the mysterious figure until dawn, my mind refused to let go of his story. It's a story about confrontation, and it calls out for our full attention. I had no choice but to confront it and try to understand what Jacob's struggle has to say to us today.

It's a story of blessing and transformation, but first, it's a story of struggle and endurance. In today's reading, we find Jacob on a journey home after twenty years away. He's returning home full of fear because he has no idea how his older brother, Esau, will receive him after Jacob tricked his way into stealing Esau's birthright and blessing from their aging father.

In an attempt to avoid facing his brother and the consequences of his actions, Jacob sends all of his belongings ahead as a peace offering, hoping that Esau will forget how Jacob wronged him. Along with everything else, Jacob sends his entire family on ahead.

The next scene is confusing, fast, and cryptic. One moment, Jacob is alone, and in the next, he is entangled in a brutal struggle with an unidentified man or force until dawn.

I imagine that when Jacob was left alone that night, his fears must have overwhelmed him. Unable to hide behind the distractions of his wealth and large family, his doubts about escaping his brother's wrath, and perhaps his shame, must have crept in. Vulnerable in the silence, Jacob could no longer hide from the truth and guilt of his deceptive ways.

I'm sure many of us can identify with an experience like this. It's often in the stillness and quietness of night—in moments of loneliness or isolation—that our defenses fail. It's in those moments of confrontation that we might crumble.

It's easier to crumble than to recognize God's steadfast presence in the mess and struggle. It can feel almost impossible to see that it's God who invites our persistence, strength, and endurance in those moments. God calls us to the edge of engagement with truth—truth about what we've done, about who we are, and about whose we are. And it's in those moments, at the very edge of our strength, when we refuse to run away, when facing it is the only option, that we take the risk of being blessed and transformed.

Instead of crumbling under the weight of his fears, Jacob grabs hold of the force that threatens to overtake him. He remains intentional in his actions, pushing past pain and fear, choosing to stay in the struggle, trusting that there must be a blessing somewhere in the mess. It's not a neat, heroic moment. It's a long, ugly struggle that leaves Jacob physically and mentally altered. His blessing comes at a cost—he is forever changed.

Jacob is no longer who he was—or perhaps, he is more himself than ever before. In his transformation, Jacob is not just physically changed—he's left with a limp—but his identity is changed. He is blessed and renamed as Israel. His blessing is not personal; it's connected to others. As Israel, Jacob is now tied to the divine blessing pronounced on Abraham. His personal struggle is forever linked to the struggle of a people.

Ellen Davis, in her book *Opening Israel's Scriptures*, reminds us that biblical "blessing" is the primary way God interacts with living beings. The divine blessing here connects Jacob to God's promise to Abraham: that he would be a blessing to all the peoples of the earth.

Blessing, Davis writes, is a "commitment of one's will to the flourishing of the other," and that is not quick or easy work. Living into and living as a blessing involves struggle, because it requires engagement, relationship, and wrestling with a difficult, messy world. Blessing is an exchange marked by both mess and transformation. It's not a reward for good behavior, but an invitation to engage with God and transform into something more. People like Jacob—trickster, manipulator, heel-grabber, as his name means—are the ones God chooses to bless.

This is good news. Because none of us are perfect. We all have growing edges, and God invites us to confront and push beyond them in the holy work of endurance. As Davis explains, "God seemingly chooses people who are susceptible to being changed by what God does in their lives." And as we witness in Jacob's long, dark night, transformation is not painless.

It is a long process that demands endurance, sacrifice, and a shift from personal desires to the liberation and flourishing of all people. It's a journey of continual effort, of continually returning to God. It's a pattern of struggle, endurance, and faith.

What are the struggles you need endurance for today? To what growing edges is God inviting you to confront?

In these pursuits, if we hold fast to the struggle, Jacob's story assures us that when we come through the other side—marked and altered—we will be transformed and blessed.

I'll end by echoing the Franciscan blessing that Rev. Mary shared in this past Thursday's newsletter, praying that we all become more like Jacob: foolish but blessed in our struggles with God and all the people of the earth. Let us pray:

May God bless you with discomfort at easy answers, half-truths, and superficial relationships so that you may live deep within your heart.

May God bless you with anger at injustice, oppression, and exploitation of people, so that you may wish for justice, freedom, and peace. May God bless you with enough foolishness to believe that you can make a difference in this world so that you can do what others claim cannot be done.

# WALKING ON THE WATER

THE REV. MARY VANO
Proper 14 – August 13, 2023

*Genesis 37:1-4, 12-28*
*Psalm 105:1-6, 16-22, 45b*
*Romans 10:5-15*
*Matthew 14:22-33*

On July 20, 1969, the world listened to those incredible words spoken by Neil Armstrong: "That's one small step for man, one giant leap for mankind." Armstrong was the first man to walk on the moon, and though many failures preceded that first success, he seemed to have nerves of steel as he made history 54 years ago.

Today's Gospel story from Matthew records another incredible feat: the first steps of men walking on water. Peter's first steps in faith were more like the wobbly first steps of a toddler than the seemingly fearless steps of Neil Armstrong—but certainly no less significant. Peter leapt out of the boat, boldly believing that as long as Jesus invited him, he would have the ability to walk with him on the water. As Peter stepped out of the boat and onto the water, he took one small step for man, but one giant leap of faith. It wasn't gravity or density that caused Peter to sink. It was fear.

Fear is the great obstacle in this story. Matthew tells us that the disciples were terrified when they saw Jesus walking toward them on the water. Their fear prevented them from recognizing their friend and Lord. This was the same teacher they had just spent the day with, the same Lord who had miraculously multiplied bread and fish to feed thousands, the same leader who had just compelled them to get into the boat. They see him on the water, and they are terrified. With Jesus encouraging them, *"Do not be afraid,"* Peter seems to overcome his fear just long enough to take his first few steps. But as soon as he feels the strong wind, his fear takes over, and he begins to sink. He cries out for help.

Fear is deeply embedded in human nature. Even infants, with no experience of the world, startle and cry when they hear loud noises. In childhood, most develop a rich imagination that tricks them into thinking monsters are lurking around every corner. We adults dismiss those fears as products of imagination, but have our imaginations really stopped tricking us? Or do the fears we project onto our future still pull us under?

The future is where most of our fears live. Will I fail? Will I have enough? What will happen if I get sick? What catastrophe is coming my way? Have I done enough to protect my loved ones? How will I survive when a beloved one dies? Our fears often live in the future. Some of them are rational, helping us make good decisions today. Others are irrational, and the more we let them blow us off course, the more we find ourselves stuck—adrift at sea—and unable to walk closely with Christ, who is not in the future, but right here with us in the present moment.

Besides Peter, the other disciples were paralyzed by their own fear and couldn't get out of the boat to meet Jesus. Jesus was on his way to them. They didn't have to get out of the boat, but risking nothing meant gaining nothing. They missed the extraordinary experience that Peter had, the chance to learn that when you follow Jesus' call, you can do things you never thought possible. You may object—Peter failed, he sank! But I say, no, those were just his first steps in faith. That was his baptism.

Thrown into the water, Peter discovered that it's never a failure to cry out for help. Jesus was there, with a swift hand and a firm grip, to rescue him from the deep. The wonderful thing about Peter in the Gospels is that he is so human. He often gets it wrong, but often enough, he gets it right. Crying out for help was the right thing to do. Peter would certainly fall again, but eventually, he would walk steadily with Christ. The first steps are always the hardest. When we live in fear of the future, we miss the opportunity to be with Christ in the present.

The good thing about fear is that it can also be a teacher. Peter did two things right in today's Gospel:

First, he relied on Christ's invitation to give him the courage to step out onto the water. Fear cannot cripple us when we know we are not alone. When we trust that God is good, that we are loved, and that we can rely on God's loving and protective presence, we can do hard things. We can step out of the boat, empowered by that holy invitation.

Second, when Peter's fear overcame him, and he began to sink, he cried out for help. Fear teaches us our need for God. We need God to give us the courage to live fully, meaningfully, and with purpose. We need God to save us when we are sinking. This is why God came to us in Jesus Christ—to meet us where we are, to calm our turbulent waters, and to save us from the deep. Christ is there for Peter, and Christ is there for us. Christ is there to grip our hands when fear pulls us down. If we only cry out in our times of need and reach for the hand that is reaching for ours, the deep waters will not overcome us.

Fear is something we all live with, but we don't have to be overwhelmed by it. While fear may pull us into an uncertain future, Christ dwells with us in the present.

We do better to live in the present moment, knowing that God is with us here. And it is here, in the present, that we discover the truth that will free us from fear: that God is good, and that God loves each and every one of us. When we know that God is good, and that God loves us, we will trust that God will save us from destruction. We will no longer be crippled by fear. Knowing that God is good and loves us, we will do things we never thought possible, as we walk hand in hand with Jesus.

Looking at the world around us, at the future, it seems like it would take an extraordinary leap of faith to get where we need to go. But know this: that extraordinary leap of faith begins with one small step in the direction of love.

# TOGETHER WE BEGIN AGAIN

THE REV. MARY VANC
Proper 15 – August 20, 2023

*Genesis 45:1-15*
*Psalm 133*
*Romans 11:1-2a, 29-32*
*Matthew 15: (10-20), 21-28*

Today, C.S. Lewis' famous quote comes to mind. When asked in an interview about which religion brings the greatest happiness to its followers, Lewis responded, "I didn't go to religion to make me happy. I always knew a bottle of port would do that. If you want a religion to make you feel really comfortable, I certainly don't recommend Christianity."

I'd like to say that I feel comfortable today, but I don't, and that's okay, because that's hardly the point. The point of our Christian faith is, in fact, the opposite. Let's take a look at today's scripture readings.

In Genesis 45, we pick up the story after Joseph—sold into slavery by his brothers—has made a success of himself in Egypt. His brothers and their families are suffering a famine in Canaan, and they come to Egypt hoping for provisions. Joseph recognizes his brothers before they realize who he is, and this moment in our reading is a turning point. Joseph has the opportunity to confront his brothers for the wrong they did him, but instead, he chooses forgiveness.

He looks at the men who threw him into a pit, took his coat, sold him to slavers, and told their father that he was dead. Do they deserve forgiveness for such a cruel act? No, they do not. Yet Joseph, having experienced God's saving hand which brought him to safety, gave him gifts that he could put to use, and allowed him to thrive. Now, he looks at his brothers who are in desperate need and knows that, thanks to God's goodness, he finds himself in a position to save them. He chooses forgiveness, a decision rooted in God's goodness, rather than callousness or revenge. There is nothing comfortable about that.

207

There's nothing comfortable about today's Gospel story, either. In Matthew's Gospel, Jesus and his disciples leave Israel—probably for a bit of rest—and encounter a Canaanite woman who recognizes Jesus and begs for his mercy on behalf of her daughter. This is a boundary-breaking story. There are boundaries between Jews and Canaanites, and between men and women. But the biggest boundary of all is about Jesus' mission of salvation and who it's for. Every time I read this story, I think the Canaanite woman must have heard about the Feeding of the Five Thousand, which we read a couple of weeks ago. Word must have reached her that Jesus not only fed thousands with five loaves and two fish but that there were twelve baskets of leftovers! She knew that Jesus could feed her, too.

Although Jesus may have wanted to focus on Israel first, she knew there was enough grace to go around. Kneeling before him, she insisted that even a crumb of grace was all she needed. Jesus could not argue with that. The comfortable boundaries could not hold the Gospel—they had to be broken.

This encounter between Jesus and the Canaanite woman set the stage for Paul's mission as the "apostle to the Gentiles." Once an enemy of Christ, Saul was transformed after encountering the Risen Lord. He became a passionate advocate for the Gospel and understood that God had chosen him to take the Good News to the Gentiles, breaking down the barriers that kept them outside the faithful community. Jesus was controversial among the Jews. The mission to the Gentiles was controversial among the Jewish followers of Jesus. But despite passionate disagreements, Paul writes in his letter to the Roman Christians to have patience, respect, and compassion for the Jews. He reminds them that they, too, have benefited from God's mercy and that God's mercy extends to Israel as well. It would be more comfortable to think that God is going to smite everyone we disagree with, but that's not Christianity, either.

Our readings today provide us with a reality check about what Christianity really is: It's forgiveness—finding the strength to weep, tell the truth, and allow compassion to bring us to reconciliation. It's boundary-breaking—embracing the Gospel so fully that it overflows the comfortable boundaries of nation, culture, race, gender, and religion, so that all may find a place around God's table of grace. Christianity is about accepting God's mercy in our own lives and extending that same mercy to others, especially those we disagree with. Forgiveness, compassion, breaking down barriers to create space for the marginalized, respecting those with whom we disagree, trusting in God's mercy—this is the uncomfortable religion we are all a part of.

Twelve years ago, I was called to St. Margaret's as your rector, and this has been the work we have been called to do together. After the beloved Rev. Peggy Bosmyer passed away, and after a difficult period of transition for this community, I entered a church with a lot of hurt and grief. Forgiveness and reconciliation—that is where we began our journey.

Along the way, God has given us opportunities to confront boundaries that keep people marginalized in our society. It's never easy to challenge cultural norms and societal prejudices. Yet, the more we embrace the abundance of the Gospel, the more we come to embrace one another. We have also found that individual differences and disagreements sometimes cause us to walk apart. When that happens, it's painful, and we must rely on God's grace to help us practice compassion and forgiveness.

Perhaps the church would grow faster if we advertised that this is a place where everyone is happy and comfortable. But if that were true, then we wouldn't be the Church. Instead, we are a community that practices forgiveness because we sometimes get hurt in our relationships with one another. We are a community that is constantly learning to breach the barriers that divide us and to respect and even love those with whom we disagree. This is who we are, because this is what it means to follow Jesus Christ.

Today, we must look to where Jesus is calling us now. With John Harmon, our bishop-elect, I believe God is telling me that I still have good and important work to do with you at St. Margaret's. I'm excited for what

God is calling us to do next, because I believe God is in our midst, offering mercy, faithfulness, and blessing. All we have to do is be willing to loyally follow God's lead, embracing the discomfort that comes with our faith.

In the same interview where C.S. Lewis was asked what religion brings the most happiness, he was also asked to define the practice of Christianity. His response was this: "A perfect practice of Christianity would ... mean that every single act and feeling, every experience, whether pleasant or unpleasant, must be referred to God. It means looking at everything as something that comes from Him, and always looking to Him and asking His will first, and saying, 'How would He wish me to deal with this?'"

At this moment, Lewis challenges us with this faithful question: How does God wish us to move forward from here? I don't know exactly, but I know that it won't be easy or comfortable as God continues to guide us toward reconciliation and grace. It's hard work, but it is holy work, and I'm grateful to be living this life of faith with all of you.

# PERSIST IN FAITH, SHARING YOUR GIFTS

THE REV. MICHAELENE MILLER
Proper 16 – August 27, 2023

*Exodus 1:8-2:10*
*Psalm 124*
*Romans 12:1-8*
*Matthew 16:13-20*

Our gospel passage today marks a turning point in Matthew's telling of the good news of Jesus Christ. So far, Matthew's narrative has focused on Jesus' moments of teaching, healing, and feeding, which have caused the crowds to wonder in amazement about who Jesus may or may not be. But in this 16th chapter, we see Jesus beginning to wonder about himself and his mission as well.

As Jesus and his disciples are traveling toward the villages of Caesarea Philippi—a place known for its shrines to Greek and Roman gods, and an emperor who deemed himself the "Son of God"—Jesus seeks to understand the truth about himself. He asks, with one of the most universal questions in human history, "Who am I?"

But Jesus starts with an easy question: "What have you heard? Who do people say that the Son of Man is?"

Can you imagine the scene? Some of us just returned to the classroom, and we may have already witnessed something like this; perhaps we even remember moments from our own school days. A teacher asks a question, and with excitement at its ease, students eagerly raise their hands to offer their answers.

"Oh, I know! Some say you are John the Baptist!" one disciple speaks up. "Others think you are Elijah." "No, they say you are Jeremiah!" counters another. "They really don't know exactly, but they say you are definitely one of the prophets!"

Jesus lets them speak freely, listening to what his disciples have heard from others. He doesn't deny or correct them. He remains silent, showing that this is where the search for truth often begins: by lifting up the stories passed down to us, by exploring and trying on the opinions and certainties of others.

This is often where our faith begins, too. We listen to the stories and perspectives we've inherited from our religious traditions. We memorize the creeds and prayers of our faith, and it is a good place to start. A safe place, even.

But then Jesus invites the disciples to go deeper. He asks a personal question, "But who do you say I am?" He wonders, "Who am I to you? How have you experienced me?"

Now, can you imagine the scene here? The silence that follows this question? The awkwardness as each disciple nervously waits for someone to speak up. And Jesus, like any good teacher, holds the silence, perhaps wondering if these closest to him have truly seen him, understood him, or loved him enough to make a claim out loud.

Eventually, Peter takes a risk and fills the silence: "You are the Messiah, the Son of the living God." In this vulnerable moment, Peter is blessed by Jesus because his confession is based on his discernment and experience of God's revelation, not just the human stories he has heard. Peter dares to articulate what he has experienced: this loving human, seeking to provide abundant life for all, is the Messiah.

At first, this answer fills our ears with relief, as it echoes familiar creedal language. But we know that it's not the end of the story for Peter.

In next week's Gospel, Jesus will upend Peter's expectations about the Messianic power when he teaches a vision of the Messiah so radically different that Peter rebukes him, trying to stop his "dizzying madness." In this brief exchange, Jesus both blesses Peter and challenges him: "Get behind me, Satan!"

Peter had hoped that Jesus would use his miraculous powers to claim military kingship—an understanding of the Messiah's role common in that time. But Jesus continually redirects the focus to nonviolence and compassion at the center of his mission. While Peter gets the title right, he is just at the beginning of understanding Jesus' true identity as the Crucified Messiah.

Yet, it is Peter—so courageous and yet so cowardly, so insightful and yet reckless, so faithful and yet inconsistent—that Jesus names as the rock upon which he will build the church. Peter's faith, his willingness to step forward into relationship with Jesus, his struggles and doubts, become our foundation. Peter persists in seeking a relationship with Christ, and this persistent pursuit is what Jesus blesses. It is this pursuit that we are called to emulate.

So, who do you say Jesus is? Do you rely on the stories you've inherited? Are some more comfortable to cling to than others? Are any of these stories harmful to the point that you need to let them go? Are you ready to answer the question? Maybe you are, maybe you're not.

The good news is that, like Peter, discipleship is a lifelong process. We are never expected to have all the answers, to comprehend all of who God is. But we are called to persist in our curiosity and wonder, to persist in our struggles and confusion, to persist in our incremental revelations and ever-deepening relationship with God.

In just two short weeks, it will be time for Rally Day—an unofficial liturgical time in the church year when we return from summer travels and rest, invited back together for the start of the church program year. Last year, we drew inspiration from St. Benedict's quote, "Always we begin again." We were invited to begin our spiritual journeys again as a community emerging from the pandemic and returning to the full expression and rhythms of the Church calendar. We were invited to explore and grow deeper in our relationship with God and to return to worship in person for nourishment in community.

This year, while that invitation continues, we are also called to step even deeper into our faith. As we prepare for Rally Day on September 10th, I invite you to think about and discern the "Gifts of God" that are present within you. What gifts has God given you, and how is God calling you to persist in offering those gifts by participating in the work of the church?

It takes 66 volunteers to offer three services every Sunday, and St. Margaret's currently operates with about two-thirds of those volunteers.

As we approach Rally Day, consider your unique gifts and current curiosities. In your lifelong formation as a disciple, what ministry is God calling you to explore this year?

In our Epistle reading from Romans today, Paul echoes this invitation and encourages us to be transformed by the renewing of our minds so that we may discern what the will of God is. Paul calls us to persist in our relationship with God and present our whole selves as an offering in response to God's grace. We are called to share the unique gifts that God has given each member of the body of Christ. We all have gifts to offer and ways to serve God through the church. Paul encourages those with gifts for prophecy, service, teaching, exhortation, generosity, leadership, and compassion.

We all have gifts to share. Do you feel called to share the stories of our faith as a lector, or to stand with a candle as an acolyte, illuminating the Word of God's good news? Are you called to bake the bread that will be broken and shared as Christ's body, or to offer the cup of salvation during communion? Maybe you are called to greet newcomers with radical hospitality or to usher and help others to their seats and toward God's table.

Take a few weeks to wonder about the gifts God has placed within you. How might God be inviting you to step deeper into relationship this year? Wonder with God, pray about it, and don't be afraid to step forward and offer your gifts.

# PATHWAY OF SUFFERING

The Rev. Mary Vano
Proper 17 – September 3, 2023

*Exodus 3:1-15*
*Psalm 105:1-6, 23-26, 45c*
*Romans 12:9-21*
*Matthew 16:21-28*

To truly understand today's reading from Matthew, we need to revisit last week's passage. Last week and today, we're hearing two parts of the same conversation between Jesus and his disciples on the road to Caesarea Philippi.

Recall what we discussed last week: it culminated with Jesus' question to the disciples, "*Who do you say that I am?*" Peter gave the winning answer, "You are the Messiah, the Son of the living God." Peter was right, in that moment he caught sight of a revelation from God and boldly gave voice to it. In response, Jesus blessed Peter, affirming his insight. But it is in the very next breath that we hear today's Gospel reading, where Peter rebukes Jesus for foretelling his own suffering and death. Jesus' response was both powerful and shocking: "Get behind me, Satan, you are a stumbling block to me." Those words must have taken the breath right out of Peter.

One moment, Peter's inspired confession becomes the foundation for the church, but in the very next moment, he's cast into confusion and sentenced to spend the rest of his life trying to figure it out.

What changed? What is the difference between these two consecutive moments in Peter's faith journey? The writer of Matthew answers this question clearly: the difference lies between the human and the divine, between death and life. In the first instance, Jesus tells Peter that his recognition of Jesus as the Messiah was revealed not by flesh and blood, but by our Father in heaven. But when Peter refuses to accept that the Messiah must suffer and die, Jesus rebukes him, saying, "You are setting your mind not on divine things, but on human things."

As startling as Jesus' reprimand is, I think it's even more startling what Peter heard just before it. Go back a few verses, and we find it: *"From that time on, Jesus began to show his disciples that he must go to Jerusalem, undergo great suffering at the hands of the elders, the chief priests, and scribes, and be killed, and on the third day be raised."*

Lurking behind Peter's sudden shift from divine insight to human confusion is the puzzle that confronts us all. It's the same one that wakes us up in the middle of the night. The same challenge that follows us like a shadow and has the power to shake our faith to its core. Peter, like all of us at some point, is trying to make sense of suffering.

Why must there be suffering? Surely, God's beloved Son should be exempt from such pain. There's a hidden hope here: If the Messiah can be spared, then maybe his followers can be too.

Suffering doesn't make sense from a human perspective. Only from a divine perspective can we begin to approach an answer to this problem.

The answer that seems most obvious to me (and the one we often prefer to avoid) is that we suffer because we are mortal. God gave us bodies of flesh and blood, through which we experience the world—taste, sight, smell, touch. We have hands to help others and arms to embrace them. We have feet and legs to journey through life, accompanying one another. On the sixth day of creation, after creating humankind, God looked upon it all and said, *"It is very good."* And it is.

Yet, no living thing is without vulnerability. Human bodies are subject to injury, disease, and aging. These bodies, fragile and finite, will inevitably experience suffering. Sometimes it's sudden; sometimes it's gradual. But until our time here is done, suffering will be a part of our human condition.

Another response to suffering is to recognize that we suffer because God loves us enough not to control us. Scripture teaches that "God is love." God's power, as revealed in scripture, is great, but not perfectly limitless. The Creator shares power with creation. God gives us free will—the power to choose. God does this because love cannot exist without choice.

So, we suffer because we sometimes choose poorly, or because others do. While we can limit our suffering by living faithfully, we will never entirely escape the pain caused by human sin and error. But to exclude the possibility of evil would also exclude the possibility of love. Love is only love if it's chosen. So, God woos us, calling us toward mutual, life-giving love. But God will not force us. We must be able to choose selfishness, to choose destruction, so that we may also choose life and love.

Another reason we suffer is because we love. Who among us has never been moved to tears by witnessing someone else's suffering? Our hearts break when a friend receives a hard diagnosis. We sacrifice for our children, we worry for our parents, and the loss of a loved one can be earth-shattering.

If we had no compassion, we might remain untouched. But we would also miss out on the relationships that make life meaningful—the strangers who open our eyes to a wider world, the friends who make us laugh when we're down, the parents who provide a safe harbor, the children who carry our hopes for the future. Maybe less love would mean less suffering, but I wouldn't trade that for the relationships that make life worth living.

Jesus didn't make that trade for any of us. I couldn't help but notice that in today's Gospel, Jesus doesn't directly answer the question of why. Peter doesn't understand why Jesus must suffer, but Jesus doesn't sit the disciples down and explain suffering to them. Instead, he tells them what to do with their suffering:

> If any want to become my followers, let them deny themselves, and take up their cross, and follow me.

Jesus chooses not to avoid the suffering of the world. Instead, he enters deeply into the suffering, for our sake, for love's sake. And he asks us to follow him.

To get there, we must first deny ourselves—giving up our own way of doing things to take on Christ's way of love. Suffering, or the fear of it, will often trick us into thinking that our way is the only way to avoid pain. But that's a trick. Not even the most self-centered people live without suffering—they often create even more suffering for themselves and others. Selfishness will not lead us to the abundant life we seek. For that, we must choose Christ's way.

Then we must take up our cross. All that sin, brokenness, anger, and injustice—it's a heavy burden. But we won't carry it alone. Together with Christ, we'll carry it to that holy hill, where God will redeem it all. Our aim is not to rid ourselves of suffering or suppress it, but to offer it. God took the Roman instrument of death and turned it into life and salvation. The pain we offer will be transformed into good.

Jesus, whom we follow, will not lead us down a path of avoidance. There will be suffering along the way, and we won't always understand it. But we don't need to understand it, because we won't be alone. Like Peter, we often get stuck on the suffering, but Jesus teaches us that suffering is temporary. "He must go to Jerusalem, undergo great suffering, be killed, and on the third day be raised."

Jesus is leading us on the pathway of love. And though we must endure suffering along the way, it always leads to life.

# WE SHOULD KNOW BETTER

DR. GREG GARRETT
Proper 18 – September 10, 2023

*Exodus 12:1-14*
*Psalm 119-33-40*
*Romans 12:9-21*
*Matthew 18:15-20*

Holy Spirit, speak to us. And may we have ears to hear.

Good morning. Welcome to St. Margaret's, Little Rock! My name is Greg Garrett, and I bring you greetings from Baylor University, where I serve as the Carole McDaniel Hanks Chair of Literature and Culture, and from your brothers and sisters in Christ at the American Cathedral of the Holy Trinity in Paris, where I am Canon Theologian. I'm here to talk with you this morning about this moment in which we find ourselves, a moment when a concern for the oppressed and marginalized is maligned as "woke," a moment when politicians in your state and in mine seem to be trying to erase the past, even though James Baldwin tells us that we are formed by our history, we literally are our history, and to deny it or run from it leaves us all in chains.

Since the last time I stood in this space over ten years ago, I have been a place or two. I've preached about race and justice and what it means to love our neighbors in the Heart of the British Empire and in the Heart of the Confederacy, have taught and listened to and prayed with clergy about reconciliation from Long Island to Louisiana to Washington State. And I have had conversations about equity and justice with all sorts of people, people harmed daily by racism, and people who do not want to think about it. One morning in Lower Manhattan, I sat down with a white Christian who loves the Lord, but who challenged me about white Christians who believe we are called to engage the issues of racism and injustice.

"Don't get me wrong," my friend said. "I love where your heart is. But what makes you think that this can ever change, given how people act, how sinful people are?"

James Baldwin, in my favorite of his books, *No Name in the Street*, feared that "it is not even remotely possible for the excluded to become the included, for this inclusion means, precisely, the end of the status quo."

Given that, it does seem impossible.

Perhaps someone has said something similar to you about any work of repair to which you may feel called. "Bless your heart," is what the beautiful old women in the church used to say to me in my childhood about something charming and probably impossible. "Bless your little heart."

But Anne Lamott tells a story about where she used to be and where she is now. "I was over there," she says, "and now I'm over here." And here's the thing, Annie notes: there is no possible way to get from there to here.

No human way, maybe.

And yet, Jesus tells us all, what is impossible for human beings is all in a day's work for God.

What our scriptures tell us today is that our call is not to pursue power and privilege, but to love each other and to hold each other accountable. Our gospel lesson is drawn from Matthew 18, a section of that gospel that scholars call Jesus' *Discourse on Life in the Faithful Community*. How are we supposed to live together, given how hard that is? I can hear my friend's voice, "Given how people act, how sinful are people?" What does it mean to be a faithful follower of the Way of Love?

The folks who assemble our lectionary have some suggestions. In today's reading from the Letter to the Romans, Paul tells us what we are supposed to be about. Rather than scrupulously following moral laws, Paul joins Jesus in saying that all of our behavior boils down to this: "Love your neighbor." Of course that means more than just loving the person next to you in the pew, although Beloved, it does mean that. But it also means those Children of God who don't look like us, or love like us, or worship like us, or vote like us.

And also—and with an appropriate sense of occasion, given the national moment of which I spoke earlier—Paul advises Christians that it is time to wake up.

What might that mean?

I believe God can and will redeem this mess, that God's irresistible grace flows out across the world like a mighty river.

But we also know that God acts in human history through the lives and persons of human beings. God asks that we participate in the work. That we wake up to human suffering. That we show up to alleviate it. That we bend our will to God's will.

That wherever God is, we will seek to be.

I come to you this morning as a professor from a Southern university founded by slaveowners whose first campus was built by enslaved people. A university chartered by a nation—the nation of Texas—that fought a war with Mexico to preserve the right to enslave people. A university that sits less than a mile from where, 107 years ago, over ten thousand good white Christian people watched and cheered as a young Black man named Jesse Washington was maimed and murdered.

It might feel impossible that somebody from Baylor University in Waco, Texas could be standing here this morning preaching the good news that we are called to be God's agents of reconciliation.

People sometimes tell me so.

And I stand here—in Little Rock—in a pulpit that is just a few minutes of drivetime away from Central High School, where 66 years ago, 1,000 good white Christians rallied and screamed to keep nine brave students from an equal education.

So maybe the presence of all of us here this morning is some kind of miracle. But it is no coincidence. Because God is here.

One last story.

Last fall, I was invited to come and speak to the clergy of the Episcopal Diocese of Mississippi about race.

221

I have spoken throughout the old Confederacy. But this was Mississippi, people. Where the Jackson headquarters of the Mississippi Episcopal Church sits literally across the street from the governor's mansion. Jefferson Davis, past president of the Confederate States of America, was a member of the vestry at the church of the seminary classmate who picked me up at the Jackson airport. The clergy conference was based at St. Paul's, Meridian, where in June of 1964, civil rights workers James Chaney, Andrew Goodman, and Michael Schwerner gave one last talk about voting rights just before they were murdered by the Ku Klux Klan.

I had been warned before I came not to get my hopes up. That although I had been talking to faithful Mississippi clergy seeking to do the hard healing work, maybe it wasn't yet time.

It is so hard to get from there to here.

But the clergy of Mississippi spent three days talking, thinking, and praying about race and justice.

We worshiped together. We sang. We ate some barbeque.

I heard both hope about the work of racial repair and fear about how this might play in the pews with white Mississippi Episcopalians.

Then, on my last day in Meridian, Mississippi, I sat in the nave of St. Paul's praying before our closing communion. I asked God to give us the courage to discover where God was so we could join in what God is doing.

And then the Bishop of Mississippi, Brian Seage, stood up to preach. He began by reflecting on a recent visit to the Civil Rights Museum in Jackson.

The bishop noticed many pictures of the heroes of the movement on the walls of that museum. He even saw some pictures of people wearing clerical collars.

But not one of them, he said, was a Mississippi Episcopalian.

I could hear the sorrow and regret in his voice.

We sat with that terrible failure for a moment. Maybe you can imagine it now. The silent church. The sting of regret.

And then Bishop Seage said this: "It is time, and past time, for the church in Mississippi to tell the truth about race."

I looked around the sanctuary, a little stunned.

I noticed that some of those seated there were in tears.

I discovered that I was one of them.

"We're going to lose members because of this," the bishop of Mississippi told his clergy, who have to submit attendance and pledging reports. "And that's okay."

God is here, he told us, and so here is where the Church needs to be.

I didn't see this coming. Maybe you didn't either. But over and over in this work of justice, when human beings show up and faithfully enter into it, when we are, as our own Dr. Catherine Meeks says, "just a half-shade braver," a way opens up where there seemed to be no way.

Something becomes possible, through the amazing grace of the living God.

Our prison doors clang open, our chains drop away, and our eyes open to a new reality, a new hope.

May it be so. Let us pray:

Jesus, our brother and companion on the way, you became truly human to embody God's peace, justice, and love to the entire human community, not just to a chosen few. Empower us to be your hands and feet and voice in this world that still desperately needs healing and reconciliation, that we might more perfectly love and serve you in the name of the one Holy and Ever living God. Amen.

# FORGIVENESS: STOP COUNTING

THE REV. MARY VANO
Proper 19 – September 17, 2023

*Exodus 14:19-31*
*Psalm 114*
*Romans 14:1-12*
*Matthew 18:21-35*

The last time I went on sabbatical was the summer of 2017. At the end of that time away, I did some counting. I visited 8 art museums in 11 cities, read 13 books, and spent 53 days resting at home. I walked over 100 miles—just in Europe. Over fourteen weeks, I traveled 13,000 miles.

Math was never my favorite subject, yet I often find myself counting. I count how many people are here every Sunday and in our Sunday school classes. I'm interested in how many children we serve in the backpack program—this year it's 40. Susy Rogers tracks how much food we give away through the Little Free Food Pantry—on average, 140 servings a week. Counting helps me see trends, measure what we're doing, and pay attention to what's happening, even when the number isn't significant.

So, when I can tell you how many people are in this room and how many days until my next sabbatical, I can relate to Peter in today's Gospel. In the passage, he's also been keeping count—not of days or people, but of sins. The conversation in the Gospel of Matthew today picks up right after Jesus' teaching on how to handle sin and discord within the community. He tells the disciples that if someone sins, they should go to them privately. If that doesn't work, they should go back with a friend. If they still don't listen, they should try again. Peter, starting to get the idea, asks, "How many times should I forgive?"

A good question. According to Jewish tradition, three times was considered appropriate. Three chances at forgiveness: "She lied. I'll forgive that. She didn't do what I asked. I'll forgive that. She said something hurtful. I'll forgive that. She didn't show up when I needed her? Nope! We're done!" But Peter, in his generosity, suggests seven times—not just three, but seven. Twice the usual mercy! He's going in the right direction, at least.

But Jesus answers in a way that changes the question entirely. Depending on your translation, he either says, "not seven but seventy-seven times" or "not seven but seven times seventy," which is 490. Some people hearing this were so startled they couldn't agree on what Jesus said. Did he really mean 490? That's a lot to keep track of! So let's just call it seventy-seven times, but even then, it's too much to count. And that's the point—Jesus is telling Peter, "Stop counting. This math is too hard for you."

To make his point clearer, Jesus shares a parable. He tells the story of a slave who owes his king 10,000 talents. To understand this correctly, we need to translate: one talent is about 15 years' worth of salary for an average Israelite in the first century. So the slave owes 10,000 talents. It's unimaginable and utterly impossible. The slave begs for forgiveness, and the king, ignoring the tally sheet, forgives him the entire debt—a debt equivalent to 150,000 years of wages.

What does the slave do with this grace? He goes out and refuses to show mercy to another slave who owes him 100 denarii. A denarius is a day's wage. While a meaningful sum, it's nothing compared to the 10,000 talents he's just been forgiven. The first slave fails to pass on the grace he's received. Jesus tells us that the king revokes his mercy for the unforgiving slave.

The character in this parable couldn't see that each tally mark he made to keep track of debts and sins was just building the bars of his own prison. Jesus is asking us to see how we do the same. We tally up every sin and offense as if those marks could ever fully capture the reality of a person's worth. We keep counting, and we push people out of our lives, making our worlds smaller and our hearts weaker. We fail to forgive, and we lock ourselves into the pain of the past, blind to our own need for mercy.

Now, I don't want to oversimplify. Forgiveness is hard, and relationships are even harder. Our ultimate aim is not just forgiveness, but reconciliation—to restore right relationships with those we share this world with. Reconciliation requires more than one person's actions; it requires mutual commitment, a shared desire for justice, and a willingness from everyone to do their part. We can't control others, but we are responsible for our own actions.

This is where it's simple—not easy, but simple. Jesus gives us the key to the prison we've made for ourselves, and that key is forgiveness. It is always our choice, always within our power to let go of the past, stop keeping tally marks, and instead approach each relationship from one moment of mercy to the next.

This past Thursday, September 14, was Holy Cross Day, a reminder that the foot of the cross is where we need to gather—week after week—to leave all those tally marks behind. The cross is our path to peace. It is the only way out of the cycles of violence, to the freedom that lies outside our prison walls. It's the cross upon which our Savior, Jesus Christ, who had been betrayed by his friends, rejected by his community, tried by authorities, beaten by onlookers, and crucified for all to see, looked out upon the world and prayed, "Father, forgive them."

# FAIRNESS IN THE PARABLE
# OF THE LABORERS

THE REV. MICHAELENE MILLER
Proper 20 – September 24, 2023

*Exodus 16:2-15*
*Psalm 105:1-6, 37-45*
*Philippians 1:21-30*
*Matthew 20:1-16*

Revealing God in the places where we encounter the world—this is the work we are all called to as members of the Body of Christ. Our collect today helps us admit the difficulty of this work and the need to ask God for strength and guidance.

We pray that God helps us not to be anxious about earthly things—not to be tied to the world or define our lives by the values and power structures of society, but to love things heavenly, to be free in the knowledge of God's abundant grace, so we can frame our perspective in the ways of God. The world is indeed passing away and can often feel scarce, but God's real and active presence in our midst is everlasting and abundant.

Our collect today helps us prepare for the gospel word we share this morning. It helps us understand that as Christians in this world, we live in the midst of two frames or perspectives, which the gospel message high-lights—the perspective of society and the perspective of God. It's true, we are a people nested in and caught by our context in the earthly world. And God does not call us to abandon this context, but we are called to know and reveal the ways of God within it. As members of the Body of Christ, this is our unique purpose in the world.

And it is hard work. First, we confront and admit the areas in our own lives where we have placed society's ways above the ways of God, seeking repentance and forgiveness. Then, turning to confront the ways of society, we are to point out and dismantle the ways of power and oppression that allow individuals to set expectations and make claims of superiority and privilege over others.

In this, we make our witness and proclamation about the ways of God—the abundant economy of God's grace. This is the word of God that we hear today. This is the Kingdom work that we are called to today. And this Kingdom work is hard work.

Living out God's ways on earth has always been difficult. How do we know? Because our readings today are full of complaining and grumbling! In Exodus, we hear the story of God's people discovering and living out God's ways in their corner of the world. They are trying to embody God's alternative way—an alternative way to the power structures of slavery and oppression that they left behind in Egypt.

It is hard work to confront and leave behind familiar patterns and structures, even those that are unjust and cruel, and choose, instead, to live out the liberating and life-giving ways of God, where God provides enough for all. This becoming comes with growing pains ... and, obviously, some complaining.

Embodying this alternative is also slow work. By the time Jesus arrived on the scene, there was still more work to be done. In his life, Jesus often called his community to this work with parables—stories about the Kingdom of God that radicalize societal expectations. These parables often demonstrated a leveling of societal structures—where the mighty are brought down, and the lowly are brought up; where the last will be first, and the first will be last. Today, in the Gospel from Matthew, we hear one such story—the parable of the laborers. In it, we find another clue about God's alternative way.

In the parable of the laborers, we hear the story of a landowner who hires workers for his vineyard at different times throughout the day. He hires workers in the first hour who work all day with an agreed contract to be paid the usual daily wage. Throughout the day, the landowner hires four more rounds of workers, all having agreed to receive whatever is right. At the end of the day, the manager hands out the wages, first to the last-hour hires and then to the full-day workers.

Here comes the hinge that holds our two frames—the way of society and the way of God—in tension! Every worker receives the usual daily wage! When the last-hour workers are paid the same wage as those who worked all day, the first workers, who had labored from the beginning, expected more for themselves. Maybe we did, too! With their equal payment came grumbling. Maybe we would like to grumble here, too!

At first, our reaction to this payment might be, "Hey, that's unfair!" This payment does not fit our understanding of fairness in the economy, as it is constructed by society. With work output should come equal reward input! The parable doesn't follow our expected ending—and it is at this upset of expectations that our clue resides.

Let's first look at the exact words of the grumbling workers. They say, "These last worked only one hour, and you have made them equal to us." It's important to note here that they aren't complaining about receiving an unjust pay. As the landowner points out, their agreed contract was honored, a just payment was given, but they are upset about being made equal in status and treatment to those hired last.

Their grumbling is a statement of belief about the last-hour workers' worth and value as human beings. This action of surprising generosity and grace challenges what they think they are entitled to because of their long hours of labor. They believed they could claim superiority over the others simply because they worked longer. But the landowner's payment, given in grace, denies that claim to privilege and superiority.

Now let's pause and think about who these workers may represent. The first-hour workers could be those who fit easily into the status quo of society—those with power, privilege, and societal acceptance. And those hired last? Surely, they weren't lazy—they were just overlooked, deemed unworthy by society's standards. They could have been disabled, sick, elderly, or simply those who didn't speak the "right" language, have the "right" nationality, or fit into the "right" culture. They were the rejected, forced to the edges of society until the landowner found them and offered them the same opportunity.

The first-hour workers grumbled against being made equal to these marginalized people. They expected to claim superiority over those deemed unworthy, but the landowner's grace shattered that expectation. The landowner's model is one of abundance—not scarcity. It is not that some must have less so others can have more, but that all receive enough to thrive.

This is the alternative economy of God's grace—a grace that is enough for all. God's economy is not about excess or lavishness, but about sufficiency—everyone has enough. And isn't that, in itself, the most fair?

This parable challenges us to reframe our expectations and understanding of fairness. It asks us to divest from the economy of scarcity upheld by societal power structures and embrace the economy of grace promised by God. This is the work of God's Kingdom that we are called to participate in as Christians.

This work is not easy. As history shows, we will grumble and complain as we divest from the status quo. But let us remember, as we work to embody the alternative ways of God, that this work is a gift from God. It may be hard, but it is the work we are called to. The ways of society and the ways of God are not always clear in daily life, but in moments like this, let us refocus and hold fast to God's abundant grace.

Let us pray:

*God of grace and abundance, grant us not to be anxious about earthly things, but to love things heavenly. And even now, while we are placed among things that are passing away, help us to hold fast to those things that shall endure. Amen.*

# THE SAME MIND AS CHRIST JESUS

The Rev. Michaelene Miller
Proper 21 – October 1, 2023

*Exodus 17:1-7*
*Psalm 78:1-4, 12-16*
*Philippians 2:1-13*
*Matthew 21:23-32*

What does it mean to live with the same mind that was in Christ Jesus? This question confronts us today in the Epistle, where Paul prays that the same mind, the same spirit of love and humility, that was in Christ live among the Philippians.

This prayer echoes within us today as it causes us to wonder, does our life together reflect the same mind that was in Christ? What would it even look like if it did? In the Epistle, Paul goes on to illustrate Christ's mind of love and humility as he quotes the Christ hymn, what would have been common words for that community as it encompassed their theology and understanding of the gospel story:

> *Let the same mind be in you that was in Christ Jesus, who, though he was in the form of God, did not regard equality with God as something to be exploited, but emptied himself, taking the form of a slave, being born in human likeness. And being found in human form, he humbled himself and became obedient to the point of death—even death on a cross.*

This mind of Christ is an understanding and practice of humility, life-giving love, and liberating service to others. This mind led Jesus, though he was in the form of God, to empty himself of power to take on a posture of servanthood that gave life to others. This mind led Jesus to embrace a spirit of humility and a practice of nonviolence that allowed him to live into the uncomfortable places of service—healing, feeding, and liberating others with compassion.

What does it mean and look like for us to live with this same mind that was in Christ Jesus? As I meditated upon this question, I was transported in my thoughts to a tall, narrow, redbrick townhouse in St. Louis at a time when seven young housemates learned how to sacrifice a bit of their individual identity and personal comfort for the good of the larger community.

Ten years ago, I spent a year living in an intentional Christian community in St. Louis, Missouri with the Episcopal Service Corps. I lived in a house with six other young adults in their early twenties. Fresh out of college, we were all so eager to start this year of communal living and community service. After all, the built-in community of the program provided a soft landing place, and serving others sure sounded like the right thing to do.

Within the first week of the program, we were charged with the task to write a shared Rule of Life to serve as a guide for our community values and practices. Our program director sat us down in front of a large poster board divided into three columns labeled: Stability, Conversion, and Obedience. We sat in silence for a brief moment, staring blankly at him. Our director went on to clarify that these three words, Stability, Conversion, and Obedience, were the monastic vows of Benedictine Spirituality that upheld the Rule of St. Benedict, which was the first model for a communal Rule of Life.

To explain these vows, Stability refers to a commitment to wherever and with whomever we find ourselves in each moment. This involves trusting that God brought us there to be together. It is trusting that if we notice someone or something, God is inviting us to enter into relationship or get involved.

In this way, Stability leads into the practice of Obedience, which isn't blind obedience for obedience's sake. Instead, Benedictine Obedience can be understood as a deep listening and looking; a noticing of the other's needs and taking it seriously enough to respond in the unique ways that we are able, trusting that our offering is enough in that moment.

These together—Stability and Obedience—ultimately lead to the third value, Conversion of Life, which is a transformation away from the ego's way of comfort and isolation towards God's way of love and liberation. This vow holds that the faith conversion is a continual experience because we live always in the presence of God, who lovingly and unceasingly tries to open our hearts and minds.

These vows of Stability, Obedience, and Conversion of Life invited us to practice mindfulness, social responsibility, and continual openness to God's call upon our lives—vows that echo Paul's prayer that we take on the mind of Christ.

As these seven new housemates sat for hours exploring how these vows would manifest in our emerging community, I remember sensing the dawning of reality. Suddenly, committing to a year of service and communal life in St. Louis, a year of intentionally striving to take on the mind of Christ daily, felt like a weighty undertaking. I mean, I had a whole new city to explore, adventures to go on ... and only one year to do it! I felt a great tension arising between living into these vows of Stability, Conversion, and Obedience and my own desire for comfort and control.

In that moment, I saw two paths emerging before me that mirrored the brothers from our Gospel passage this morning. On one path, like the first brother, I wondered if I could tell my housemates that this all felt like it was asking too much. I wondered if I should just say "No" and plan to walk away. Or, like the second brother, I remember thinking to myself, how easy it would be to tell my housemates and God, "yes, sure, I'll do all this," even as I slowly pulled away from and abandoned the community and the vows of our life together. It would be easy to only give lip service to these vows and program expectations; living them out would take a lot more, like a change of heart and mind and a release of personal privilege and comfort.

Today's Gospel passage echoes back through these thoughts to convict me and all of us in our quest to take on the mind of Christ because we live in between the realities of these two brothers' words and actions. Both of these brothers exist within each of us at every moment as we are constantly presented with opportunities to reveal and build the Kingdom of God in both great and small ways in our corner of the world.

So often, instead of embracing the challenge that comes with the daily commitment to follow Christ, to love our neighbor, and struggle for justice, we all too often choose personal comfort, control, and power. Like the second brother, we may offer up hollow words about what we believe is the right thing to do but end up not living it out or acting upon our beliefs. On the other hand, like the first brother, we can also be honest about how difficult and seemingly impossible this Kingdom work is, and yet, not look away from the need that remains and allow God to change our hearts and minds as we learn how to eventually respond with God's help.

It is part of our baptismal vows to serve others and meet needs with dignity. And while many of us have publicly made these promises, I'm sure there are many ways in which we have not yet changed our lifestyles to live into these vows. I hold this up not as a way of shaming each other, but rather in recognizing that living out our vows to God requires daily commitment and a community of loving and gentle accountability holders to help us live beyond mere lip service.

During my year in the Episcopal Service Corps, house meetings every Friday morning renewed and refocused my fickle efforts to abide in community and live a life of service. This weekly and intentional effort to re-center our lives and minds around our commitments to live out our Christian identity on a daily basis was a necessary obligation as we strove to cultivate amongst ourselves the mind that was in Christ, our ultimate example of humility and loving service.

Nowadays, as I live into community with all of you at St. Margaret's, I will point to how we all go through this same process of weekly review and renewal every Sunday during the Eucharist. It is in the breaking of the bread that we too are crumbled and broken open each week, so that we may confess our sins. It is in the eating of the bread that we are nourished and able to turn back to God with renewed energy to try again and do better.

As we return to God, we re-member and become the Body of Christ in the world. It is in our release and self-emptying of privilege, personal comfort, and power that we will begin to embrace the same mind that was in Christ, so that we may develop ourselves as better vessels of God's greater love. It takes intentional effort to empty ourselves out for the common good and to live into the uncomfortableness of service so that our hearts and minds may finally be opened as Christ's. Through all this, we must also trust Paul's final words in our Epistle that it is God who is at work in us, enabling us to will and to work for God's good pleasure.

# GOOD, CARING TENANTS

THE REV. MICHAELENE MILLER
Proper 22 – October 8, 2023

*Exodus 20:1-4, 7-9, 12-20*
*Psalm 19*
*Philippians 3:4b-14*
*Matthew 21:33-46*

It has been an interesting few weeks at St. Margaret's! Now, many people might call the word "interesting" a nonword—and I can agree that it reveals very little—but I choose it on purpose. My experience has been as broad as the word can possibly imply. There have been extraordinary highs and frightening lows, and a mix of curious and mundane moments throughout.

Mostly, though, while our beloved and incredible Rector, Mary Vano, has been on sabbatical, there have been many learning moments for me. I have seen ever more clearly the intentional work that goes on behind the scenes to connect people in this community—and beyond—with the love and care of Christ. I continue to be grateful to be a part of this particular outpost of God's Good News.

One of the most exciting new aspects of my role has been my new job title: Preschool Chaplain. It has been a lot of fun! The minds and opinions of preschoolers are definitely ... interesting!

On Tuesdays and Wednesdays, I journey downstairs to our Early Childhood Center and join each age group for a short lesson or chapel time. With the youngest infants, I join them in play on the floor, read a story, pointing out animals and colors, and wonder with them about God. With the 2-year-olds, I lead a story time during their snack. And for the 3- and 4-year-olds, I invite them to the Catechesis of the Good Shepherd Atrium for a chapel service.

During chapel, we light a candle to remind us of God's light and love surrounding us. We strike a singing bowl before the lesson and before we pray, helping us listen quietly and pay attention. We read from a storybook or the Bible and wonder where they see themselves in the story, what part they think is most important, and what it teaches us about God. We close with prayers before taking turns to snuff out the candle.

Through these new, holy rhythms, we are building the foundation of our faith journey together. I've wondered a lot about how to build a good faith foundation, how to introduce these little ones to Christ—the rejected life-giving and liberating cornerstone of our Christian faith. There's a lot to learn about God, and much that we can never fully imagine. These little ones are curious sponges and quick learners. I take this foundation-building work very seriously, wanting to offer them care and intention as they encounter God's expansive creativity and unconditional love.

For our lesson last week, we explored the Creation story. I read from a children's Bible, but there was a line I couldn't read aloud. The story said, "God created the world for us." I couldn't read that. It didn't align with what I understand and believe about God. So I changed it. I said, "God created all the world and us humans to care for it." Then I asked, "What a big job, huh? To care for all the big, huge animals that God created? And all the teeny-tiny animals? And all the plants and water places all over the world? We're going to have to work together, huh?"

It is a big job, and one that we humans often get wrong—just as if we were raised with that simplified version, that the world was created for us. Likely, many of us were raised with this understanding, but it's too easy to perpetuate this false story that the world was made for us.

In my adult Sunday School class, we've been exploring biblical Creation stories and studying Doug Tallamy's *Nature's Best Hope*. We learned that in the first Creation story, we are reoriented to the truth that God didn't create the world for humans, but created us to play a specific role within Creation.

The dominion God gave us wasn't about control; it was about care and protection, to keep the good balance of Creation in right relationship with God. This responsibility is made clearer in the second Creation story, where God places humans in the Garden of Eden to till and keep it. Our original purpose is to serve and preserve God's Creation.

Too often, we who are stewards and tenants of the land act like owners. We live upon it, extract from it, and destroy it without any accountability. We live like the wicked tenants in today's gospel, who, when the landowner sends messengers and his son to collect the fruits of the harvest, respond with violence and abuse of their entrusted authority.

Debbie Thomas, a theologian and biblical commentator, reflects on this passage and clarifies the analogy:

*"Have we not, like the tenants in the parable, deluded ourselves into thinking that we 'own' the earth and all that is in it, when in fact, we are meant to be stewards only? Have we not, like the tenants, assumed that God is absent, or apathetic, or uninvolved—and hoarded the beauty and bounty of creation for our own selfish ease, gain, comfort, and convenience? Have we not, like the tenants, ignored and even maligned the countless messengers who have warned us over the past many years that our rapacious relationship with the planet will lead us to destruction?"*

We forget, ignore, and even reject our created role as stewards of God's vineyard—this creation, and all our human and more-than-human neighbors who live within it. In doing so, we also reject and turn away from our relationship with God.

Is there a way to turn back? Can we reorient our lives away from the false sense of ownership and return to our vocation as good tenants and stewards of God's vineyard? Can we cultivate a life-giving harvest for the world that we can return to God with thanksgiving?

Our reading from Exodus calls to us here. As God offered a life-giving way to live to his people in the wilderness, God continues to extend a way of loving guidelines to us today as we stagger through our own wilderness of creation's destruction.

God's Ten Commandments guide us to live lives of balanced relationship that produce the good fruits of justice, grace, and dignity. They call us to value two relationships: vertically, as we love God, and horizontally, as we love our neighbor and all of Creation. The hinge that binds these two is the commandment to respect the Sabbath rest.

Sabbath is the hinge that allows us to live the Way of God. It enables us to care and give of ourselves, and it allows the earth to rest, grow, and produce abundant fruit. In the beginning, after God created and named all of creation as good, God rested and delighted.

Through Sabbath, God asks us to rest so we can delight in our vocation as stewards, and to preserve the land so it can rest and delight. Sabbath leads us and all of Creation to produce the good fruit of God's life-sustaining love.

So, wonder today—how can we become God's good tenants, taking rest seriously so we can delight as we live to love God and all of Creation as ourselves? Can we reorient our perspective, remembering that the world was not made for us, but that we were made to care for Creation? Can we rebuild our foundation upon the true cornerstone of Christ, producing good fruit? Can we live in peace with the reality that all we are and all we have is a gift from God?

May it be so.

# PUTTING ON CHRIST'S WAY OF LOVE

The Rev. Michaelene Miller
Proper 23 – October 15, 2023

*Exodus 32:1-14*
*Psalm 106:1-6, 19-23*
*Philippians 4:1-9*
*Matthew 22:1-14*

"Let's just admit it: this is an ugly parable." That's how one biblical commentator described today's passage from Matthew's Gospel, and I agree. The details of Jesus' parable about the Kingdom of Heaven being like a great banquet are unique to Matthew's Gospel, and it's a parable that takes us through some harsh, unsettling moments. Without the proper context, we might find ourselves asking, "Wow, that was really harsh, Jesus."

There's a similar story in the Gospel of Luke, which ends on a note of grace when the guest list is opened wide. In Luke's version, the invitation is extended to everyone—the poor, the crippled, the blind, the lame—those who would have been marginalized. But Matthew's version contains violence and judgment. The original guests reject the invitation, even going so far as to kill the messengers sent by the king. And when a man shows up without the proper garment, the king has him thrown out into the darkness. It's a harsh parable, and it's not easy to find the good news in it at first.

When compared to Luke's version, Matthew's seems to lack grace. However, to truly understand the message, we need to look at where this parable is placed within Jesus' ministry and the audience he's speaking to. In Luke, the parable occurs earlier in Jesus' ministry, while he's still traveling, healing, and teaching the crowds. But in Matthew, we find ourselves in the city of Jerusalem during Holy Week. Jesus is teaching in the temple, addressing the religious leaders with increasing critique.

The day before, Jesus had entered Jerusalem on a donkey, in stark contrast to the Roman leader on a warhorse. He cleansed the temple of corruption, driving out the money changers and healing those in need. Our parable comes on the next day. Jesus remains, occupying the temple, debating and responding to the temple authorities who demanded to know by what authority he was doing all these things. This parable is the third and final story in a series where Jesus is responding to this one question as he directly addresses and critiques them—the religious leaders in his midst, his colleagues in ministry, and the keepers of his own Jewish tradition.

We have held and confronted each parable in the series these last few Sundays. In the first, we will remember that there were two sons who were asked by their father to tend to the vineyard—one brother responded with the proper "yes" but did not go, and the other one said "no" but ended up changing his mind and going.

In the second parable, there were tenants who were entrusted with and supposed to care for the fruits of a vineyard but instead killed the servants who came to collect the fruit and thought that they could just keep it all for themselves.

In this parable today, Jesus highlights how the original guests refuse the invitation to celebrate in community, prioritizing instead their own business and money-making ventures as better things to do.

In all of these parables, Jesus prophetically pronounces woe upon those in power. In the first parable, Jesus highlights the disconnect between the leaders' promised words and subsequent actions. In the second Jesus points out how they have forgotten their roles as tenants and caretakers of God's people. In the third, Jesus critiques how the leaders prioritize their own power and resources over community care.

This is a prophetic call for the religious leaders to reform. They had the opportunity to stand up against the oppressive Roman Empire but chose violence and their own power over the wellness of their community; over God's invitation to care for His people and build the Kingdom of abundant life where all can flourish.

The message and pronouncement of this Palestinian Jewish man echoes throughout the ages to our world today. Today, Jesus remains standing and teaching in the temple of that holy city of Jerusalem, prophetically crying out and calling to all leaders throughout time and space who have aligned themselves with the death-dealing, oppressive forces of empire in order to protect and serve their own power by hoarding resources instead of caring for the larger wellbeing of the community; by prioritizing their own business over preserving the dignity of who they promised to care for and neighbors who God entrusted them to tend as tenants of his beloved Creation. Jesus weeps. Jesus continues to cry out today.

The message isn't just for the religious leaders of Jesus' time; it extends to us today. Jesus continues to stand in the temple, crying out to all leaders throughout history who have aligned themselves with oppressive powers to protect their own wealth and influence. This message calls out to all of us who hoard resources instead of sharing and who choose business and power over caring for others.

But Jesus offers another way: a way of love, peace, and dignity. The invitation to this way isn't just about showing up to the banquet—it's about transformation. The guest who shows up improperly dressed is cast out because, in Matthew's Gospel, it's not enough to accept the invitation; we must also transform ourselves to align with the values of the Kingdom of God.

The "proper garment" symbolizes the transformation required to fully embrace Christ's way of love and nonviolence. We must put on the garment of Christ's love, not just as an outward sign but as a daily practice that reshapes our lives. The transformation isn't only spiritual; it impacts how we interact with the world and care for one another.

So, what does this transformation look like in our daily lives? Lauren Grubaugh Thomas, an Episcopal priest and tender of soulful revolutions rooted in Jesus' way of nonviolence, points out the importance of turning to spiritual practices in our aim to embody Jesus' ethic of love. She explains,

> Spiritual practices can help make space in our imaginations for a love that transgresses the boundaries our brains tend to create between whom we like and is like us, and whom we dislike and is unlike us. ... Amidst the relentless, violent assaults of the world, spiritual practice is a means of coming home to ourselves. Here,

we gather the strength, the perspective and the courage to stay human.

Spiritual practices help us respond, not react, to the chaos of the world. They give us the strength and courage to prioritize healing alongside strategic disruption of oppressive systems. We become more capable of holding paradox, more skilled at living with the seemingly unbearable tensions of the human condition, while distilling what work of justice is ours to do today and with whom we will do it.[27]

Spiritual practices are what empower us and help us to accept Jesus' invitation to change our hearts and minds, turning from society's ways of isolation and violence to Jesus' way of love and nonviolence. Spiritual practices help us review, reflect upon, and reform our lives. Spiritual practices help us take on a new identity in Christ as we put on Christ's way of love and community care, so we are able to fully love God and God's Creation—our human and more than human neighbors as ourselves.

One such spiritual practice is the daily examen, where one looks back at the day's end to examine where God felt close or far away, to notice where God is calling us to live most alive or what might need more care. Let us close by sharing this practice—reflecting on some questions from John O'Donohue's take on the daily examine, called "At the End of the Day - A Mirror of Questions" Through this practice and others, may we repeatedly accept the invitation to the banquet while clothing ourselves in our best robes of love.

Let us take a moment to reflect on our daily lives, using a spiritual practice. John O'Donohue offers a beautiful set of questions to guide us in the examen, which we will share now:

Where did my eyes linger today?

Where was I blind?

What differences did I notice in those closest to me?

Whom did I neglect?

Where did I neglect myself?

What did I do today for the poor and the excluded?

Where could I have exposed myself to the risk of something different?
Where did I allow myself to receive love?
What reached me today? How deep did it imprint?
Who saw me today?
What did I avoid today?
From the evidence—why was I given this day? [28]

These questions invite us to examine where we've lived into Christ's way of love and where we might need to do better. As we continue to respond to Jesus' invitation, may we be empowered to transform ourselves and the world around us, putting on Christ's love, nonviolence, and care for all creation.

# GLIMPSES OF IMAGE BEARERS

The Rev. Michaelene Miller
Proper 24 – October 22, 2023

*Exodus 33:12-23*
*Psalm 99*
*1 Thessalonians 1:1-10*
*Matthew 22:15-22*

There are many things about Jesus that I admire and seek to emulate in my own life. As a human, Jesus was deeply caring, generous with grace, and had an unflappable moral compass set on justice. In all of this, Jesus was fully aligned with—and thus revealed—God's renewable energy of love. It was this never-ending reserve of love that powered Jesus' mission and movement in the world.

In today's gospel lesson, we get a glimpse of Jesus' unflappable moral compass. Even when faced with great tension and challenge, He remained clear-headed. And let's be honest, that kind of clarity is something I wish I had in moments like this—when I can only replay a conversation over and over in my head and think, "Ah! *That's* what I should've said."

This level of cleverness and clarity is something I wish I could access in moments of conflict. It's something I work on with my therapist when I find myself thinking, "How can I see things more clearly and name what's going on here?" Jesus, however, is always clear. He sees the world with complete clarity, and in this moment, He demonstrates this wisdom and cleverness in His response to a tricky challenge.

You may have noticed, if you've been following along with the Gospel these past weeks, that this conversation with the Pharisees and Herodians is particularly intense. We are standing with Jesus in the temple in Jerusalem during what we call Holy Week. The shadow of the cross is looming. Jesus has already made a statement by entering the city on a donkey in contrast to the Roman ruler entering on a warhorse. He cleansed the temple, overturning the money changers' tables, and has been in intense debate with the temple leaders. It's no wonder they now try to trap Him with this question: *"Is it lawful to pay taxes to the emperor or not?"*

This question is loaded with danger. The Pharisees and Herodians are two groups who, on the surface, seem to be at odds with each other. The Pharisees oppose the Roman Empire and its oppressive taxes. The Herodians, on the other hand, support the Empire to further their own interests. It's a tricky question that could ensnare Jesus no matter how He answers.

But Jesus doesn't fall into the trap. Instead, He asks them for a coin. *"Show me the coin used for the tax."*

And, by this, Jesus lays out a roadmap for us to follow. We see him lay this same roadmap over in the gospel of John as well. There, in another tense scene in the temple, the scribes and the Pharisees brought forth a woman who had been caught in adultery; and, pointing out how the law Moses commanded [them] to stone such women, they again put Jesus to the test asking what he would have them do.

And likewise, Jesus sees the trap clearly and he pauses. He slows down the conversation. He takes a moment to sit in the test and, here, actually bends down to draw in the dirt before flipping the tables; saying, Let anyone among you who is without sin be the first to throw a stone at her.

This clever practice of slowing down is a way that would help any of us remain present in difficult situations and calm in challenging times. It is a practice of responding rather than reacting. It is a practice of the wise and self-possessed. It is a practice that goes well beyond what many of us are able to do in a situation like this. Here, Jesus is not seeking to merely win the argument. He is seeking to reveal the truth, simply and profoundly.

By asking for a coin used for the empire's tax, Jesus reveals how his pockets are empty while exposing the truth about his questioners, who produce the coin upon demand. Jesus begins to reveal how they are more enmeshed, and likely complicit, in the oppressive economics of the empire. All those watching this scene unfold, begin to see more clearly what Jesus has seen from the start.

And, slowing the conversation down again with another question, he pushes the clarity even further. Whose head is this, and whose title, he asks about the coin. With this he points to how it is his questioners, not himself, who possess a coin bearing the idolatrous image of Caesar and his blasphemous title stamped upon the coin naming him the son of god.

And then, finally, after this clarification, Jesus answers their original question—Is it lawful to pay taxes to the emperor, or not? In the midst of the unfolding truth, he gives an answer that is between the lines, between the traps that the Pharisees and Herodians have set for him. Give therefore to the emperor the things that are the emperor's, and to God the things that are God's.

By this, once again, Jesus reveals truth that reaches well beyond merely winning the argument. By this statement, Jesus places the situation and the wider world into perspective. By this, he brings down the mighty and lifts up the lowly.

Sure, Jesus says, give unto Ceasar what bears his image. This coin, this small piece of metal that holds the power that we, as in the larger society, assign to it. This little piece of metal is what Caesar has created. The mighty is brought low.

But to God, give what bears God's image. Give unto God what God has created. And with this, the world is put back into perspective. With this, truth is revealed. With this, the preciousness of life and the land and the dignity of all those oppressed under or cast out by society are brought up—as precious bearers of God's creative spark.

These words—those spoken by Jesus here and those implied between the lines—call us all back to the beginning. And God said, let us make humankind in our image, according to our likeness. Upon each of us is stamped the image of God—the Imago Dei. So, to give unto God what is God's? Here is our truth: to God we give our whole being—our heart, soul, mind, and strength; our whole precious life as we also turn to notice the preciousness of the image bearers beside us and all the fingerprints of God upon Creation.

At Camp Mitchell, the 6th Rule of Life states that, when we honor the fingerprint of God upon Creation, we become more Christlike. When we honor ourselves and our neighbors as image bearers of the Divine, and when we recognize God's reflection in all of Creation, we become more Christlike. As we become more Christlike, we become more able to respond vs. react, we are able to slow down, we are able to seek and reveal truth. We too begin to emulate Jesus and become deeply caring, generous with grace, and set our moral compasses on justice. Stepping into this truth, we also receive and reveal God's renewable energy of love as we continue Jesus' mission and movement in the world. May it be so.

# LUNCH TIME AT JUNIOR HIGH

THE REV. ROB LEACOCK
Proper 25 – October 29, 2023

*Deuteronomy 34:1-12*
*Psalm 1*
*I Thessalonians 2:1-8*
*Matthew 22:34-46*

Good morning.

Thank you all for welcoming me back this morning. My name is Rob Leacock. I know many of you already. If you don't know me, I'm the chaplain at the Episcopal Collegiate School. I'm so pleased to be with you all this morning. Being a school person, my analysis of this portion of Matthew's gospel has led me to label it as the Junior High School cafeteria part of the gospel. That's my own designation as opposed to any well-reasoned scholarly title.

Stay with me; I'll explain: What we have in this section of Matthew's gospel is several episodes where groups or cliques confront this edgy new kid at school. He seems to be quite popular with some kids at school. But he also isn't abiding by the established rules and social order. So these different groups at different points confront the new kid in the cafeteria while everyone is watching and they try to zing or diss or burn him. They try to catch him being lame or suss, as the kids at my school would say; they want to destroy his credibility in order to maintain their own status. They try to trick him into saying something dumb to try and humiliate him in front of the school. First it was the Chief priests and the elders. Then the Pharisees and the Herodians. Then the Sadducees. They all try to trick or confound or shame Jesus.

So the Pharisees circle back to try Jesus once more with one of their questions. Now there are other moments in the gospels where people question Jesus. This isn't the first or only time someone questions Jesus. In lots of these places, it's genial and respectful. Sometimes the people who question Jesus end up liking his answer. But here? Here, it's lunchtime at Junior High, and the gloves are off. The Pharisees are coming in hot. It says that they send a lawyer; we might interpret that as they sent their top theologian. It says that they do this to test him. It's the same Greek word used when the Devil tempts Jesus in the wilderness. This isn't a friendly debate.

In ancient Judaism, it was common for Rabbis to debate parts of the Torah—and not necessarily to come up with a definitive answer. They would often pose difficult-to-impossible questions just to engage with their sacred laws in order to understand and appreciate the sacred covenant they shared with God. This sort of thing was a spiritual discipline, a means of deepening one's relationship with God.

The Pharisees' theologian asks Jesus, "Can you sum up the whole Torah—all 613 commandments in a single commandment?" It's an interesting thing to consider but not easy to answer. On the one hand, Jesus could say "I don't know." He could hem and haw and equivocate and stumble his way through a non-answer and end up looking foolish. And they could say "Oh, I guess you aren't a real teacher, are you?" On the other hand, he could offer an answer that seems to cherry pick a part of the Torah and effectively reject the rest. And they could say, "Oh! So, you would just toss out the rest of the Torah in favor of this one commandment?!"

Jesus doesn't shy away from the challenge. *"You shall love the Lord your God,"* he says, *"with all your heart, and with all your soul, and with all your mind. This is the greatest and first commandment. And a second is like it: 'You shall love your neighbor as yourself."* Boom. Jesus isn't telling the Pharisees anything they don't already know. The first commandment comes from a part of the book of Deuteronomy called the Shema—a well-known prayer in ancient and modern Judaism. It would have been the sort of verse that even those who were not experts in scripture would have likely known from memory. It's Jesus's way of saying, "Shouldn't you know the answer?" Then he hits them with a second commandment, which quotes a verse from Leviticus which sums up a section on how we should treat others: *"You shall love your neighbor as yourself."* Another verse the Pharisees would have been able to recite without looking it up. Then, Jesus says, *"On these two commandments hang all the law and the prophets."*

Now, Jesus isn't just winning the battle for Junior High Cafeteria superiority. He's making an essential, but complex theological point—not just to the Pharisees but to those who would take up their cross and follow him. Do we love God? Well, it's academic. We want to take it as a given. But it's more complicated. Do we love God with our whole self, with every aspect of our being? How do we demonstrate our love of God with our heart? Or with our mind? How do we love God with our soul? How do we love God continually and with all of our being? And friends, I think that's the easy one! The second one gets pretty complicated!

Is it easy to love our neighbors? How do we define "neighbor" a question Jesus famously answers in another gospel? Do we do a good job on a consistent basis with that? If our regard for our neighbors is a reflection of our love for ourselves, do we even know how to love ourselves? Do we love ourselves in the right way? Do we love ourselves as well as God loves us? Do we understand and truly know what it means to be beloved of God?

These two commandments are inextricably linked. We can't do one without the other. We can fulfill one only by fulfilling the other. Jesus himself says it: everything depends upon these two. It's simple and lovely to hear Jesus say it. But living it out? That's another matter entirely.

There's this next little bit of this gospel, which may or may not be entirely related to the first part: Jesus turns the tables a bit on his interlocutors by asking a strange, nitpicky, trick question. Honestly, part of me interprets this as Jesus is maybe over the whole Junior High battle.

Again, Jesus here is very much in the normal accepted vein of intellectual debate among Rabbis. There's nothing unusual about him posing this kind of question. He asks about whose son is the Messiah. A seemingly simple question, but actually it brings to bear a lot of complex views of that time on who and what the messiah would be and do. It's a leading question. The most likely answer is, as the Pharisees respond, "The son of David." Which was a perspective on the Messiah established in the prophets.

Prior to this whole Junior High series of confrontations, Jesus himself, on purpose, chose to evoke the image of David by riding into Jerusalem on a humble donkey while people shouted, *"Hosanna! To the son of David."* So don't let's pretend that this is an innocent question. Jesus is really asking them a question about himself, and though it doesn't explicitly say so in the text, these Pharisees probably understood that. The messiah, he is the son of David. Jesus using a bit of rhetorical and exegetical jiu jitsu quotes the opening verse of Psalm 110. This is a confusing bit. What Jesus is saying here is that if David is the author of Psalm 110, how can David say, *"The Lord said to my Lord, sit at my right hand."* The argument here is that the first Lord is the Lord, God Almighty. The second Lord is supposed to be the Messiah. So why would David refer to his son as "my Lord." Wouldn't David say, "My Lord said to my SON," if the Messiah was the son of David? It's a pretty silly argument. Jesus shutting down one silly debate with an even sillier one.

This gospel lesson is, at best, a peculiar encounter in the gospel, the kind of which may leave us with more questions than answers. It's maybe the kind of passage that leaves a preacher asking, "What am I going to do with this?" Don't worry, I'm going to press on.

The main issue with these different groups of people who confront Jesus is that they think they know what Jesus is about. They think they have his number. Clearly, they do not, but it may speak a bit to our own misunderstandings of Jesus and our own attempts to cast Jesus in an image we find palatable rather than truly follow him. These kinds of encounters between Jesus and the Pharisees point to our own attempts to reduce authentic faith to religious questions and semantic debates. Sometimes, we aren't asking the right question.

The response to all of it is the real answer: love. But we're talking—or rather, Jesus is talking about love of the highest order. Capital "L", love. The sort of Love that surpasses our understanding. The sort of Love that we neglect and forget and lose track of in so many ways. The love that underpins our entire being is the very meaning and purpose behind God's creation of us and choosing us to be God's beloved. Loving God, loving one's neighbor—it's the heart of our faith. Everything else hinges on this.

Speaking rather famously about this Love, Paul reminds us that many things we uphold as important come to an end or are incomplete. Prophecy and knowledge will come to an end, he says. We can prophecy only in part; we can know but only in part. Something else, something more, is required. All sorts of things are incomplete or come to an end but Love never ends.

Like the Pharisees and these other groups, we are often caught up in the incompleteness of truly knowing—knowing God, knowing ourselves. We do not quite understand how truly we can love God, not with all our heart, mind, and soul. We are incapable of loving our neighbor—or even ourselves—the way God calls us to love. It's not the sort of thing we can argue our way out of. It is Christ himself who is the answer, the fulfillment of our questions, our deep, unarticulated longing truly to know God. Jesus, the Christ, the long-awaited and much-debated Messiah, the Word made flesh—the very Love of God incarnate, who by his passion, cross, and resurrection is the very demonstration of the Love to which we are called. It is that love that will make up for all our incompleteness and shortcomings. It is that Love on which we can hang all our fears, all our arguments and debates, all of our hopes.

# THE PRESENT MOMENT

THE REV. MARY VANO
All Saints Sunday – November 5, 2023

*Revelation 7:9-17*
*Psalm 34:1-10, 22*
*1 John 3:1-3*
*Matthew 5:1-12*

Today, I begin again. I want to thank you all for giving me the space to take a sabbatical. It was a restful and restorative time. It was a time for me to reflect on where my journey has taken me, to slow down, to be present to myself and my family, and to listen for God's call as I move forward. That time was exactly what I needed so that today, I can begin again.

Today, you can begin again. Today, we celebrate All Saints' Day—a day when we remember the communion of saints who have gone before us. It's a day when we remember that we, too, are members of that same communion of saints, called to be instruments of God's grace in our own time and place. As saints of today, we build the bridge for those who will come after us, even as we baptize one more into this communion.

Our readings today remind us that we have both a past and a future. John's Revelation speaks of a multitude of people gathered before the throne of God, clothed in white. Who are they? They are the ones who have come through the great ordeal, who have faced hunger, thirst, suffering, and sorrow. They have a past. They also have a future—a future of beautiful diversity, singing, and praise, where their thirst is quenched with the water of life.

When Jesus preached the Sermon on the Mount, he began by saying, *"Blessed are the poor in spirit, blessed are those who mourn, blessed are the meek."* Nine times he repeats this phrase, enough for us to know that he could go on. It's enough to know that there are blessings for everyone, and each of them has a past. Like the Galileans who climbed the Mount to hear Jesus, death, need, and shame have brought us here, too. And, Jesus reminds us, we have a future ahead of us—comfort, mercy, and fulfillment.

We have a past and a future, but most importantly, we have a present. Jesus didn't say that we will be blessed; he said that we are blessed. Nine times he says "are." There is enough blessing for each of us, and for every single day. To be blessed is to be honored by God—not just when we've achieved something, but now. To be blessed is to be loved by God—not just when we prove ourselves worthy, but now. *"Beloved, we are God's children now."* (1 John 3)

This present moment matters more than any other because it's in the present blessing that we are connected to the calling that moves us onward. Our past suffering and the pain we carry today can propel us toward a future of comfort, mercy, and fulfillment, but to reach for those things, we'll have to let go of our grip on what was. We'll have to cling less tightly to what is. It's not easy, and we'll need a good guide and a supportive community, but you've already taken the most important step.

In your baptism, you gave your life and your heart to God in Christ, and you can give your past to Jesus, too. You can give your pain to Jesus. You can begin again with your hand in Christ's, who will lead you to the love and peace for which we were made. You can begin again.

Today, we can begin again, too. For those who might not know, All Saints' Sunday marks the anniversary of St. Margaret's. We held our first worship service in a movie theater on the first Sunday of November in 1991. We are 32 years old now, and as a community of saints, we find that every day is a new opportunity to move toward God's vision for us— something I've spent a lot of time reflecting on recently.

What captivated me in today's epistle reading from 1 John was the passage that reads,

> *See what love the Father has given us, that we should be called children of God; and that is what we are. The reason the world does not know us is that it did not know him. Beloved, we are God's children now; what we will be has not yet been revealed. What we do know is this: when he is revealed, we will be like him, for we will see him as he is. And all who have this hope in him purify themselves, just as he is pure.*

Equipped with God's love. Known as God's children. Though the world may not understand us, we are still on our way to becoming what we will be. The author calls us to "purify ourselves, just as Christ is pure." As I read these words, I wanted to understand more about what this meant. It could be taken to suggest that we should throw out all the sinners and keep only the perfectly righteous. But I'm not sure who among us would be left. The English Standard Version translation continues with, "*everyone who makes a practice of sinning also practices lawlessness.*" But you can't do this if you're a child of God. The next verses say, "*Whoever practices righteousness is righteous, as Christ is righteous.*" Our aim is to practice righteousness rather than sin, allowing our faithful practice to attune our hearts to what pleases God. Do we fail sometimes? Yes. Is there forgiveness? Yes! Do we keep practicing? Absolutely. "*Blessed are the pure in heart, for they will see God.*"

As we blow out the candles today on our 32nd birthday, we—St. Margaret's—can begin again. We can listen, practice, and hope. We can begin again.

Today, I begin again—so blessed already by the love of God that I know here in this community. You can begin again with me as you recommit your heart to God, moving with faith, hope, and love into the future. And, St. Margaret's, we as a church community can begin again, supporting each other in practicing our righteousness, so that together we will see God. Today is a blessed day. Let's renew our baptismal covenant and begin again.

# REFERENCES

[1] Episcopal Church. (2006). *Revised Common Lectionary Episcopal Edition (NRSV): Pew/Desktop Edition.*

[2] Amadeo, K. (2022, April 20). What does income inequality look like in the US? *The Balance.* Retrieved from https://www.thebalancemoney.com/income-inequality-in-america-3306190.

[3] Davis, E. (2019). *Opening Israel's Scriptures.* Oxford University Press.

[4] Working Preacher. (n.d.). Commentary on Lamentations 1. Retrieved from https://www.workingpreacher.org/commentaries/revised-common-lectionary/ordinary-27-3/commentary-on-lamentations-11-6-4

[5] Brochard, P., & Newton, A. (2022). *Vital Christian Community: Twelve Characteristics of Healthy Congregations.* Church Publishing.

[6] *A Heart for Justice.* (2010). A Franciscan blessing: May God bless you with discomfort, anger, tears, and foolishness. Retrieved from https://aheartforjustice.com/2010/10/07/a-franciscan-blessing-may-god-bless-you-with-discomfort-anger-tears-and-foolishness/

[7] Luke: Ancient Christian Commentary on Scripture, NT Vol 3. (2002). InterVarsity Press.

[8] King, M. L., Jr. (1963). *Letter from a Birmingham Jail.* Stanford University. Retrieved from https://kinginstitute.stanford.edu/encyclopedia/letter-birmingham-jail

[9] Hardingham-Gill, T. (2022, September 12). Canadian family taking world tour before children lose their vision. *CNN.* Retrieved from https://www.cnn.com/travel/article/canadian-family-retinitis-pigmentosa/index.html

[10] Wagoner, David (1999) *Lost.* Retrieved from https://grateful.org/resource/lost-david-wagoner/

[11] Ó Tuama, Pádraig. (2015) *In the Shelter.* Broadleaf Books, Minneapolis p. 9.

[12] Thomas, Debie (2019) *Into the Mess.* Retrieved from https://www.journeywithjesus.net/essays/2484-into-the-mess

[13] L'Engle, Madeleine, *First Coming.* Retrieved from https://theadventusproject.wordpress.com/resources/poetry/madeleine-lengle-first-coming/

14 Oliver, Mary. *The Spirit Likes to Dress Up*, Retrieved from https://kkmeow.word-press.com/2012/11/04/poem-the-spirit-likes-to-dress-up-by-mary-oliver/.

15 Stone, Rachel Marie, *Birthing Hope*. Referenced in https://www.ivpress.com/Media/Default/Press-Kits/4533-press.pdf

16 Roosevelt, Eleanor (1958) Remarks to the United Nations. Retrieved from https://ironline.american.edu/blog/our-basic-human-rights/

17 Whyte, D. (n.d.). *Half a shade braver*. Retrieved from https://www.davidwhyte.com/half-a-shade-braver

18 Matt Skinner. (2023). Sermon Brainwave. *YrA.E5.2023*.

19 O'Donohue, John, *Blessing for: The Interim Time*. Joyful Business. Retrieved from https://joyfulbusiness.com/blessing/

20 Nathan. (2020, January 23). History of Memento Mori. *Daily Stoic*. Retrieved from https://dailystoic.com/history-of-memento-mori/

21 The Emperor's Handbook. (n.d.). Retrieved from https://www.goodreads.com/quotes/1221731-your-days-are-numbered-use-them-to-throw-open-the

22 Episcopal Church. (1979). *The Book of Common Prayer Chapel Edition: Red Hardcover*. Church Publishing, Inc. p. 265.

23 Krulwich, R. (2011, April 26). Nature's living tape recorders may be telling us secrets. *NPR*. Retrieved from https://www.npr.org/sections/krulwich/2011/04/26/135694052/natures-living-tape-recorders-may-be-telling-us-secrets

24 Bishop Curry. (2017). Sermon at St. Mark's Alexandria, Diocese of Virginia. Retrieved from https://www.youtube.com/watch?v=4mDKPlAMmXA

25 Gulick, T. (2017). Sermon at St. Mark's Alexandria. Diocese of Virginia.

26 Oliver, Mary (1992). *The Summer Day*, Retrieved from https://www.loc.gov/programs/poetry-and-literature/poet-laureate/poet-laureate-projects/poetry-180/all-poems/item/poetry-180-133/the-summer-day/

27 Thomas, Lauren Grubaugh. (2023). Then We Will See Face to Face, Retrieved from https://laurengrubaughthomas.substack.com/p/then-we-will-see-face-to-face.

28 O'Donohue, John. (Doubleday, 2008). To Bless the Space Between Us: A Book of Blessings, p. 98.

# ABOUT THE AUTHORS

*The Rev. Mary Vano* is the Rector of St. Margaret's Episcopal Church in Little Rock, Arkansas. A graduate of Texas Christian University, Mary then attended the Seminary of the Southwest in Austin, Texas, where she was awarded a Master of Divinity degree in 2003. After serving as a priest at St. David's Episcopal Church in Austin, Mary and her family moved to Little Rock, where she has been leading St. Margaret's since 2011.

*The Rev. Michaelene Miller* is the Associate Rector for Christian Formation at St. Margaret's. After receiving a Master of Divinity from Virginia Theological Seminary, she was ordained in the Diocese of Arkansas in 2018. Since then, she has served as Curate at All Saints in Russellville and as Executive Director of the Deaconess Anne House, an Episcopal Service Corps Program in St. Louis, Missouri. Michaelene has long felt called to build and form community, overcoming boundaries that divide. This desire to build and form caring communities rooted in God's dream for Creation remains at the center of her call to the priesthood.

*The Rev. Cindy Fribourgh* received her Master of Arts in Pastoral Studies from Loyola University, Chicago. She was ordained October 28, 2000 and served at St. Margaret's 20 of her 23 years of diaconal ministry. Cindy worked with The Rev. Dr. Christoph Keller on his creation of the Institute for Theological Studies at St. Margaret's, which offered educational programs for teens and adults from which came The Interfaith Center and SUMMA: A Student Theological Debate Society.

*Dr. Donnal Walter* has been a member of St. Margaret's since 2000, serving in numerous lay capacities. He is a retired physician, receiving his MD-PhD from the University of Kansas in Kansas City in 1976. He practiced neonatology at the University of Arkansas for Medical Sciences and Arkansas Children's Hospital from 1984 to 2021, where he remains an Adjunct Professor of Clinical Informatics.